Inculturation
and African Religion

American University Studies

Series XXI
Regional Studies

Vol. 16

PETER LANG
New York • Washington, D.C./Baltimore • Boston
Bern • Frankfurt am Main • Berlin • Vienna • Paris

Stephen Owoahene-Acheampong

Inculturation
and African Religion

Indigenous and Western
Approaches to Medical Practice

PETER LANG
New York • Washington, D.C./Baltimore • Boston
Bern • Frankfurt am Main • Berlin • Vienna • Paris

Library of Congress Cataloging-in-Publication Data

Owoahene-Acheampong, Stephen.
Inculturation and African Religion: indigenous and Western approaches to medical
practice/ Stephen Owoahene-Acheampong.
p. cm. — (American university studies.
Series XXI, Regional studies; vol. 16)
Includes bibliographical references and index.
1. Akan (African people)—Medicine. 2. Akan (African people)—Religion.
3. Traditional medicine—Ghana. 4. Medicine—Ghana. 5. Christianity and culture—
Ghana. 6. Ghana—Social life and customs. I. Title. II. Series.
DT510.43.A53093   306.4'61'09667—dc20   96-478
ISBN 0-8204-3129-X
ISSN 0895-0482

Die Deutsche Bibliothek-CIP-Einheitsaufnahme

Owoahene-Acheampong, Stephen:
Inculturation and African Religion: indigenous and Western approaches to medical
practice/ Stephen Owoahene-Acheampong. –New York; Washington, D.C./
Baltimore; Boston; Bern; Frankfurt am Main; Berlin; Vienna; Paris: Lang.
(American university studies. Ser. 21, Regional studies; Vol. 16)
ISBN 0-8204-3129-X
NE: GT

for my family
and particularly to the memory of
Akosua Abiwa,
Mary Poku,
and
Anthony Nyanor

Acknowledgements

Many people contributed immensely to this book in different ways and they deserve my heartfelt and sincere thanks.

Foremost is Professor Michael A. Fahey, S.J., whose concern and encouragement sustained me to this end. I should also put on record the bursaries awarded to me by the University of St. Michael's College without which this study would not have been a reality. Also, the financial help of an anonymous International Foundation immensely facilitated this work.

Others have helped more immediately in the direction that this work has taken. Professor Lee Cormie's patience in reading over this work many times, and his insightful discussions and critical comments helped shaped this study. My appreciation also goes to Professors Carl F. Starkloff, S.J., Harold G. Wells, Ovey N. Mohammed, S.J., Roger O'Toole, all of colleges in the University of Toronto, and Charles A. Anyinam of York University, North York.

I will be remiss not to express my indebtedness to those authors and publishers whose work are constantly referred to in these pages. I thank *Mission, Journal of Mission Studies– Revue des sciences de la mission*, Institute of Mission Studies, Saint Paul University, Ottawa, for the permission to reproduce part of Chapter 4 already published in Vol. II, No. 1, (1995), of the journal. My thanks also go to Oxford University Press, the publishers of *Human Development Report 1993*, for the permission to use some statistical data on Ghana. Table 4 is reprinted from *Social Science and Medicine*; and I thank the publishers, Elsevier Science Ltd., for the permission. Also, I thank the publisher's "invisible" reviewers, and the staff at Peter Lang Publishing, Inc., New York, for their help. Nona Reuter, the

Production Manager, deserves special mention for her invaluable advice and assistance.

Finally, my thanks go to my entire family, my friends and co-workers of the then Diocese of Kumasi, Professor Ellen M. Leonard, C.S.J., and Mrs. Sharon McGhie of St. Michael's College, Mr. and Dr. Agyemang Badu-Danso, the staff and students of the then St. Basil's College Residence, University of Toronto, with whom I stayed shortly in 1987 and also from 1989 to 1991, and all my beloved friends who were sources of encouragement and hope.

Table of Contents

List of Tables

Preface

This book, which with minor changes was presented as my Ph.D. dissertation, deals with the Akan people of Ghana and their experience of colonialism and, therefore, Christianization. The colonial officials and the missionaries introduced many changes—political, economic, religious, medical, ethical, and legal—into the Akan society. These changes have not only altered the life of the people but have also generated conflicts within the community and within the individual human person.

Concentrating particularly on the impact of cultural and religious teachings and practices on medical practices, this study affirms, through the approaches of the articulation of modes of production and the theology of inculturation, the serious conflicts which ensue when cultures meet, particularly when promoters of a foreign culture seek a dominant position in relation to indigenous people and their culture.

The concern which prompted me to undertake this study was my own experience of the conflicts and the experiences of them by my people—the Akans—and Ghanaians in general. The conflicts are reflected and much pronounced in the poverty, malnutrition, poor drinking water, infant and maternal mortality, ill-health, and lack of general well-being of Ghanaians. In other words, they are reflected in the political instability, social injustices, maldistribution of national income, lack of development and neglect of things "native" and, thus, the overdependence on the West. In this study, therefore, I have made strides in pointing out medical, religious, economic, and political dimensions of these conflicts generated through colonization and their effects on the health and general well-being of the people.

Using indigenous medical practices and practitioners as immediate cases of reference, this work shows the dominant attitude of the Western world towards Ghanaians and other peoples of developing societies and the perpetuation of Western ideological interests by some Western educated Ghanaians. Importantly, I see this study not just as a reflection on the past experiences of Akans of colonization, but rather the extension of those experiences in the present-day life of the people. Thus, I see this work as contributing to the analysis and understanding of the devastating conditions which prevail in modern Ghana and other developing societies.

Equally important, this work allows space for the losers—oppressed people of Ghana—to express their concerns and dissatisfaction over the impact of foreign political, religious, medical, and economic policies on their indigenous institutions. It also allows them space to affirm the best in their own culture. The persistence of traditional institutions, particularly religion and medical practice in Akanland, in the face of massive colonial and Christian encroachment and suppression, modernization and new forms of colonialism are indications of the strength of the traditional spirit which gives viability to the traditional institutions. The articulation of modes of production and the inculturation approaches, as used in this study, are therefore promising because they encourage the voices of the historically marginalized and silenced and empower them in addressing the problems of the present.

I see this study as part of the broader cross-cultural debates by social scientists and theologians on religious, medical, economic, and political issues. This study highlights the relevance and importance of these debates. It highlights key aspects of these debates and points to the direction that it is through these debates that resolutions will be made, and solutions found to help alleviate the precarious conditions in developing societies.

At the same time, the study adds to the voices of many Church men and women concerning the necessity and relevance of the theology of inculturation and the theology of liberation in the life of the Church in Africa, Latin America, and Asia. Specifically, this work adds to the calling on the global Church and particulary the Church in Ghana and other African societies to develop their health care services to suit the religious, economic, and socio-cultural needs of their people.

From the insights gained from the modes of production and inculturation approaches, then, this study calls on Church leaders, pastoral agents, government officials and those of the first world with responsibility for programs in Africa to formulate policies which will improve the general well-being of the marginalized and silenced peoples of Africa and also help to liberate them from the colonial forces of oppression which still persist in various forms in Africa and other developing societies.

Chapter 1

Introduction

Developing countries are in deep crisis. African countries, for example, are shoulder deep in debt. The social infrastructure of these countries is crumbling. Now more than ever, rates of unemployment, abject poverty, malnutrition and hunger, outbreaks of diseases are all growing in developing societies. These conditions have attracted the attention and interests of social scientists and theologians. They are trying to understand the causes of these devastating conditions. These efforts have resulted in many cultural and cross-cultural debates on issues of politics, religion, economics, and medicine. These debates are relevant for both the secular institutions and the Church. The proper understanding of root causes of the predicaments of developing societies would, I think, help further enlighten Church leaders and pastoral agents to see more the importance of re-shaping its theology and practices to create more suitable conditions for the implementation of proper and adequate strategies to enhance the spiritual and physical well-being of the populations of developing societies, to promote integral human development, in the words of Pope Paul VI.

This book is intended to contribute to on-going cultural and cross-cultural debates, concentrating particularly on the area of medical practice.

No meaningful contribution will be made to the understanding and the alleviation of disease, poverty, hunger, and political instabilities in third world societies if the various governments of those societies, the "super powers", benevolent institutions, the churches, and the indigenous peoples themselves do not have proper understanding of the dynamics of the processes taking place there: the processes which, in addition to their sociological, political, and economic imports, are also of fundamental religious significance. This study will seek to contribute particularly to the intersection of three sets of concerns usually kept separate in Western academic discourse: beliefs (religion), illness and health (the understanding and practices of medical science, psychology and psychiatry versus those of "traditional" cultures), and social movements, institutions and structures (the domains of social sciences). This will be done through the theology of inculturation approach and the integrating lens of modes of production analysis (emphasizing the roles religious beliefs play in the articulation), with particular reference to the present-day situations of conflict and dilemma among Akans of Ghana.

It was the vision of Ghanaians, as indeed of many other peoples of colonized societies, that independence from colonization would bring them "free-dom" and a better tomorrow. Little did they realize that the effects of colonization would long outlast liberation, or that a new system of domination and exploitation would take its place. A new culture and, therefore, new systems were introduced into the society. New institutions were introduced which displaced the indigenous institutions, and also bred new elites who, consciously or unconsciously, worked to perpetuate the ideologies of the new systems. Specifically, I propose that the inadequacies of medical treatment and the persistent abundance of poverty and disease in Ghana can be explained in part in terms of the ideological leanings of the colonial administration—(political, economic, religious, and medical)—and subsequently to the perpetuation of the colonial ideologies by the various institutions and governments and the Christian churches after "independence". It will be shown that the tragic medical and religious situations in Ghana reflect a conflict arising out of the clash of two different worldviews: one which is religious and communitarian versus one which is materialistic and individualistic.

Thus it will be shown that the encroachment of Western medical systems upon the traditional medical system of Akans[1] in Ghana through colonization, and also the Church's definition given (through her theological teachings, pastoral and social ministries) as to what is normative in terms of administering and also receiving medical treatment, have contributed immensely to the generation of this conflict (conflict within individuals, and also conflict within the community in general), and therefore to the health hazards, among other things, of Akans.

In Ghana, as it is now, there has been neither any proper development of the indigenous medical practice, (it has no developed institutional framework and little support), nor its replacement with an adequate "Western" system, nor integration of the two. It will be shown that this lack of proper development of the former and its integration with the latter stems from neo-colonialism on one hand, and the complex conservative/dynamic roles of both the Christian religion and the indigenous religion on the other hand.

The rapid growth of Christianity in Africa has been attested to in theological and social science literatures. The new religious movements in Africa (African Independent Churches) have been generally seen as one of the major factors for the growth of Christianity in the continent in recent years. And one of the most frequently cited reasons for the spread of the new religious movements, often called spiritual healing churches in Ghana, is their healing activities based on the integration of African traditional elements with Christian approaches. Thus, it will be shown that the numerous and still rapidly growing indigenous spiritual healing churches in Ghana, and for that matter Africa in general, are but one indication of the population's resistance to key aspects of Western medicine, as part of its resistance (however unconscious) to Western cultural and religious imposition in general, and specifically to the "individualism" and "materialism" characteristic of Western approaches to development and an effort to sustain "traditional" culture, especially in face of the lack of an alternative system.

In my view, in the Church the theology of inculturation offers the greatest promise for addressing the suffering and conflicts arising from conflicting modes of production embodying different cultures and religious sensibilities. In the theology of inculturation, theologians offer a solution to the problem of conflicts resulting largely from the dominating attitude that the promoters of a foreign culture take, and the resulting resistance on the part of the indigenous culture(s). This study, therefore, emphasizes the need and relevance of inculturation in the life of the Church in Africa.

I propose that if there is to be any breakthrough for adequate and proper distribution of health care, and indeed if the Church is to contribute meaningfully towards the World Health Organization (WHO) program—health for all by the year 2000—and, also, if this program is to be a reality for all Ghanaians and peoples of other developing societies, then there is the need for the mission churches to reconsider their theologies, and for those in the first world with responsibility for programs in Africa, and indigenous officials themselves, to shirk off their strong ethnocentricism which does not augur well for dialogue, integration, and acceptance and, therefore, the spiritual wholeness and general well-being of humanity.

The proposed methodology for this study requires the examination of literatures pertaining to the articulation of modes of production, the concepts of illness, health, and healing in both Western and Akan traditions, and also the theology of inculturation. The preliminary examination of these literatures will require a clear understanding of the issues within their own contexts. Thus, it will require looking at the structure of the Akan traditional society and religion, changes introduced by colonization, and subsequent changes.

Second, the literatures must be analyzed for their social science and theological imports, indicating areas where theology and social science complement each other, and where they can cooperate and work to help alleviate some of the deplorable health and other conditions of Akans of Ghana and third world societies in general. Theology and social science help to clarify why indigenous traditional practices are, even today, still marginalized. Again, theology and social science help to clarify why numerous new religious movements are cropping up in Akan and other third world communities.

In the following chapter I will present a brief background review of the social science arguments regarding theories of development. I will expound the concept of modes of production and develop its relevance for analyzing medical systems.

In Chapter 3 I will review the theology of inculturation and its promise vis-a-vis other proposed approaches like adaptation, incarnation, contextualization, indigenization, acculturation, and enculturation. I will also link the concept of inculturation to the concept of the articulation of modes of production and to medical practice/healing.

In Chapter 4 I propose to reconstruct the structure of Akan traditional society and religion. The idea here is to give a picture of the practices and institutions of Akans before their encounter with Western culture and Christianity. I will also reconstruct and set forth the structure of Akan traditional religion as comprising the nature and structure of the spirit world, the practice of magic and medicine, and the nature and roles of religious functionaries.

I will review in Chapter 5 key changes introduced under colonization, indicating in particular the new cultural and religious elements that were introduced into the Akan society.

In Chapter 6 I will look at the concepts of illness, health, and healing in both the Western and Akan traditions. The aim is to indicate the different views which the two traditions represent in terms of those concepts.

In Chapter 7 I propose to show the current situations of Akan traditional medicine, Western medical practice, and the Christian religion vis-a-vis Akan traditional religion. This will shed light on postcolonial developments up to today. The purpose here is to show the conflicts resulting from the contacts between the Western worldview and the Akan worldview. In the context of mutual respect and dialogue, both sides have much to learn from the other. In this spirit, some of the weaknesses of both Western and indigenous approaches to health and healing will be shown.

To conclude, in Chapter 8 I will draw together the discussions of the approaches to medical practice and show the need for theologians and Church leaders to reconsider theological teachings on healing and other medical methods. I will emphasize the need and relevance of inculturation if the Church, particularly, is to contribute meaningfully to the WHO program—health for all by the year 2000—in Ghana and to its own internal renewal. Thus, I will address the implications of this study for the Church's pastoral and social ministries. I will indicate some challenges that both the articulation of modes of production and the inculturation approaches face.

Chapter 2

Modes of Production

The Concept of Articulation of Modes of Production

To place the study in a proper perspective and also to introduce the kind of theoretical framework we shall lean towards, it is proper to review briefly here competing theories that have been used in the analysis of African and other third world societies. Among the competing theories is the theory of development. Briefly, this theory, which is structural-functionalist in its framework and elaborated in its most systematic form by Parsons, proposes that for third world countries to develop they must necessarily journey through the path through which advanced capitalist countries journeyed; in this view the penetration of third world economies, as was characteristic of both periods of colonization and neo-colonization, are essential prerequisites for the development of those nations. These theorists argue that colonialism was a positive force and a necessary stage[1] for the development of societies like those in Africa, Asia, and Latin America.[2]

Another competing theory is the underdevelopment theory. Briefly, this theory is seen to have originated from the writings of Sweezy,[3] Baran,[4] and Frank.[5] In fact Taylor calls them the underdevelopment theorists. According to Leys, 'underdevelopment' meant, at one time, in UN parlance, 'insufficiently developed', or what is now called 'less developed'. It was thought that the state of affairs in the 'underdeveloped countries' was due to "a lack of capital, know-how and other inputs which had led to the 'development' in the advanced industrial countries." This view was criticized. Critics argued that, on

the contrary, "the predicament of the 'underdeveloped countries' was due to the application to them of western capital,
know-how and political power, often over several centuries, in
ways which had structured (and continue to structure) their
economies and societies so as to continually reproduce poverty, inequality and above all, political and economic subordi-
nation to the interest of western capital."[6] According to Leys,
even if Andre Gunder Frank might not be said to be the first
person "to subvert the original meaning of 'underdeveloped'
by writing of the 'development of underdevelopment' he was
certainly responsible for condensing the essential argument
involved in this succinct polemical form."[7] The underdevelopment theory, thus, conclusively asserts that the development
of third world societies is attendant on the removal of capitalist penetration.

> Its conclusion that indigenous development is attendant upon the
> removal of capitalist penetration can be premised upon the claim
> that the latter does not bring about the potential state, and that it
> fails to do this because it does not promote what (from within the
> potential state) can be defined as 'indicators' contributing to this
> potentiality. On this basis, it can be argued that all that has to be
> done is to remove the penetration. Such a conclusion is ultimately
> premised on a comparison of the given with the potential, and the
> further assertion that capitalism alone retains the given.[8]

The underdevelopment theory, then, according to Taylor, rejects and argues to the contrary the views of the Parsonian
modernization sociology.[9]

Dependency theory, which is a version of structural theory
(and "of course has been enriched by contact with and stimulus from Marxist economics")[10] and which has been applied to
political economy, offers other insights in the analysis of third
world societies. Briefly, the theory, which has its original formulation in Latin America,[11] explains that the political and
economic underdevelopment of third world countries and the
high accumulation of capital by more advanced countries are
results of the fact of the former's extensive but asymmetrical
contact with the latter. There is an uneven transfer of surplus
value from the underdeveloped countries to the developed
capitalist countries, and thereby, bringing about uneven development. In other words, those countries which lose their sur-

plus value tend to stagnate into underdevelopment while those appropriating countries continue to develop and expand.[12]

Another approach which is from within the historical materialism theory, and which, in my view, is particularly illuminating, is the now quite common concept of an articulation of modes of production. Briefly, this concept holds the view that in the development of a society modes of production do not replace each other; "instead, a new mode of production can develop—can 'establish its dominance'—on the basis of the continued functioning of older, 'subordinate' modes of production."[13] Thus the old mode(s) of production continues to reproduce itself. In other words, the new (capitalist) mode of production does not destroy the old (non-capitalist) mode(s) of production; rather they co-exist alongside each other, although the old mode(s) is dominated. However, the relations of their 'co-existence' are themselves relations of conflict and struggle: the reproduction of the non-capitalist mode and its elements tend to set limits and barriers on the capitalist penetration.

> To establish its dominance over the non-capitalist mode, *capitalist penetration utilised the existing mode only to attempt to destroy it at a later (imperialist) stage of penetration.* Yet, because of its past actions, and because of the resistance put up against imperialist penetration by the non-capitalist mode (depending of course, on the particularity of its dynamics), either this mode or elements of it continue to be reproduced—even when the capitalist mode becomes dominant . . .

Among other instances, Taylor says this of Latin America:

> In Latin American formations . . . we are continually faced with a situation in which two different modes of production are reproduced concomitantly. Whilst the capitalist mode of production has gained predominance in industry . . . and is attempting to penetrate parts of the agricultural sector, and whilst imperialist penetration has tried both to reduce the political power of the landowning class and to persuade it to accept at least limited capitalist reforms, it still remains the case that semi-feudal mode of production continues to reproduce itself alongside the increasingly dominant capitalist mode.[14]

Pointing to this same conflict arising when capitalist and non-capitalist modes of production clash, and also hinting at the complex relations among classes amidst conflicting modes of production, Simonse notes that when capitalism encroaches upon other modes of production, as happened during the colonial rule in Africa, two types of tensions are generated: i) "between the basic principles of the respective logics of the two conflicting modes of production"; and ii) "within classes as defined by each of the two modes of production."[15]

> Normally the capitalist and the pre-capitalist modes of production do not continue neatly to confront each other according to all the rules of the gentle art of fencing, until such time that one will have slain the other. On the contrary, all sorts of cross-connections emerge between both modes of production. The basic principles of the two systems intertwine to such a degree that social intercourse is increasingly governed by a logic that is internally contradictory. In addition to this, the classes as defined by both modes of production may enter into complex relations, one of the most common of these being an alliance between the dominant classes of both modes.[16]

Comaroff neatly sums up this process:

> . . . as the ethnographic records show, the extension of capitalism into the Third World was by no means a replay of the history of the modern West. The transformation of preexisting modes of production has seldom been a smooth, undirectional process . . . and, far from sweeping all before it, and replacing indigenous cultural forms with its own social and ideological structures, the advancing capitalist system has clearly been determined, in significant respects, by the local systems it has sought to engulf. . .[17]

Though not myself a Marxist,[18] it is my view that recent reformulations of Marxian frameworks in interpreting the present day African situation are very relevant. I am concerned that one cannot fully grasp the various changes—social, religious, political, and economic—taking place in African societies today if one does not take cognisance of and relate the relations of production which existed in the continent before colonization to those which have prevailed since. In other words, we are saying that there is the need for a theory that can provide us with a "rigorous basis for analyzing the existence, forms, or effects of the various types of capitalist penetration within societies" like those in Africa which were "dominated by non-capitalist modes of production."[19] There is need for a theory that can enable us to relate many different kinds of changes and, also, see in a larger framework the wholeness of African social formations. Looking at the theory from the anthropological point of view, and relating it specifically to situations in Africa, Geschiere and Raatgever write, and I quote them at length:

> . . . it is . . . [the] complicated intertwining of old and new contradictions that has shaped the confusing diversity in present-day power relations and in the performance of the ruling classes in contemporary Africa. In this sense, the model of an articulation of production may provide a general perspective by which to analyse the complexity and variability of present-day politico-economic developments on the African continent.
>
> At the same time this model can serve as a new stimulus for anthropological studies. The traditional anthropological preoccupation with such subjects as kinship, bridewealth, witchcraft or prophetic movements does not necessarily betray, in this view, an antiquarian interest in phenomena doomed to disappear. On the contrary, these phenomena derive from old relations of production which can even generate new forms during their inevitable transformation under capitalist dominance.

They continue:

> Therefore the study of these old structures and their modern transformation continues to be indispensable if social scientists are to gain insight into . . . the wide range of effects of capitalist expansion in Africa. In its perspective, for example, it is easy to understand why, along with the anthropologists, virtually all the segments of the Africa population, including westernized elite, are still preoccupied with 'traditional'—in fact often 'neo-traditional'—ideas about kinship, bridewealth, witchcraft and so forth.[20]

At the same time as these developments in the theories of dependency and modes of production were occurring, other theorists have been revising Marxist approaches to religion. A circumstance whereby Marxian theory of religion has been reformulated and used in the concrete analysis of a current social situation of conflict resulting from the combinations of a new (capitalist) and old (non-capitalist) modes of production is Latin America. Latin American sociologist Otto Maduro uses the concept of modes of production to analyze the conditions (religious, social, economic, political, cultural) prevailing in Latin American communities. From one point of view, Maduro clarifies in Latin America what historically transpired between colonizers and the colonized; in particular he de-

scribes how a society which has once been colonized continues to bear the yoke of colonization even after its "independence". Maduro shows this in terms of the clash between the
mode of production (religious and social) which accompanied
colonization and which was superimposed on the traditional
modes of production of the indigenous peoples.

Speaking about the religious field (and by implication the
religious mode of production) as it pertains to Latin American societies today, Maduro says, historically, the subjugation
of the Latin American continent by the "empires of Spain and
Portugal was accompanied by setting up of Catholicism as *the*
official religion. There is . . . at least one indisputable trait: in
the Latin American religious field, Catholicism is the predomi-
nant religion."[21] And this religion, which is still the dominant
religion in the continent, and whose functionaries are in the
majority of European origin, has been contributing, unconsciously, to the perpetuation of domination and suppression.
In other words, because this body of religious functionaries
belongs to a particular group of people, this group, like any
other human group, has its own mode of production by which
it organizes itself. And the way this group (religious functionaries) organizes itself, perceives "its socio-natural surroundings, and hence its behaviour, individual and collective, in these
surroundings, are limited and orientated by its [Western]
worldview." In this sense then, Christianity in Latin America
is performing, against its best intentions, a conservative function in terms of preserving capitalist hegemony. Thus Christianity is, through the activities (religious practices, teachings,
etc.) of its functionaries who are from the dominant class, con-
stituting, though unconsciously, an obstacle to the development
and the autonomy of the subordinate classes.

From another point of view, Maduro specifies how religion,
as well as society, can be a vehicle of change. It is not always,
he says, that religion performs "purely conservative function
with respect to conflictive social relationships of dominance."

> Religions do not necessarily constitute an obstacle to the autonomy
> of subordinate classes, or to their alliances against domination. . . .
> [Rather] under determinate social conditions, and in the presence of
> a determinate internal situation in the religious field, certain reli-
> gious practices, teachings, and institutions perform, in class societ-
> ies, a role that is favourable to the autonomous development of cer-

tain subordinate classes, and to the reinforcement of their alliances against domination.[22]

Such a "revolutionary" role that a religion can play depends less on the religious agents' consciousness and intentions than it does on "the objective microsocial and macrosocial conditions in which such agents are operating."[23] The religious agents make reference to the principal form on which they situate and orientate themselves, and act in their socio-natural milieu. Social groups or communities which find themselves subjected to a relationship of dominance, which find themselves reduced to a subordinate position, tend to develop an *autonomic strategy*—"a strategy of autonomy with respect to this dominance, and to strike alliances against it." And in those communities and groups whose worldview is preponderantly a religious one, the "development and unfolding of this strategy" is "determined by the *religious conditions* in which this strategy unfolds and deploys itself."[24]

Maduro thus points to religion's twofold performance as a conservative force and as a revolutionary (dynamic) force. In other words, religion can be a medium of constructive, even radical change, as well as a source of support for continuing domination. And the role which religion plays, Maduro emphasizes, is often played unconsciously by its agents.

Maduro specifies, also, that a collectivity of human beings share a worldview, which (among other functions) limits and orientates the society which they, the social group—knowingly or unknowingly—produce. It is the worldview that enables any human group to produce, reproduce, or transform its social relationships; it is that which also limits and orientates the possibilities which it has opened up for the production, reproduction, and transformation of social relationships. And religion, according to Maduro, plays a very important function of shaping a determinate worldview. Religion does this by transforming the "socially lived" into the "socially thought". Religion "reconstructs subjectively the objective experience of the social groups of believers in a particular manner."[25] In this process it defines the social group's activities: what is useful, possible, desirable, urgent, thinkable and important; and makes it possible for its adherents to act upon their socio-natural surroundings. In sum:

> Every religion, inasmuch as it organizes in a comprehensible and com-
> municable manner (that is, as it gives meaning to) the collective expe-
> rience of a social group, thereby constitutes a fundamental element
> (and in some cases the very nucleus) of the believing group's *con-
> sciousness* and *identity*. Believer's *know* the world—perceive it and think
> it—*through* their religious worldview. By that very fact their activity
> upon that world is guided and directed by this perception of the world
> that their religion makes possible, limits, and orientates.
>
> Likewise, believers *know* themselves—perceive and think them-
> selves—*through* their religious view of the world (of which they form
> the center). They are held together and identified in their activity by
> this perception of themselves made possible, limited, and oriented by
> their religion.[26]

The worldview of pre-Columbian communities, according
to Maduro, was religious. Though each had its own single religious system, "religion in those communities does not present
itself as a differentiated institution, separate from the other
dimensions of collective life—economic dimensions, for instance, or political, or military, or family. On the contrary,
religion appears inextricably bound up with these other dimensions."[27] This was due to the kind of social organization
or mode of production each of the communities exhibited.
Latin American societies today are characterized by political,
religious, and economic conflicts, which can be explained in
terms of the (natural and sometimes even unconscious) resistance post-Columbians are exhibiting against their having been
placed in a forced relationship, under the domination of a new
mode of production.

Maduro's analysis of both pre-Columbian and post-
Columbian religious and social situations results in a picture
which, in my view, parallels to a large extent most African societies which have experienced colonization and therefore capitalist encroachment. Elements of 'conservatism' and 'dynamism', and also resistance and conflict, permeate the different
institutions of those societies. And these conflicts can be illuminated in terms of the articulation of modes of production.

For example, in *Peasant Consciousness and Guerrilla War in
Zimbabwe*, Terence Ranger shows concretely how a religious
worldview played a crucial role in a people's resistance to colonization. Ranger's historical analysis of the Zimbabwean guerrilla war against capitalist domination demonstrates the dynamic function of a religion in shaping peasants' radical

consciousness. "Peasant religion", as he puts it, "formed an indispensable part of the composite ideology of the war."[28] Even before the war, according to Ranger, spirit mediums exercised a very considerable influence among the peasantry. Among other roles they played in their communities, the spirit mediums were the custodians and 'owners' of the land. They gave orders and directions to the peasants as to when and which land was to be tilled and how the land was to be used. And when the lands were taken from the hands of the peasants by the whites to establish commercial farming and ranching, the spirit mediums, not only alerted the peasants to the consequences of their alienation from the lands which belonged to their ancestors and spirits and from which they had their livelihood, but also, by their (the spirit mediums') 'ritual' avoidance or acceptance,[29] represented the peasant grievances (over lost lands and administrative coercion).

> Spirit mediums were significant to peasant radical consciousness precisely because that consciousness was so focused on land and on government interference with production: above any other possible religious form the mediums symbolized peasant right to the land and their right to work it as they chose.[30]

In other words, the spirit mediums played a vigorous role in resistance to the state's enforcement of agricultural rule, (new intensive cultivation)—which contrasted sharply with the way the ancestors of the peasants, and the peasants themselves, used land.[31] And when the war came:

> the mediums proved ideally fitted to play another and crucial role. It was they who offered the most effective means of bringing together peasant elders, who had hitherto been the local leaders of radical opposition, with young strangers who entered each rural district, armed with guns and ready to administer revolutionary law.[32]

Not only the peasants drew heavily on the religious elements within the composite ideology of the war, but also most of the guerrillas themselves. The adherence to the demands of the ancestral spirits as pronounced by the spirit mediums helped to bring about discipline and morale within the liberation movement. In fact the pace, the strategies, and also the success of the war were heavily influenced by an African religious worldview which had 'survived' the encroachment of Western, and for that matter Christian, ideology.

Ranger's historical analysis of the Zimbabwean guerrilla war, in my view, substantiates Maduro's theoretical hypothesis that in communities or social groups whose worldviews are pre-ponderantly religious,

> to transform the conditions of . . . [their] existence, to place obstacles in the way of the hegemonic strategy of dominators, and to grow in strength in order to set up opposition to a dominating social bloc, depends upon . . . [their] ability to develop a worldview that will be independent of and different from the worldview of the dominant classes. The transformation of the subordinate classes' worldview into one that is autonomous and distinct from that of the dominant classes is the indispensable condition for creating the objective possibility of transforming the material conditions of their own existence, and thereby ceasing to be subordinate classes.[33]

Maduro also insists:

> . . . these groups will not be able to develop their class consciousness without religious mediation—that is, without religious changes per-mitting them to situate and orientate themselves differently from the dominators and in open opposition to their domination (which will in turn open to them the possibility of acting against the domina-tion). Only in the antecedent or concomitant presence of religious transformations can such groups situate and orientate themselves, and act, in opposition to dominant classes.[34]

The Zimbabwean guerrillas articulated their own stance with reference to the traditional religious worldview of the people which helped them to solicit the unflinching and enduring support of the spirit mediums and the peasants in their suc-cessful war against alienation, discrimination and oppression.

Another example concerns the Zeruru of Southern Rhode-sia (Zimbabwe). Speaking about the Zeruru, Peter Fry shows how religion was used by the nationalist leaders as a reference and a base for the transformation of the people's condition of existence, (and thereby situating and orientating themselves differently from their white dominators, as Maduro would put it). Peter Fry points out that much emphasis was placed by the nationalist leaders on 'traditional institutions', especially spirit-mediumship. The struggle which was a political one became a religious struggle. Many of the people who belonged to the

Christian churches returned to their 'traditional' religious rituals. Thus, "not only were the white political institutions under
attack, but also many of the premises of their culture."[35] Attacks were launched by the people on the churches in Rhodesia for "having condemned the indigenous Shona religion that
they found." Christianity had forced the people to forget "the
efficacy of the prayers they had one time addressed to their
spirits." However, the people were in doubt now as to the efficacy of the new (Christian) religion. And with heightened political conflicts entering the arena, Christianity was no longer
acceptable to many and was "opposed for being a peaceful
way of perpetuating colonialism. . . . Africans lost faith in the
religion they could not fully understand. They now look back
with admiration to their old ways which Christianity forced
them to forget."[36] Fry quotes Nathan Shamuyarira as putting
"the general case succinctly:

> The NDP [National Democratic Party] was concerned to find a spiri-
> tual and cultural base for African Nationalism. The party encour-
> aged its supporters to value those things which were African customs,
> names, music, dress, religion and food and much else. . . . In religion
> young Africans increasingly rejected the view encouraged among their
> elders by missionaries that worshipping ancestral spirits or gods of
> idols was heathen superstition. . .Africans feel they can worship most
> effectively through the intermediary of ancestors they know . . .
>
> In rural areas meetings became political gatherings and more—
> social occasions where old friends were renewed and new ones made,
> past heritage was revived through prayers and traditional singing with
> African instruments, ancestral spirits were evoked to guide and lead
> the new nation. Christianity and civilisation took a back seat, and
> new forms of worship, and new attitudes were trust forward dramati-
> cally . . . the spirit pervading the meetings was African and the desire
> was to put the twentieth century in an African context. (1965: 68,
> 69).[37]

We have stated above that in the process of establishing itself as the dominant mode of production a new mode of production does not replace the older mode(s) of production;
rather, they co-exist alongside each other although the old
mode(s) is dominated; and the reproduction of the old mode(s)
and its elements tend to set limits on the penetration of the
new mode. This insight is going to be the guiding principle
for our discussions of conflicts in the area of medicine. It is

therefore particularly worth noting Peter Fry's observation
about the political and religious trends among the people of
Chiota. The Chiota people, who had been exposed to white
administration and Christianity around 1892, were involved
in the 1896 bloody rebellion by a number of Shona groups in
Central Mashonaland against white settlers. The white settlers
had installed themselves in the region in 1890, following Cecil
Rhodes Pioneer Column that year. Before the rebellion and in
the years immediately after the rebellion Christianity had made
little headway in Chiota. The great breakthrough (of Christianity) seemed to have "occurred in the 1930s when there was
increased demand for education which was provided by the
missions."[38] The Anglican, Roman Catholic and Methodist missions opened many schools and churches. Women's and men's
bible study groups and also women's clubs were encouraged
especially in the Methodist church. The practices of African
traditional religion and traditional rituals were strongly for-
bidden. So during the thirties, forties and fifties, Christianity
and education flourished in Chiota. "But all this", Fry writes,

> was at the level of public and social behaviour on the wider stage that
> had been set with the inclusion of Chiota in a wider society. The be-
> liefs themselves did not die out, nor did they cease to be used; they
> went underground and the open collective rituals associated with
> spirit-mediumship gave way to more secretly held consultations with
> the herbalist/diviners. . . . Although the white missionaries may have
> thought that their converts had been totally weaned from their origi-
> nal beliefs, this had not in fact occurred. Indeed even after the rise of
> mediumship in the late fifties I was able to observe that some Meth-
> odist evangelists continued to keep a foot in both camps. They at-
> tended church in the public and worshipped the ancestors indirectly
> by contributing in cash or kind to the cost of rituals.

Peter Fry continues:

> But the situation of overt Christianity with traditional religious forms
> more or less kept underground was to change dramatically in the
> early 1960s.[39]

In the early 1960s, the people demonstrated their dissatisfaction with missionary Christian imposition and white domination in general. They did this through political activity (pro-

tests) which mainly took the form of acts of aggression against churches, churchmen and people who had taken sides with the whites.

These observations about the Chiota people, and the Zimbabweans in general, I think, confirm the articulation of modes of production theory. Firstly, they point to the impossibility of a foreign worldview, no matter its strength and force, completely destroying and in the process replacing an indigenous worldview; thus they point to the conflict and struggle that arises out of the relations of the 'co-existence' of dominating and 'subordinate' worldviews. Secondly, they point to the complex conservative/dynamic roles of religion—religious beliefs and rituals affirming the continuity with the past or promoting change in the existing social order.

So far, we have been speaking about the conflict between two worldviews (reflecting different modes of production) mainly in terms of politics; we have not yet referred to medicine and health which we have proposed as our areas of concern. However, at its deepest level "medicine", as Virchow says, "is a social science, and politics is nothing more than medicine on a larger scale."[40] In other words disease and health, as Virchow defines them, are "products of the social and economic situation."[41] And as we have illuminated above, social and economic situations are strongly shaped, especially in the African context, by religious beliefs, ideas, and practices.

According to Virchow, the best guarantees for the enduring health of people are education, prosperity and freedom.[42] It is essential that every human population has the freedom to develop their innate (spiritual and moral) potentialities and also live their own natural lives as their cultural and religious beliefs, ideas, and practices dictate. Imposition of external ideas, beliefs, relationships, and institutions on a people not only minimizes their choices and hinders their development and, thus, their prosperity, but also places them in a situation of dilemma, conflict and anxiety which are not conducive to human well-being. The Christian beliefs, teachings, symbols, and the Western sociocultural order which were superimposed on the traditional African ones have multiplied internal contradictions within the African societies and also within the human individuals themselves. People who have been "abruptly wrenched from their human and spiritual contexts, are no longer able to recognize or realize themselves."[43]

Education is fundamental in the lasting health and well-being of people. But the question is: what kind of education? Is it the education concerning the importance and superiority of one worldview (approach to medical practice and healing) over another, or the education on the mutual acceptance, recognition and integration of different worldviews? In his article on the people of Tamale in Northern Ghana, J. P. Kirby points to the roles religions (Islam and African Traditional Religion) play in the field of health care. He also argues that education should involve the acceptance and integration of different worldviews.

As a person in the field, Kirby observes that education is a weak link in African rural health care programs. He notes that, despite the intensive campaigns by Primary Health Care (PHC) workers to educate villagers in Northern Ghana in, for example, water sanitation for the prevention of guinea worm and other water-borne diseases, "there has been little change." Kirby accepts the fact that in changing something as basic as people's eating and drinking habits more time is needed, but, he argues, "the high level of resistance in N. Ghana to such rudimentary measures like boiling and filtering drinking water leads one to suspect that there is a cultural-based nexus of miscommunication here."[44]

> In Tamale area, for example, borehole water, which is quite potable, is rejected for 'more tasty' (but less wholesome) river or 'dugout' water. But the deeper, underlying reason for not drinking this 'safe' water is that in the minds of the people it is contaminated with the spirits of the ancestors. The white sediment in the water confirms their suspicions.

Kirby continues:

> The scientific principles fundamental to Western health care are not at all basic to the thinking of rural Africa. African traditional thinking processes, including those surrounding the cultural complex of illness management, are both strong and resistant to change.[45]

So, how and where does education come in, and who gives and who receives it? Kirby proposes that:

Greater progress and longer results might be achieved if less time were spent trying to get Africans to think like Westerners and more time spent trying to discover how the basic elements of Western-medical knowledge . . . can be incorporated into traditional systems of thought and action so that they make sense from the perspectives of the local people.[45]

The underlying reason for the villagers' rejection of the borehole water can be looked at in a much deeper way. On the basis of my experience as an African and a Ghanaian, I suggest that it is the people's way of saying that their ancestors would disapprove of their rejecting the river and 'dugout' water, which nourished them and their ancestors for many years, for something new and foreign. In their view, the spirit of their ancestors, and the spirit that takes its abode in the river or the 'dugout', would be angry with them for such rejection. Further it is easy to imagine that the idea that the borehole water is contaminated with the spirits of the ancestors is being promoted by a spirit medium or a medicine person or a diviner. We come face to face, once again, with a situation where a people are articulating their resistance to foreign imposition in religious terms.

Instances whereby the people have rejected Western services and treatments, observes Kirby, do not mean that "there are no inroads being made." Where Africans see Western services and treatments as an "improvement over existing techniques for problem solving and illness management" they readily adopt them "on a 'self-help' basis. . . .

But, most importantly, their use does not require the acceptance of the entire Western medical institution or even a change in worldview. . . . Such isolated changes in practice rarely lead to a revision of one's basic premises regarding the dynamics of illness and health.[47]

In these instances, we witness the conflicts arising from the clash between two modes of illness treatment and management. As Kirby has indicated, if the Primary Health Care (PHC) program in Northern Ghana is to be successful, then its objective should not be to change the people's whole way of thinking— "to eventually get people to think in Western bio-medical categories,"[48] but to dialogue with the people's beliefs and practices. In other words, there should be mutual respect between Western medical practitioners (on whose practice the PHC program in Ghana is based) and African traditional practitioners if the benefits offered by the former are to gain acceptance.

S. K. Bonsi[49] has also pointed to the resistance an indigenous mode of production poses to an advancing new mode of production and conflict concerning medical practices which results. According to Bonsi, the impact of Western pressures on traditional institutions has been recognized by contemporary writers on social change in Ghana. Some "see modernization as a destructive mechanism or a technological "processing" that assaults traditional institutions." And some analysts have further suggested that "because of rapid social, economic, and educational changes traditional social structures will disintegrate and with them the ideas and practices which they support." Bonsi, however, disagrees:

> The introduction of western institutions and values in Ghana has definitely given rise to new sets of interests and values that are incompatible with and threaten traditional social forms. However, traditional norms, values and beliefs still persist and, in most instances, interweave with the new. Hence shifting attitudes and conflicting alliances that often result from the interaction of different and sometimes opposing sets of interests and belief systems characterize modern Ghanaian social life. But while these inconsistencies and conflicts are part of the social process in Ghana, there is evidence of reconciliation and synthesis of both the old and the new forms.[50]

In Bonsi's analysis, the traditional values and the way of life of the people of Ghana have been profoundly transformed since contact with European civilization in the 18th century. The people's way of life and work have been deeply influenced by the patterns of Western politics, economics, education, and social life. One of the most important influences has been the establishment of Western medical institutions. The introduction of Western medical practices into traditional life of Ghanaians inevitably involved "new sets of ideas, interests, concepts and medical theories which oppose traditional medical concepts and practice. . . . People no longer have to be completely dependent on the traditional medical practitioners, but have become oriented toward the use of Western medical facilities." So with the impact of Western influence, and notably with the strong support of Christian missionaries who through the establishment of educational and health institutions sought to change both the spiritual and material values of the indigenous people, traditional interpretive frameworks, practices and institutions have been challenged. The traditional medicine has been portrayed by Westerners as therapeutically less effective and powerless. The prestige, credibility, and influence of traditional practitioners have been undermined with the result that they are less able to compete with Western medical practitioners for clients.

This encroachment upon their occupation by Westerners pushed the traditional medical practitioners to resist. But their capacity to resist was limited. For example, in the 1920's, Governor Gordon Guggisberg made an attempt to eliminate traditional medical practice from the cities. The traditional practitioners successfully resisted "but they could not secure an official mandate and their practices were circumscribed." Since the traditional medical practitioners were opposed by the colonial government and their practice was prohibited, they had to continue their practice in obscurity. They practised their trade this way until independence of the country in 1957, "when interest in traditional culture and institutions found expression in Kwame Nkrumah's Africanization policies and programs." This new era that dawned with independence called for a response to social and cultural conditions of the colonial situation. There was a quest for a new orientation and emphasis on material and nonmaterial elements which could distinguish the African approach to the world from that of the West. Consequently, a move was initiated by the government to improve and promote traditional healing.

> . . . Thus, . . . the political revolution of the 1950's was at the same time a social and cultural revolution. There was the desire to search for and revive symbols of cultural and historical heritage which would contribute to the new African image. This drive for nationalism and cultural awareness resulted in the formation of the government-sponsored Ghana Psychic and Traditional Healers Association in 1963. This association established a school which has now developed into the Institute for Scientific Study into Plant Medicine.[51]

Contemporary native healers have been influenced in some respects by modes of medical diagnosis and treatment procedures and practice from Western medical sources. However,

Bonsi argues, ". . . the impact of this borrowing has not been a total assimilation of western medical culture, but a rediscovery and reassertion of traditional values and a search for some form of synthesis and modernization." Traditional beliefs about health and illness which are embodied in the traditional cosmology still exist. And as is a common knowledge now, this traditional cosmology, of which health and illness form a part, is religious. In this cosmology, framework and dimensions are central in addressing health issues.

> In considering the individual's health behaviour . . . four elements are essential: the importance of the spiritual world; the particular order that links the individual with this spiritual world; the medical theory based on the legitimacy of the ancestral supremacy in the affairs of men; and the relationships between the individual and his fellow man. The individual is constantly reminded of his dependence on the other members of his group, his ancestors and other spirit entities. He comes to believe that illness and death are some of the inevitable consequences of deviant behaviour. Hence, the individual lives and operates in a religious universe in which natural objects and phenomena which occur in his environment are closely associated with gods and spirits. For him, the physical and the spiritual are two dimensions of one and the same world.[52]

In considering the resistance of the traditional healers to the colonial government in the 1920's, and which they continue against the encroachment of Western medical institutions and practices upon traditional medical institutions and practices in Ghana, we will need to concede the fact that, however implicit it might be, religious factors had a major role to play. The traditional medical practices and institutions which are based on religion resist the individualism and reductionisms of Western medical frameworks and practices. In other words, by insisting on their practices, the traditional healers were developing an *autonomic strategy*—"a strategy of autonomy with respect to . . ."[53] Western domination. That is, the indigenous healers were opposing encroachment of Western "materialistic" way of life upon their own way of life. The persistence of the traditional healers and the resistance they pose to Western practitioners also affirm what the concept of the articulation of modes of production helps us to see: a new mode of production does not simply replace an existing mode(s) of production, they continue to exist alongside each other though in conflict and resistance.

In particular, the presence and growth of the healing churches—African Independent Churches—in the African continent illustrate the conflicts concerning health frameworks and practices resulting from the clash of modes of production.[54] Christianity, which is couched in Western modes of thought and which was introduced to Africa alongside colonization, has not replaced the traditional religions of the indigenous peoples. The traditional religions still exist and are practised now in some sectors of Africa; elements of these cultures (drumming, dancing, etc.) have also found their way into the activities of the mainstream churches—now promoted in the new theology of inculturation. African Independent Churches also clearly illustrate the complex dynamics of the intersection of two modes of production.

In this sense then, John Sivalon is correct in affirming that:

> Religion, rather than being insignificant or a mere ideological reflection, is presented here as a factor in a dynamic social whole. This social whole is made up of various elements that shape and reshape each other in an historical process. The dynamics become even more complex when various modes of production encroach upon one another through a process of articulation mentioned above. New religions, old religions and various mixtures of the two can through various historical circumstances either foster or actually help shape new relations of production or support resistance to and frustrate the growth of new relations.[55]

In summary, then, we wish to emphasize two points. The imposition of a new mode of production on one or more old modes of production results in conflict and resistance; and "religious" factors play different roles in the developing strategies of different groups in the new conditions fostered by capitalist encroachment.

The Concept of Articulation of Modes of Production and Medical Systems

Little attention has been given by the theoreticians of the concept of modes of production to health issues. The connections between disease, traditional medicine and religion, (to put it broadly, medicine and religion), and the analysis of the co-existence of the traditional African medicine and the Western medicine have generally been articulated in structural func-tional terms. And even here, in their ethnographical studies in Ghana, and elsewhere in Africa, many anthropologists placed the focus of their studies on the socio-cultural aspects of the culture, and especially their religion. And even with religion the focus was placed on magical practices and rituals. Simi-larly, traditional healing was seen as comprising only magic and ritual performances.[56] Very little attention was paid to the dynamics of the religion and the conflict which has arisen out of the co-existence of traditional African health care and Western medicine and their consequent effects, positively or negatively, on the populations.

In this work I propose to use the concept of articulation of modes of production to illumine important aspects of medi-cal discourse and practices of the Akan people of Ghana and their encounter with Western medicine and medical practice,[57] basing ourselves strongly on the Christian theologies and the Akan traditional religious beliefs and practices. The relevance of the religious beliefs, teachings, and practices cannot be over-emphasized. In the first place, the religious, social and other changes that swept and are still sweeping all over Africa, south of the Sahara, cannot be understood without reference to the teachings and activities of the Christian missionaries. In fact, the inroads of colonization were largely dependent on Chris-tian theologies and missionary activities. What Comaroff has said of the people of southern Africa can be said of all Africans:

> A century and a half ago, Christian missionaries served as the van-guard of colonialism among the peoples of southern African inte-rior, introducing a mode of thought and practice which became en-gaged with indigenous social systems, triggering internal transformation in productive and power relations, and anticipating the more pervasive structural changes that were soon to follow. . . . Indeed, Christian symbols provided the *lingua franca* through which the hierarchical articulation of colonizer and colonized was accom-plished.[58]

This conclusion has been affirmed by Chief J. O. Lambo in speaking about colonialism and its impact on African cultural heritage, referring particularly to the practice of herbal medicine in Nigeria. He pointed out that one of the important weapons the colonialists used to destroy the African cultural heritage was religion. The missionaries, who had been inspired by the famous missionary explorer of Central Africa, David Livingston, came to Nigeria professing to make the education of the people and the rendering of some medical services their main duty.[59] David Livingston is reported to have declared that "in the glow of love which Christianity inspires, I resolved to devote my life to the alleviation of human misery."[60] And his approach in alleviating "human misery" in Africa is best described in what Lambo says about the activities of another distinguished person, Thomas Birch Freeman. Freeman came from England with several missionaries to preach on the west coasts of Africa. But they did not limit their activity with preaching the Gospel. They waged war on things native.

> In the field of therapy, they branded the Herbalists as witch doctors and their methods of healing as rural, unscientific and unhygienic. . . . Thus they gradually changed the mentality of the majority of the people. Those who have the full knowledge of African science, began to forsake them in the interest of religion. The sick began to run away from the Herbalists and those who know the ability of the Herbalists in the field of Therapy would go to them at night. . . . Synthetic medicine replaced the natural drugs and the people did not take any trouble to find out and compare the efficacy of the two methods.[61]

Bonsi also drives the point home when he says this of the colonial expansion in Ghana:

> . . . the missions exerted an influence through education and sought change in both spiritual and material values of the indigenous people. . ., the traditional beliefs and values were assailed by the educational aims and ethical views of the Bible. Fellowship in the Christian faith demanded complete conformity to the Christian doctrine. This involved a rejection of traditional beliefs, rituals, and other non-Christian observances which form an essential part of traditional medicine. . . . The converts could not simultaneously share in the details of both the traditional and Christian world-views.[62]

As will be shown in this study, the prevailing attitudes of Africans today towards the reception of health care (both Western and African traditional health care systems) are very much dependent on the religious beliefs of the people. Christian theologies have become a large part of the spectrum through which Africans view healing and life in general. In this study, therefore, we will note particulary the tremendous impact the (healing) theologies of the mission churches and the new religious movements (African Independent Churches) in Africa have on medical reception and medical practices.

Chapter 3

The Theology of Inculturation

The Concept of Inculturation

Finding an adequate framework(s) for analyzing what happens when two or more cultures meet has been not only the preoccupation of the discipline of the social sciences, but also of theology. In recent years, many theologians have been preoccupied with finding models for analyzing the evangelical methodology or methodologies of the Christian missions that went from Western Europe to other continents in past centuries. This concern has arisen partly as a result of the mission churches' awareness of the often shallow impact of their teachings in those cultures. In particular the concern is a result of the complaints of third world peoples, particularly Christians, of the kind of Christianity that was brought to them by missionaries and colonial administrators. There is also the concern over the rapid growth and expansion of the new religious movements.

The concept of inculturation has recently become very influential among theologians seeking to respond to the concerns indicated above. "Inculturation" signals a new stage in analyzing Christian missions and in seeking to make the Christian message more relevant and livable in the context of a given cultural situation. It will be useful to set this approach in the context of others. There are other theological and sociological approaches which have been proposed as conveying what inculturation involves.

"Adaptation" has been perhaps the most widely used term in the past. The term was used interchangeably with another term, "accommodation", in the Vatican II documents.[1] It is used to refer to a more creative approach to mission. The missionary or the pastoral worker tries to fit "the Christian life in the fields of pastoral, ritual, didactic and spiritual activities" into the customs of the faithful among whom he or she works. The "adaptation" and "accommodation" approaches have been criticized and discarded recently on the grounds that they "express the external aspect of the encounter between Christian faith and different cultures."[2] These terms are criticized for containing within themselves "the seeds of perpetual Western superiority and domination."[3] The Christian faith is made to fit into a particular culture without the former being open for change.

Another approach is "contextualization". This concept focuses attention on "context" rather than "culture". Its proponents seek to interweave "the gospel with every particular situation. Instead of speaking of a particular culture, whether traditional or modern, it speaks of contexts or situations into which the gospel must be inculturated."[4] By so doing its proponents promote awareness that every particular context or situation "calls for creative theological reflection. . . . [It] also shows greater awareness of the historical development and change that is ongoing in all contexts."[5] This approach, however, is criticized for defining faith and church in foreign terms.[6] There is also a danger that the "term . . . may overemphasize the present context to the detriment of continuity with the past. Others say that its emphasis on the ever-changing particular context results in a chameleon-like theology that lacks constancy and solidity."[7]

"Indigenization" is another approach. The words "indigenization", "indigenous", "indigenuity" derive from a nature metaphor, that is, of the soil. "Indigenous" means to be native of a particular place or land, to be born into a particular culture. An individual who is born into a particular culture is not an outsider. He or she belongs there. In this sense, the indigenization of the Christian message is to articulate from the perspective of the native, the insider. The indigenization of theology means then that while the local church community does not cease links with the universal church, and is encouraged and guided by it, leadership is taken by indigenous people. The creative development of teaching, liturgy, and practice become the primary responsibility and task of the local church.[8] However, the "indigenization" approach is rejected for it has, in some languages, an "all too restricted meaning." It restricts itself to the work of the insider, the native, while little room is given to the contribution of the expatriate, the outsider, except at the beginning and at key stages. Also it has the inherent "danger of being past-oriented and falls short of expressing the dynamic changing aspect of culture."[9] In other words, it has the tendency to view culture as static. The natives may know the culture from inside out, "but they may not be sufficiently aware of the ongoing changes in the culture that are affected by modernization, technology, education, et. al."[10]

Another approach is "incarnation". This is a term which has direct reference to theology. It takes its reference from the mystery of incarnation, the divine taking human form, God the Son becoming man. "Incarnation refers to the entire Christ-event—the coming, birth, growth, daily life and struggle, teaching, healing, resting, celebrating, suffering, dying, and rising of Jesus Christ."[11] Thus the term "incarnation" situates the Christian message in a particular context or culture. It makes the message a particular cultural event. Jesus Christ was born into a particular cultural situation. "He learned the language and customs, and in and through these he expressed the truth and love of God. He . . . instinctively took part fully in the culture he was born into, and then critically affirmed and challenged that culture in the light of the Spirit."[12] Those promoting "incarnation" therefore call for the identification of Christian life "with the culture, people, and history we are part of", challenging and affirming both the Christian message and the culture in the particular cultural context. In short, the gospel is to be 'incarnated' in particular cultures and contexts. Pinto has cautioned that, to use the term "incarnation" to signify inculturation could be questionable in that "there was only one incarnation of God the Son, which took place in a given culture of Palestinian Judaism in the person of Jesus."[13] However, as Pinto himself

has countered, "we could speak of "incarnation" to signify inculturation by way of an intrinsic analogy, which is
proper" even though the "primary Incarnation is that of Jesus
Christ."[14]

"Acculturation" is also a term which has been widely used.
It is a term from the social sciences[15] which has been closely
associated with the theological concept of inculturation. "Acculturation" is the encounter between two or more cultures
and the ensuing changes. It is a concept which "comprehends
those phenomena which result when groups of individuals
having different cultures come into continuous first-hand contact, with subsequent changes in the original cultural patterns
of either or both groups."[16] In this sense, the term "acculturation" which is synonymous with 'culture-contact' according to
Roest Crollius, poses some difficulties when adopted in theology. First of all, the relation between the Church and a given
culture is not the same as the contact between cultures. The
Church, "'in virtue of her mission and nature, is bound to no
particular form of culture.'"[17] Moreover, the process that has
to be described is not just any kind of "contact," but a profound insertion, by which the Church becomes part of a given
society.[18] "Acculturation" is also criticized by some as imply-
ing an element of aggressiveness, and not conveying the
aspects of dialogue and mutual fusion which are ideal for
some.[19]

A term which brings us closer to the term "inculturation"
which is our focus here is the recent concept of "enculturation".
This social science concept has often been used by theologians
as an analogy of the theological concept of "inculturation".
But in order not to confuse both terms, it has been suggested
that, the term "enculturation" be technically used in social
science context and "inculturation" in theological contexts.
"Enculturation" is a concept which indicates "the cultural learning process of the individual, the process by which a person is
inserted into his or her culture."[20] In other words, it is a process by which a person (as a kind of *tabula rasa*) is introduced
and gradually learns and grows into his or her culture. This
process is often referred to as "socialization". But the terms
cannot be used synonymously since the term "socialization" is
more limited, referring to the process by which a person is

introduced into a society as its member and induced to play his or her roles. The concept of "enculturation" goes beyond that; it refers to the process whereby the person learns how to think.

> While the process obviously includes formal teaching and learning, it is very largely an informal, and even an unconscious, experience. To a great extent the individual teaches himself through a process of adaptive learning, the rules of which are given by the society. The images or symbols of a culture are in themselves didactic, and they teach the individual to construct his own categories and even to transcend them in the very act of constructing them. Thus the manner in which an individual apprehends experience is essentially culture-bound.[21]

We now arrive at the theological concept of "inculturation". The term "inculturation" was apparently introduced into theological circles by the members of the Society of Jesus.[22] As we have indicated above, the term "inculturation" is slightly different from the term "enculturation". While the social science concept of "enculturation" denotes a process by which a person becomes inserted in one's own culture, its theological form of "inculturation" denotes the process by which the Church becomes inserted in a particular culture of a people. According to Roest Crollius, we need to note that the difference between enculturation and inculturation does not consist only in the change of subject, "in consequence of which we speak of the insertion of the Church in a culture, and not of the individual"; more basically each of the terms is used in a different system of language.[23] The usage of "inculturation" in theological discourse is different from the usage of "enculturation" in social science discourse. "The theological discourse corresponds to the consideration of the salvific event in Jesus Christ. The theology of man—and culture—considers human reality in relation to this event."[24] Thus, while theological anthropology acknowledges facts, relations and attitudes in human history in relation to the saving acts of Jesus Christ, the salvific acts of Jesus are not relevant to cultural anthropology.

Emphasizing the difference between enculturation and inculturation, Roest Crollius argues that enculturation denotes that the individual does not yet have a culture; the person acquires his or her "culture in the process of enculturation, whereas the Church, though it is bound to no particular culture, does not enter into a given culture unless already linked with elements of another culture." He says that even when we look at "culture", and depending on how we define culture, there are several elements in the definition which can be predicated of the Church. In other words, there are several elements which belong to the very nature of the Church which are of a cultural character. "Therefore, from an anthropological point of view, the process of inculturation has also the characteristics of a process of acculturation."[25]

What is the concept of inculturation then? Roest Crollius defines the process of inculturation:

> the inculturation of the Church is the integration of the Christian experience of a local Church into the culture of its people, in such a way that this experience not only expresses itself in elements of this culture, but becomes a force that animates, orients and innovates this culture so as to create a new unity and communion, not only within the culture in question but also as an enrichment of the Church universal.[26]

In a similar spirit, Azevedo says it "is the dynamic relation between the Christian message and culture or cultures; an insertion of the Christian life into a culture; an ongoing process of reciprocal and critical interaction. . . ."[27] In this sense, the inculturation of theology is not a one-way process whereby the Christian faith and Christian living are superimposed on a culture; rather the Christian teachings and practices are integrated into the given culture, and the local culture and practices in turn integrated into the Christian message. In other words, there must be a mutual and critical dialogue and integration. In particular, the advocates of inculturation denounce cultural and spiritual domination. They call for a mutual and fruitful dialogue between an already existing—and therefore incultured in particular ways—form of Christianity and another culture with its own forms of religious experience and sensibilities. Thus, they call for a mutual and fruitful dialogue between the Christian message and culture or cultures on the basis of dialogue between equals.

Inculturation and its relevance are summed up by David Nazar in summarizing the affects on both the evangelizer and the evangelizee. I quote:

Affect on the Evangelizer

- open to conversion and to the discovery of God in the local culture

- seeks the history and the terms of God's presence locally

- seeks dialogue at the level of faith between the gospel + Christian tradition and local faith + its tradition

- carries the structure and theology of the church lightly

- open to local acceptance/ rejection of traditional Christian practice

- open to new articulations of the Christian dispensation in view of other experiences of God

- open to new theologies and new church structures

- identifies "culture" as a locus for evangelization

Affect on the Evangelizee

- culture and local experience of God are respected

- seeks to further the local experience on its own terms

- conversion to and from past ways happens according to locally viable principles

- local definitions of faith and of God obtain

- Christianity is received in local terms

- autonomy is left in the local culture, except for the invitation to dialogue

- cultural and spiritual integrity are maintained

- theology and church will grow out of local symbols

- local faith is challenged on its terms: change would proceed intelligibly[28]

In general terms, Nazar concludes:

1. This "model" is heuristic, aiming at the experience of God to date in the culture. It seeks to understand and to initiate a conversation between that experience and the Christian experience of God. It allows and encourages the local articulation of this experience and the furtherance of it throughout the culture. Its hermeneutic is controlled as much as by an orthodoxy of process as of content: faith seeks faith; religious tradition dialogues with religious tradition. The conversation is one of equals.

2. This evangelical approach is universally applicable. All that is at issue is acceptance or rejection of the dialogue.[29]

The concept of inculturation is, thus, an all-embracing concept which recognizes conflicts which ensue when different religious traditions and cultures meet and also sets a stage for the resolution of those conflicts in dialogue and mutuality. In so doing the proponents of inculturation go beyond and also fill in some of the inadequacies of the other concepts we have discussed above. They seek the kind of evangelization which will make the Christian message or Christianity relevant to the evangelized culture. The cultural or religious elements embodied in each system coexist in mutuality. Thus, there is a mutual exchange which comes about through dialogue and acceptance. Cultural and spiritual domination have no room in the process of inculturation. As will be shown later in this work, inculturation reflects concern about the feelings of self-worth and dignity at the heart of total human development. In this sense, inculturation is not only about theology and liturgy, but also about catechesis, medicine, law, politics, etc. In a word, inculturation concerns the integration of the Christian message into a particular culture. It is the Christian message finding a 'home' in a particular culture. It is being truly Christian in a given cultural situation. Inculturation reflects openness to a process of interpreting and reinterpreting the Christian message in an ongoing process of mutually respectful dialogue among Christians in different contexts and cultures in the global Church.

The Concept of Inculturation and the Concept of Articulation of Modes of Production

It is important, at this point, for us to look at the concept of inculturation in relation to the concept of the articulation of modes of production discussed above. This will clarify the common concerns underlying the choice of these approaches and the logic of their use in this study.

In the Church the development of "inculturation" as an approach offers the greatest promise for addressing the suffering and conflicts arising from conflicting modes of production embodying different cultures and religious sensibilities. In the theology of inculturation, theologians offer a solution to the problem of conflicts resulting largely from the dominating attitudes of the promoters of a foreign culture, and the resulting resistance on the part of the indigenous peoples with their own cultures. Thus, in advocating inculturation, theologians are seeking to find solutions to correct the unequal relations between Western culture and cultures of Africa and other third world societies. They also affirm that an alien religion, in our case Western Christianity, has not completely destroyed or replaced indigenous religions; they recognize, rather, the continuing coexistence, though in a conflictual manner. Inculturation, thus, in my view, points to the same dynamics as the concept of mode of production as we have understood it in this study. The modes of production framework suggests that when two or more cultures meet conflicts abound, contributing to poverty, hunger, ill-health, etc. in the subordinated culture(s). As indicated above, these conflicts and inequalities cause undue sufferings to the people in the dominated culture(s). And it is these sufferings that the proponents of inculturation seek to resolve. Their aims are dialogue, reconciliation, and mutual acceptance.

> What characterizes inculturation therefore is the drive leading to a "praxis" which is destined to reconcile the contradictions now arising in a society, whose traditional system has been deeply shaken by the new needs [and oppression, exploitation, and repression] revealed or introduced by the presence of the foreigner.[30]

The concept of inculturation, thus, sets a new stage in dialogue, respect, solidarity, and more promising experiments in search for solutions. In other words, it sets a new stage for the re-examination of relationships among different cultures and religious traditions.

It is my hope that solutions could be found, probably not permanently since the process of inculturation is an on-going one, if peoples of different cultures and religious traditions learn to accept the cultures and religious traditions of others. In other words, peaceful and beneficial coexistence among peoples of different cultures and religious traditions would be achieved if they meet in dialogical and reconciliatory attitudes, rather than in arrogance. Each could enrich the other, for every culture has its own virtues. In short, the believers of cultures and religious traditions should shirk off their ethnocentricism to facilitate acceptance, enrichment, and peaceful, and mutually beneficial levels of existence. Similarly, there is the need for repentance, conversion and a transformed universal Church leadership for the Church to be enriched by different cultures and religious beliefs.

Inculturation and Medical Practice

As in the case of the articulation of modes of production,[31] the inculturation approach has not been developed in relation to medical practice or healing. Whenever the issue of inculturation comes up, what often comes to mind, both in experts' (theologians) and lay circles, is inculturation of liturgy—drumming, vestments, songs, dancing, etc.—and of the sacraments—baptism and confirmation and eucharist. So far debates about medical practice or healing have not been informed by the insights associated with the inculturation approach.[32]

To speak of medical practice and of healing in relation to inculturation is appropriate. In theological terms the subject matter of inculturation, as indicated above, is Jesus Christ, who embodies true healing and well-being. In fact Jesus is often pictured as the medical practitioner, the healer par excellence. He demonstrated this in his ministry, culminating in his death and resurrection which brought spiritual and physical redemption (healing) to the whole world. Indeed, it is the belief of Africans, and peoples of other cultures and religions, that it is God who heals. For them, the healing arts must not be restricted to the use of technology and chemicals alone; the healing power of God must be emphasized.

Liberation theology which places greater emphasis on Jesus Christ as liberator, as we know, was born out of Latin Americans' experience of abject poverty and hunger stemming from injustice, inequality and massive oppression. The liberational character of Jesus and of his ministry is stressed in the face of these evils. Latin Americans draw inspiration from Jesus the liberator whose love for justice, freedom, peace, and equality impels them to work against anything that is to the contrary. Inculturation, the insertion of the Christian message into a particular cultural situation, has thus found proper and innovating expression in Latin American communities. Latin Americans are working to bring about transformation in the inhuman situations in which they find themselves by analyzing the cultural contexts in which the situations occur and confronting them with the gospel and the Christian tradition and popular pressure for social change.

In Africa, perhaps more obviously than in parts of Latin America, the dynamics and structures of oppression and exploitation also have cultural and spiritual dimensions. Fear, insecurity, ill-health, premature death, poverty, and other misfortunes are all interpreted in indigenous terms as reflecting the influence of evil spirits. These are areas where the inculturation framework can help. The commitments reflected in the inculturation approach require respect for these claims, and openness to the possibility that they may point to aspects of these dynamics which are unrecognized or underemphasized in Western theological and medical approaches. The healing aspect of Jesus' ministry can be emphasized. Emphasis on Jesus Christ as the healer and as one who dispels demons and their atrocities resonates powerfully with African traditional themes. After all, African beliefs of evil spirits appear very similar to those of first century Palestinians, some of whom were reported healed by Jesus. (Cf. for example, Mk.1:39; 3:20-27; 5:12-13; 9:14-29).

Some kind of inculturation in this area has already begun. It has begun not by the mission churches in West Africa, though, but the African Independent Churches. We will return to this point below, and also point out some areas in the Catholic teachings and practices where inculturation in this direction can be done. Africans learn to see Jesus Christ as a healer, as Latin Americans have seen Jesus, and rightly so, as a liberator.

Inculturation has been defined as the insertion of the Christian message into a given cultural context. In this sense, the concept seems to suggest "merely the transfer of faith from one culture to another. . . . In short, it seems to suggest that the process of mission or evangelization is a one-way process."[33] This impression, Shorter insists, is unfortunate. However, we may rectify this unfortunate impression if we recognize that the faith that is being transferred to another culture is not an obscured or dormant faith; rather it is an explicit faith, a faith which is already being practised by a people. And in our case, it is the Christian faith, the faith which is held by the Church, the people of God. For this reason we can speak of the faith in terms of the Church. And the Church, as Roest Crollius has pointed out, "though bound to no particular culture, does not enter into a given culture unless already linked with elements of another culture."[34] Indeed, the Church, from its earliest establishment, has been influenced and shaped by different cultural systems.

> The Church, for all its claims to catholicity, partakes of the character-
> istics of a cultural system or subsystem, beginning as a Jewish phe-
> nomenon, then achieving an act of transcendence from that system,
> only to enter into another determination—the Greco-Roman, then the
> Frankish and Anglo-Saxon, all of which have deeply influenced its
> development.[35]

For this reason, we can speak of inculturation in connection with medical practices which are aspects of cultures. Western medical practices were introduced in most African and other third world societies through missionary evangelization (which, as indicated above, had already been influenced and shaped by different cultural systems). The bearers of these medical practices generally rejected dialogue with the indigenous medical practitioners, concerning virtually all the other aspects of the indigenous culture. Indeed, as has been pointed out in the previous chapter, the newcomers sought to eliminate the indigenous medical practices. But as the concept of modes of production underlines, such an endeavor was, and still is, and will always be resisted, and the cost is great. Traditional beliefs and medical practices still exist alongside the dominating Western medical practices. But for the enrichment of both practices, and for the well-being of humanity, particulary the indigenous peoples whose cultures have been encroached upon, bearers of both practices should dialogue, so that the practices find proper expression in inculturation.

Also, as the modes of production approach insists, conflicts, exploitation, resistance, and sufferings generate when a new culture and religious tradition are imposed upon an indigenous culture and religious tradition. And the impact of the conflicts, exploitation, and resistance upon the people of the indigenous culture and religious tradition is immense. They inhibit development and general well-being of the indigenous people. So, for peoples in African and other third world societies to develop suitable systems for their specific needs and conditions, institutionalization of historic patterns has to change. In other words, relations of power between the dominant and the dominated have to change; and exploitation has to be stopped. There should be equity and justice in all situations, else no amount of benevolence and/or food and medical aids will help peoples of developing societies. For example, the provision of suitable, adequate, and sufficient medical services for health care needs of Africans will be an illusion, if their own therapeutic approaches are not considered by first world officials with responsibility for (health) programs in third world societies. The theologies and pastoral practices of the Church also have to be changed by Church leaders to suit the religious and cultural sensibilities of peoples in Africa, Asia, and Latin America. Thus, the dialogue which the theology of inculturation calls for can be initiated by the Church, since the Church is the bearer of the foreign message; and it is the Church which defines what is normative to her faithful in terms of administering and receiving medical treatment.

The agitation for inculturation by third world peoples, particularly Africans, may be appreciated more fully when we look at the peoples' traditional modes of existence—social life, politics, religious beliefs and practices, customs, ethics, and also the history of colonization and Christianity in those societies. The knowledge of these will provide us with the necessary background for understanding, and also help us find strategies for resolving the precarious conditions prevailing in third world societies. In the following chapters, then, we turn our attention to the encounter of these traditional elements with those of the Western world.

Chapter 4

Reconstructing the Structure of Akan Traditional Society and Religion

A Short Overview of Akan Traditional Society

The Akans are a group of people who occupy the southeastern part of the Ivory Coast and the southern half of Ghana with the exception of the southeastern part. They occupy mostly the equatorial forest and the coastal areas that lie between the Black Volta River in the north, the Guinea Coast in the south, the Camoe River in the west, and the Volta River in the east. This group of people who have never had a common polity are, however, culturally and ethnically closely related. They are composed of the Fante-Agona, Ahanta, Kwawu, Ashanti, Brong (Bono), Akyem, Wasa, Akuapim, Nzima-Evalue, and Assen-Twifo.[1] They share the same customs, beliefs, social organization, and the same language (which comprises dialects that have slight variations but each of which can be understood by every Akan). Among the languages and dialects—Twi, Fanti, Nzima, for example—that they speak, Twi is the commonest among the Akans in Ghana. It has almost become the lingua franca of Ghana.

Because they dwell mostly in the forest areas, the Akans are predominantly farmers, with some fishing done in the coastal areas. Although traditionally Akan farmers are subsistent farmers, today, having been integrated into the global economic and political systems—which, of course, do not favour them—they produce, among other crops like cola, plantain, cassava, yams, rice, pineapples, bananas, oranges, maize, tomatoes, coffee, etc., about half of the world's supply of cocoa. Akan farmers are usually craftsmen as well and they engage in crafts- manship as a hobby. However, today craftsmanship is taken up as full-time job by some Akans. Some of the people are em- ployed in government services, others in private services, while others are engaged in trading. It must be mentioned here also that the vast territory which the Akans occupy is also very rich in minerals—gold, bauxite, manganese, etc.—and so mining activities are also a source of employment for the people.

The Akan society is a matrilineal society; lineage is traced from the mother's line. By virtue of one's birth one becomes entitled to all the rights and privileges of the lineage. And being also an exogamous society (a society where one marries outside the clan and family), an Akan does not lose his or her membership rights and status in a lineage through marriage or migration. Among the Akans succession, inheritance, and political allegiance are determined by matrilineal descent. For this reason, an individual's maternal uncles and aunts form the inheritance group. And for this reason also, real control and jural rights over the individual come from the head of the lineage (*abusua panyin*) and the maternal uncle (*wofa*) respec- tively. This is so because among the Akans, marriage confers rights in uxorem but it does not confer rights in *genetricem*. "A child's *genitor* is not necessarily his *pater*. In other words when- ever a man marries a woman, and brings forth offspring by her, the man is the biological father but that does not neces- sarily mean that he is the sociological father. In terms of social relationship, the child's maternal uncle has rights of the so- cialization of the child."[2] The father's responsibility to the off- spring, and thus to the "nuclear family" (which includes the wife), is the provision of shelter and food. "As the children grow older, their father's responsibilities to them decrease, but during their childhood the father is the person upon whom the children may depend."[3]

The idea of the matrilineal descent is derived from the Akan conception of human personality. It is the view of the Akans that the individual is a composite of physical (*Mogya*) and spiri- tual (*Sunsum* and *Okra*) entities. The physical entity, *Mogya* ("blood"), is received from the mother. It is the belief of the

Akans that it is the *mogya* which makes the child a human being, and hence where the child receives his or her lineage identity and membership. In other words, it is the transmission of blood from the mother to the child which forms the base of the lineage (*abusua*). The *abusua*, and here one's maternal lineage, is a localized group of both men and women who trace their physical descent through the female line to a common ancestress. This lineage is located in a chiefdom which it regards as its home. The head of the lineage, who is usually an older male member of the extended family, is responsible for making economic, political, and social decisions which affect the group as a whole and its individual members. He settles disputes and conflicts among members. He is the custodian of the morals of the group and the property rights are invested in his authority. He represents the group on the chief's council. As we have indicated above, succession to an office or inheritance of property are determined by a person's matrilineal descent.[4]

The spiritual entity, *Sunsum* or *Ntoro*, is transmitted by the father to the child. The Akans believe that the *sunsum* entity, transmitted by the male, mingles with the *mogya* element of the female partner and "gives rise in the first instance and after the sexual act, to conception, and moulds and builds up the embryo."[5] However, it is thought that the *sunsum* from the father moulds the child and is the source of the individual's personality and character: ". . . a person is believed to have the same temperament as his father. From spirit come his distinctive personal gifts and virtues. Thus, the Akan proverb *Oba se ose nanso owo nkyi*, meaning, "The child is like the father but he has his kinship ties.""[6] It is believed also that a child "cannot thrive if its father's *sunsum* is alienated." This explains why "a priest sometimes traces the cause of a child's illness to the grief of its father's *sunsum*."[7] This point brings out the need for a further clarification of the father's position in the "nuclear family." As Manoukian has pointed out, although legally the father's position in the "nuclear family" is a weak one because of the fact that it is the "blood" tie, the *abusua*, that really counts, "the supposed power of the father's . . . *ntoro*, which protects his children, helps to mitigate the importance of the *abusua*, so that in practice the father is a good deal more than the mere figurehead in the family which he might seem to be theoretically."[8] The upbringing of a child in the Akan community, then, as we shall see in this work, becomes the responsibility of the maternal, as well as the paternal families. And since the Akans traditionally live in small communities, a child's upbringing becomes a communal affair.

The *Okra* ("soul") is a life principle. It is a small indestructible part of God which is given, and with it one's destiny (*nkrabea*), to the individual on conception by God, the Creator. The *Okra* is considered the most important part of the human being because in the first place, it is the divine spark in the individual which makes one what one is. In other words it gives meaning to life. In the second place, it is the most important part because it is immortal. When a person dies, the *okra* does not die, but lives on. It returns to join its creator and the ancestors. Since the Akans have a very strong belief in reincarnation, it is said that an individual who considers his or her work on earth unfinished may decide to come back in a different shape, but with the same fate, and finish it. Thus, for the Akan, death is not an end to life, but rather its extension. "The eternal existence of the *okra* is expressed by the Dormaa [people] with the following words: *Onyame nwu na mawu* or *Onyame bewu na mawu–Onyame* does not die, therefore I also will not die; or if God dies, I will also die; but since God is immortal, so am I."[9] So for the Akan, since God is immortal and the *okra* ("soul") is a part of God given to the individual on conception, the *okra* too is immortal. The belief in the immortality of the *okra*, and its association with its creator, gives rise to the veneration of ancestors, which in turn, as we shall see shortly below, gives religious character to traditional institutions, particularly chieftaincy.

The Akans organize their society around the system of chieftaincy. Chieftaincy in Akanland has two separate offices: the office of the chief (male) and the office of the queen-mother (female). The chief occupies the central position in the society. He is the focus of unity in the society. The chief is so regarded for several reasons. One is that the throne which he occupies "is the symbol of the local community's or the nation's unity. It enshrines the religious and cultural identity of the people and links the living with their dead ancestors. . . The chief, or king, is the manifest embodiment of the ancestors. . . ."[10] Another reason is that it is the chief's duty to reconcile the interests of the various lineage leaders for the common good of the society, rather than each of them pursuing only the interests of his own lineage. So the chief, with the aid of his Council of Elders (most of whom are heads of the lineages), controls the administration of the society. The social and political organization of the society, therefore, is his responsibility. Attack on chieftaincy, then, means interference or disruption of the administrative machinery of the people.

The queen-mother is constitutionally regarded as the 'mother' of the chief; but more often she is the sister or mother or niece (sister's daughter) or mother's sister, and so on, of the chief. In short, the Akan society being a matrilineal society, the ascent to both the thrones or stools of chief and queen-mother is by matrilineal descent. It is only people who are born into the royal house who have claim to the throne. The queen-mother "is expected to advise the Chief about his conduct and may scold and reprimand him in a way not permitted to his councillors."[11] She is consulted in matrimonial affairs within the royal lineage. She is regarded as the authority on kinship relations in the royal lineage. And when the throne of a chief is vacant, and families of candidates are vying for the position, she proposes a successor; however, the final choice of the candidate to the throne is the consensus decision of the council of elders who represent the people. The process of choosing a chief, then, is in many respects democratic. Traditionally, a chief or any leader cannot be installed or dethroned against the will of the people, as it happened during the colonial period.

As indicated above, the throne of the chief, or king, enshrines the unity of the community or nation and also the ancestral power and, so, it is sacred and religious. It is therefore expected of the one who occupies it "to be pure in heart and to hold high ethical and moral standards." It is the belief of the Akan that "the ancestors bring peace and harmony to the society through the monarch's upright and spiritual rule. The success and fertility of the monarch are believed to influence the fertility of the people and their land and animals—infertility casts suspicion on the moral, religious and ethical life of the chief."[12] Thus, for prosperity, peace, unity, and harmony to reign in the land, the chief must be a responsible individual and a person of integrity. A chief who does not prove to be mature, and whose period of reign may be filled with widespread disease, drought, famine, and other economic, political, and religious calamities may be dethroned by the people. Such a chief is seen to have lost his spiritual potency, the mainstay of his office.

The spiritual character of chieftaincy, derived from the ancestral spirits, embodies and gives meaning and force to all other traditional institutions. This spiritual character of chieftaincy, as we shall see in the next chapter, was a major reason for the Akans' chagrin of the colonial administrators' meddling with chieftaincy. Thus, it was a rallying force in the people's resistance against the colonizers' encroachment on their land and traditional institutions. In other words, religious factors played a role, however subtle, in the Akans' resistance against colonialism.

The Akans believe that the ancestors are the actual owners of the land. The chief, who is the manifest embodiment of the ancestors, is the custodian of the land. As one who holds the general interests and welfare of the community at heart, the chief is responsible for the fair distribution and proper utilization and care of the land. The land is administered by him and his elders on behalf of the people. It is the right of every member of the community to have land for one's use—to farm or build on it. But the land does not become the private property of the individual. Strangers who do not belong to the community (i.e., residents who do not belong to the lineages which fall directly under the rule of the chief), can have access to the land only by permission of the chief. In that case the user rents it. And any agricultural products and buildings that the individual puts on the land are the individual's properties; but the land itself and any minerals which may be on it belong to the chief, and thus to the stool which symbolizes the community. The land can be taken away from the user any time by the chief and his elders. Thus, strictly speaking, it can be said that the Akans have "farm tenure, not land tenure in the classical meaning of the phrase."[13] It is not difficult, then, to see why in the wake of colonialism, Africans, with some perception of the colonial officials impulse—taking over their land, and interfering in their modes of life—resisted.

The above is the brief description of Akan traditional society. Akan society represented earlier modes of production. And like any other modes of production, there were internal conflicts and struggles between the elements—economic, political, social, and religious. In other words, it is not hard to imagine, in the Akan society, internal conflicts, wranglings and struggles between and among family members, chiefs, chiefs and elders and vice versa; misappropriation of stool and family properties by some chiefs and elders, and so forth. However, these cannot be compared to conflicts and struggles increasingly generated, interference, and disintegration of a people's worldview and, thus, the devastating impact on their general well-being, in the event of a clash of their social, economic, and political institutions with a different mode(s) of production.

The Structure of Akan Traditional Religion

As previously indicated, African traditional institutions thrive on religion. Religious beliefs and practices are essential components of the peoples' modes of production. Some knowledge of their traditional religions is, therefore, necessary for understanding further their cultural, economic, political, and social organisations.

Academic discourses on African peoples frequently and necessarily touch on the religion. Numerous studies have been undertaken exclusively on the traditional beliefs and practices. However, confusion still persists among both African and expatriate thinkers on whether the continent of Africa has one religion or many religions. While persistently addressing some distortions and misinterpretations of African traditions, and particularly the religion, and arguing that the religion be given due recognition among other religions, some thinkers tend to base their claim on conformity rather than recognizing variations in African cultures, customs, social formations, religious beliefs and practices. It is necessary, in this part of this study, to address this issue.

It is the argument of Nadel, Idowu, Dopamu, and the others that the religion of Africa can be spoken of in the singular. The argument, in the words of Idowu, is based on the fact that

> a careful look, through actual observation and comparative discussions with Africans from various parts of the continent, will show, first and foremost, that there is a common factor which the coined word *negritude* will express aptly. There is a common Africanness about the total culture and religious beliefs and practices of Africa. . . . With regard to the concept of God, there is a common thread, however tenuous in places, running throughout the continent. . . .it is in fact this one factor of the concept, with particular reference to the 'character', of Deity which makes it possible to speak of a religion of Africa.[14]

It is the claim of this study that it is true that there are similarities among the traditional lives and ideas of the peoples, and also that the similarities are much more evident in the traditional religions and particularly in the aspect of the concept of God. However, we cannot speak of Akan traditional religion, for example, as representative of African traditional religion, nor as representative of West African, nor even as that of Ghanaian traditional religion. This is so because,

> . . . there is a plethora of African cultures. Partly as a result of hard geographical and physical conditions, there is a gulf between Africa north of the Sahara and Africa south of the Sahara, between East and West Africa. To confound the issue, within West Africa and even within one country, like Ghana, there are remarkable differences based on tribal background. Thus the Akan groups of Ghana are by and large matrilineal, while the Ewe and the Ga groups of Ghana are patrilineal. Again in some tribes, e.g., the Akan of West Africa, the spirits of the ancestors are very important, while among others, e.g., the Masai of East Africa, they are no use.[15]

Since it is Akan religion, it is unique to the Akan. Commenting on the generalizations that are often made in representing one traditional religion as the traditional religion of all Africans, Assimeng writes:

> The obverse, and equally insufficient illuminating pattern of this presentation about single countries, is where Akan traditional religion, for example, is often taken perhaps unconsciously to typify the cosmological thought of the whole of Ghana, as the writings of Busia (1954), Sarpong (1974), and Gyekye (1987) seem to indicate. Even

more controversial is the situation where Akan cosmology is assumed to represent that of Africa, as appears to be the case of Abraham's (1962) characterization of the 'mind of Africa'; or in *Osofo* formerly (Reverend) Vincent Damuah's attempt to present the theology of what he calls Afrikania religion (cf. Damuah, V. K., *Afrikania Handbook; Reformed African Traditional Religion*. Accra: 1983). A similar assumption seems to underlie K. O. K. Onyioha's conception of Godian religion in Nigeria (cf. his *The National Church of Nigeria, its Catechism and Credo*; and *A New Civilization from Africa*. . .[16]

This is not to say, however, that it would be inappropriate, when speaking of a particular people, to draw examples from other peoples of the continent where such examples are common to them.

Also, I wish to emphasize here that the differences in African religious beliefs and practices must not be viewed in any way as offsetting the uniqueness and meaningfulness of African traditional religions. Thinkers must acknowledge that there are many traditional religions in Africa just as there are many customs and cultures in the continent.

Another area where there is little agreement among commentators is the area of the scope and content of the structure of African traditional religions. This disagreement is one of many which arise out of critical responses of new scholars (both African and expatriate) to colonial scholarship, which often failed and continue to fail to give accurate presentation and interpretation of African traditions and practices. This also shows how colonial scholarship failed to see the interconnectedness of African belief systems, and the role the beliefs and practices play in the mundane life of the peoples. In analyzing the structure of the traditional religions, Idowu accepts with reservations the four elements which Talbot says appear, though compounded, to be the main elements of the religion of the inhabitants of Southern Provinces of Nigeria; the elements are polytheism, anthropomorphism, animism, and ancestral worship. According to Idowu, we can accept the element 'polytheism' "with reservation as an element in the structure of the religion, if we are thinking only of the pantheons of the divinities. For it is only in this connection that we can predict pluralism at all of the religion." Talbot is right, according to Idowu, "in saying that 'polytheism' is a compound part of the whole structure."[17] But the question is, can we accept polytheism as an element of the traditional religion even if it is "a compound part of the whole structure", or even when we are "thinking only of the pantheon of divinities"? It seems Idowu is being too accommodating here! It is true that the traditional religions make room for a "pantheon" of divinities, but the religions are not polytheistic, as the word is understood in its modern usage.

'Polytheism' is defined by the Webster's Encyclopedic Dictionary of the English Language as "belief in or worship of more than one god". If we accept this definition, then the word cannot be ascribed to any traditional religion in Africa. As Max Assimeng notes,

> Arguments have been raised as to whether African religion as a whole should be seen as monotheism or polytheism. We believe, however, that one could perhaps answer the question, whether the West African traditionalist worshipped a single god or multiplicity of gods, by stating clearly that he worshipped the one god through the many gods created by the one god. This is not an unclear statement, as it appears to be at first.

He goes on to quote Dzobo, who in analyzing the traditional Ewe society in Ghana, has written:

> The Anfoega-Ewe in their religious life may appear to be worshippers of many gods but in their own thinking they are not, because they believe in one supreme god called *Se* whose varied attributes find embodiment in different other gods on earth.[18]

Idowu rejects the element 'anthropomorphism'. As he rightly puts it, 'anthropomorphism' is only a way of making a conceptualization of the Divine Power and powers and therefore cannot be regarded as being "a separate component element in the structure." For there is nothing really 'cultic' about it. 'Anthropomorphism' "is a prevailing atmosphere of religion at every level, in every place."[19] We wonder if anybody would attempt at all to reckon 'anthropomorphism' as an element of the structure of Judaism, and for that matter Christianity, or Islam.

Another term which has been commonly used for the so-called "primitive" religions, and which Talbot classifies as one of his four elements of the structure of African traditional religion, is 'animism'. This word can be traced to the work of E.

B. Tylor who used it extensively in his book *Primitive Culture*. The word has its root in the Latin word *anima*, which means breath, life, soul. Tylor and his followers imagined that "primitive" people saw this *anima* as existing in every object—plants, rivers, stones, etc. In other words, "primitive" people perceived every object as having its own soul; and therefore for them the world was filled with 'spirit beings'. This led Tylor, who considered the evolution of religion as having its starting point with "primitive" thought, to define 'belief in spirit beings'. We need not labour over this theory. Is the definition applicable to African traditional religions, and for that matter other traditional religions of other parts of the world? According to Idowu, we accept 'animism' as an element in the structure of the traditional religion "only in the strict sense that it signifies the recognition and acceptance of the existence of spirits, often in an uncharacterized sense, with cults existing in consequence of the recognition and acceptance."[20] Mbiti, on the other hand, does not seem to be satisfied with Idowu's conclusion. He insists that:

> . . . African people are aware of all these elements of religion: God, spirits and divinities are part of the traditional body of beliefs. Christianity and Islam acknowledge the same type of spiritual beings. The theory of religious evolution, in whichever direction, does not satisfactorily explain or interpret African religions. Animism is not an adequate description of these religions and it is better for that term to be abandoned once and for all.[21]

The last defining element of the traditional religion which Talbot puts forward is ancestor worship. There is absolutely no question concerning the centrality in Akan religion of the concern for the relationship between Africans and their departed relatives. While accepting the relationship between the peoples and their departed relatives as "definitely a component element in the structure," as Idowu says, there is need "to examine whether the term 'ancestor worship' is appropriate or not."[22]

After examining other authors' analyses and classifications of West African Religion and the religion of the Ashanti, Idowu suggests five component elements which go "in reality . . . into the making of African traditional religion." In his view, the elements are "belief in God, belief in the divinities, belief in spirits, belief in the ancestors, and the practice of magic and medicine, each with its own consequent, attendant cult."[23] While accepting some parts of the structure as Idowu has sketched it, I would like, however, to make a modification. I prefer to place the belief in God, the belief in the divinities, the belief in the spirits, and the belief in the ancestors under one heading, viz., the spirit world. I do not in any way say that they are the same, nor am I confusing them. I firmly believe, as do Idowu and others who have seriously studied traditional religion, and as do Africans themselves whose traditional religion it is, that these categories of beings are different entities, though not unrelated. Also, I add to the structure another element which has often been overlooked: the element of religious functionaries. I think that it is not doctrine (or faith) alone that makes religion. For a religion to function it needs rituals. And it needs cultic figures (priests) and cultic participants who express their acknowledgement of the divine through beliefs and practices. It seems that if we speak only of God, ancestors, divinities, spirits, magic and medicine in African traditional religion, then we are touching only on the belief system, and on only a tiny aspect of the cosmic structure of the religion.[24]

I thus set forth the structure of the Akan traditional religion as comprising: i) the nature and structure of the spirit-world, ii) the practice of magic and medicine, and iii) the religious functionaries. I will describe each component of the structure with the aim of setting the stage for a proper understanding of later discussions in this study of the religious and medical situations in Ghanaian society today. In other words, a fuller comprehension of the dynamic structural unity of African traditions, particularly religious beliefs and practices and medical practice, will help us see more adequately the force behind the constant reproduction of traditional elements and, also, the effects of "traditional" colonialism and neo-colonialism in modern Africa.

The Nature and Structure of the Spirit World

The Akan depends very much on the spirit-world. The Akan believes in the spirit-being whom he or she commonly calls Nyame (Onyame) or Onyankopon. It is the belief of the people that this spirit-being is the greatest of all beings; he controls the whole universe; he is the Supreme Being; he is before and above all things. *Asase tere, na Onyame ne panyin,* 'The earth is wide but Onyame is Chief.' We can call this Supreme Being God. The explanation of the names which the Akan gives to God affirm how supremely he is regarded. The name Onyame is connected with the root *onyame,* which basically means 'shining' or 'brightness'. Nyame or Onyame means a bright, glorious God. Onyankopon is derived from *Nyame-koro-pon* (Nyame—the One—the Great).[25] The Akan calls God Twereduampon—the general sense of which is the God in whom one may put all trust. The Akan believes that God is the creator of the universe; he sustains it and he is the final authority in everything. He has power over life and death. The power and authority of God is recognized by Akans. "Atheism is foreign to the Akan because, as his proverb puts it, *obi nkyere abofra Onyame*—since God is self-evident, no one teaches a child to know God."[26] The attributes which the Akan gives to God are pointers to his or her concept of God. The Akan, like other Africans, recognizes the eternity, loving-kindness, omniscience, omnipresence, omnipotence, immanence, holiness, justice, mercy, faithfulness, and transcendence of God.[27] The nature and attributes of God are frequently heard in the every day conversations, songs, poetry, and drums of the people.[28] In every day conversation if one asks the old Akan man or woman, for example, *"Wo honam mu e?* 'How are you?' [he or she] will probably reply, *Nyame adaworoma, me ho ye,* 'By God's grace, I am well.' Similarly, when anyone in trouble is asked how his affairs are progressing, he will often answer, with an appropriate gesture, *Nyame nko ara,* meaning that the future is in the hands of 'God alone'."[29]

I do not need to belabour the fact that the Akan, and for that matter the African, has strong belief in God and sees Onyame as the highest and greatest of all beings. There have been many repudiations by both expatriates and Africans of assertions by earlier writers like A. B. Ellis that the people of Ghana's conception of God

is really a god borrowed from Europeans and only thinly disguised. . . . To the negro of Gold Coast [now Ghana], Nyankopon is a material and tangible being, possessing a body, legs, arms, in fact all the limbs, and the senses, and faculties of man . . . no sacrifice was offered to

him. . . . There were no priests for Nyankopon . . . consequently no
form of worship of Nyankopon was established.[30]

The Akan regards God as a Supreme Being; and God, being
such a powerful and supreme being, is not to be approached
lightly or bothered with trivialities. He has therefore given
authority to other beings—*abosom* (spirit powers, as I prefer to
call them), and the ancestors who act in his place. They are,
therefore, the vehicles, intermediaries, through whom the
people encounter God.

The ancestors, or the living-dead (as Mbiti prefers to call
them), are the deceased members of the clan, lineage, family,
who led virtuous lives while on earth and who are now dwell-
ing with God. It might be useful here to discuss the Akan conception of the ancestor, which is widely shared throughout
Africa. It is the belief of Africans, and thus Akans, that a person becomes, soon after death, "a living dead—he is a 'spirit'
in the sense that he is no longer in the body, yet he retains
features which describe him in physical terms. He retains his
personal name, so that when he appears to human members
of his family, they recognize him as so-and-so. He is counted as
part of the family in many ways, even though people know and
realize that he has forsaken them."[31] Though the person is dead,
he or she is regarded as still alive; form and will are attributed
to him or her. The individual still has personality and "he retains features which describe him in physical terms" (form).

> So far as Form is concerned . . . the dead . . . lead a shadow life; the
> fixed outlines and concrete substance of Form have given place to
> something quite nebulous and misty. . . . The dead, again, cannot be
> grasped, but can be seen through; they have no bones. Occasionally
> they are imagined as being smaller than the living. But even though
> the form has disappeared to a great extent, it is still there: the dead
> man resembles the living; he can be recognized, seen and spoken
> to.[32]

In fact the Akan regards the ancestors as 'people', they are
bilingual: "they speak the language of men, with whom they
lived until 'recently'; and they speak the language of the spirits and of God, to whom they are now drawing nearer
ontologically."[33] It is believed that these ancestors come back
to their families, from time to time, to symbolically share meals
with them, ". . . they inquire about family affairs, and may even

warn of impending danger or rebuke those who have failed to follow their special instructions. They are the guardians of family affairs, traditions, ethics and activities."[34] In other words, the ancestors are factors of cohesion in the society.

So far, we have come to understand that the ancestor, the living-dead, is a 'person' who still 'lives' among his or her family members, has dealings with and influence over them—he or she can rebuke some members who fail to go by his or her instructions. In this regard, the dead then are "more potent than the living: their will imposes itself: it is irresistible. They are superior in strength and insight. . ." Thus the ancestors are seen to have power and authority; and their requests and injunctions must never be refused or disobeyed. The Akans believe that the power and authority which the ancestor has are derived from God. The ancestor has the power and authority precisely because he or she is closer to God, and also, and more importantly, because God has made him or her an intermediary between himself and the people. The ancestors are expected to relay the requests of the people to God, and sometimes carry God's response back to them. The ancestors can use the power they have to harm or to help. Many evils are attributed to the work of the ancestors. They can bring drought or famine. They can bring upon the people sickness and death. Calamities that befall the people are believed to have been caused by the ancestors in disapproval of the misdeeds of their relatives. On the other hand, the ancestors can bring blessing and abundance, health and healing upon the descendants. They can cause rain and also give fertility to the earth to facilitate the growth of crops. Fortunes that come peoples way are believed to have come from them.

> One ancestor may indicate to one of his own people the remedy to an illness in his dream. . . . Another may see to it that the girls of his lineage are endowed with fecundity. . . . Thus the ancestral spirits are continuously involved in the affairs of the living; but they manifest their powers and interest characteristically in the unforeseeable occurrences which upset the normal rhythm of life.[35]

It is important to note here that not all who die become ancestors; there are conditions to be fulfilled while the person is alive. The influence one enjoyed during one's life-time, and the circumstances under which one died are some of the con-

ditions under which one become an ancestor. "In virtue of
their rank, for instance, tribal leaders usually possess power
after death also, and there are even cases where continued life
after death is limited to the bearers of power. . . ."[36] To be regarded as an ancestor, one must have lived to a ripe old age
and lived in an exemplary manner and done much to enhance
the standing and prestige of the family, clan, or tribe. ". . .[The]
deceased must have a reputation which gives them power and
respect among the living. This reputation is one of having fulfilled the ideals of their society . . ."[37] i.e., the individual must
have led an exemplary life, by tribal standards.

> A person who does not cause unnecessary troubles, or abuse his el-
> ders, juniors or equals, especially in public, is a good person. . . . A
> thief is a public menace; nobody wants him in his company. His spirit
> is unreliable. A bully, especially if he is a man who threatens women,
> a person who takes other people's wives, a talkative, an alcoholic and
> an excessively extravagant person are all considered evil persons.
> Laziness, refusal to work when you are strong, and cowardice are also
> frowned upon. Anyone who is known to be consistently indulging in
> these evils cannot hold a responsible office, and no one will name a
> child after him. He is not a person to be imitated. He cannot be an
> ancestor, for if a living person is not good, his "ghost" cannot be good.
> But it is a good "ghost" who blesses his people.[38]

The conditions which, when fulfilled, make one an ancestor
form the basis for the attention, respect and veneration the
Akan gives to the ancestor. A person can be "canonized" an
ancestor only when he or she was virtuous while alive. Because
the ancestor is one who had an unquestionable moral, spiritual and social life while alive, the Akan believes that his or
her departure from among his or her clan, tribe, and family
members brings him or her "nearer" to God than an ordinary
person would be. The ancestors are regarded as the friends of
God. They are seen by the Akan as mediators between him or
her and God. Therefore the attitude of the living towards them
is nothing more than reverence. The ancestor is not regarded
as God, and therefore is not worshipped. The ancestors are
revered and venerated. They are considered "intermediaries,
divinely given channels of contact with the supreme being or
ultimate reality however conceived."[39] Explaining the veneration given to ancestors, Shorter writes: "ancestor veneration is
comparable to the Christian cult of saints in so far as it is an

expression of the moral ideals of society. . ."[40] An individual is made a saint in the Christian tradition because the person lived the moral ideals of the Christian faith, ideals similar to those of Akan traditional religion.

Another aspect of the spirit-world is the spirit powers—spirits and divinities, which the Akan calls *abosom*. The etymology of the word, *abosom* is not certain. *Obo* in Akan means stone or rock; *abo* is the plural meaning stones. *Som* means serve or worship. Thus *abosom* literally means the worship or serving of stones or rocks. The confusion surrounding this word has led Williamson to say that ". . . as trees and rivers and other objects can be *abosom*, this derivation is either false, or the word is of so ancient an origin that a word once narrowly applied has grown a wider significance."[41] Commenting on the same issue, Pobee writes, "it appears the word which originally describes an act has been transferred to the object of the act. Whatever the etymology, gods are not always in the form of stones or rock. . ."[42] And in fact, as Pobee has indicated, the most popular and widely recognized ones in the Akan society—Bosomtwe, Tano, Bea, and Bosompo—are not in the form of stones; Bosomtwe is a lake, Tano and Bea are rivers, and Bosompo is the ocean. So the "etymological association of the god with a rock may be a hint at the security found in the gods, rock being a symbol of stability and strength, albeit derived from the Supreme Being."[43] It is essential to note of the *abosom*, as Pobee and also Williamson point out, that they are derived powers. They are regarded as the children of God. They are also the voices of God through whom God speaks to and also receives messages from human beings.

The *obosom* can be in the form of any natural phenomenon—a stone, a tree, a river, a mountain, a lake, the ocean, and a hill. It should be noted that the *abosom* are not the hill or the ocean or the tree or the stone itself, but they may from time to time be contacted at a concrete habitation, though they are not confined therein. Mbiti emphasizes this when he writes:

> Where some natural phenomena or objects are personified, or thought to be inhabited by spiritual beings, it is possible that people may address their prayers to them. In such cases, the prayers are addressed to the "divinity" or "spirit" and not the object or phenomenon as such.[44]

Some of the *abosom* have wider reputations, others have local significance only, while others are tutelary deities of towns, villages, or families. Like the ancestors, the *abosom* can be harmful and also benevolent; they take interest in the welfare of human beings, and they punish when the occasion demands it. Like the ancestors, the *abosom*, though without physical bodies, have "personalities, namely their values, attitudes, and thoughts" which are likened to those of human beings. Thus they command the attention and respect of human beings. The similarities between the roles the *abosom* and the ancestors play may tempt one to think they are the same. But, they are not. The ancestors, as we have explained above, are the spirits of departed (once loving, caring, devoted) relatives, while the *abosom* belong to the "race" of spirits; and "whereas the gods may be treated with contempt [and rejected] if they fail to deliver the goods expected of them, the ancestors, like the Supreme Being, are always held in reverence. . ."[45]

It is important to raise here the issue of terminologies that have contributed to the confusion surrounding the debates over the monotheistic nature of African traditional religions. Here, I am referring specifically to the terms 'god' and 'lesser god'. From the time Europeans first came into contact with Africans to this day, that spirit being which Akans call *obosom* has been referred to by Europeans and also Akans as 'god' and 'lesser god'. In my judgement, this terminology is inappropriate and misleading. Because the Akan language (and probably African languages and dialects in general), and the Akan people do not refer to and regard the *obosom*, in any context, as a being whose power is absolute and complete in itself as the word 'god' seems to connote. Its power is derived from and regulated by Onyame. People approach it because they see it as an envoy of God. In fact the closest the two come to bearing a similar title in the Akan language is when each of them is referred to as Nana, or when each of them is spoken of as a *tumi* (a power). And even then Onyame is unambiguously distinguished from the *obosom* by being referred to as *tumi-nyinaa-wura* (literally, 'possessor- or creator-of-all-power') or having the proper name attached to the title Nana—Nana Nyame. The point here is simply that foreign categories should not be forced on the African. The *obosom* is never 'god' or 'lesser god' but a spirit power or being, or simply *obosom*. And since African traditional religions are not polytheistic, proper and adequate terminology must be used to refer to the *obosom*.

The Akan traditional religion also recognizes the existence of evil powers (which Assimeng prefers to call *honhom fi*). If there is any hierarchical structure among them, then their chief would be *Sasabonsam*. *Sasabonsam* is said to be a forest monster who is in league with sorcerers and *abayifo* (witches), the latter being his chief agents. The powers of these evil beings are not derived. They are beings who are inimical to human beings; they frighten people, cause disasters, afflictions—illnesses, poverty, deaths, barrenness. They can influence people to do bad things. In short, these beings are harmful and dangerous, and therefore are neither loved nor revered; the Akan holds them in contempt. The fact that evil powers can cause people to do evil things does not absolve human beings from the evil they commit.

According to Assimeng, this issue of *honhom fi*, which for him is the "central focus of religious activity in African traditional societies. . .", has not been taken seriously by students of traditional religion in Africa. It is worth quoting him at length.

> It has been a general practice in the analyses of traditional religion, to pursue issues concerning the concepts of gods, their attributes, and the destinies of men. It has often been asserted that the religious activities of men are directed ultimately either to the High God, or to any of the several spiritual intermediaries according to specific needs and situations. Rather, however, I believe the central focus of religious activity in African traditional societies seems to be the warding off of what the Akan calls *honhom fi* from the affairs of men.

He continues:

> This preoccupation of the traditional believer appears to me to be the central basis, although as yet under-investigated domain, of traditional religiousness. Consequently I prefer to label the process as the constant enactment of the ritual of redemption. . . .What one has to consider, is that what men look for in religious behaviour, without exception, are security and satisfaction in their day-to-day world of experience.

He then goes on to quote Simon Patten: "religion begins not with a belief in God but with an emotional opposition to removable evils."[46]

In my view, the discussion on *honhom fi* is very important because African societies are pervaded by this belief of a powerful evil force which causes all kinds of afflictions and misfortunes to human beings. In fact the Akans, and for that matter other Africans, do not see events happening without some involvement of the spirits. Thus for Akans, there are no merely "natural" explanations. Every mishap is to be investigated to find out how and, more importantly, why it is happening to one person and not to another. It would be premature to say, and Assimeng himself does not claim, that *honhom fi* is the central focus of the Akan traditional religion. However, I believe that it deserves further study; it could be a basis for the content of theodicy in Akan traditional religion. As Assimeng suggests,

> It seems . . . no adequate understanding of symbolic classification in traditional religion in West Africa is, therefore, possible without an attempt to clarify and locate the nature, source, and manifestation of this entity of *honhom fi* which is believed to pervade society's cosmic universe. It is this entity which gives rise to the several and elaborate attitudes and actions that are directed towards the understanding of life, its meaning and its drama. In search for fertility and for plenty, and the general survival requirements for societal existence, the notion of *honhom fi*—the unpredictable, unseen, vital force with its attributes of strength, power, and action—is very pertinent.[47]

Evil powers remain a concern of Akan society. These concerns help to explain the rapid growth and popularity of the African Independent Churches, which continue the tradition of conceptualizing life in terms of evil powers in the lives of the people and therefore work to find solutions to them.[48]

However, traditional African religiousness should not be simplified with the issue of *honhom fi*. Because even granting that the warding off of *honhom fi* from the affairs of the peoples is "the central focus of religious activity in African traditional societies", it does not, however, neutralize that fact that "religious activities of men are directed ultimately either to the High God, or to any of the several intermediaries. . ." For, in my view, Africans are not unaware that the religious acts they perform are directed to a more powerful being who can ward off evil and grant them the satisfaction and security they are seeking. For example, the Akans, as indicated above, call that being Twereduampon or Tumi-Nyinaa-Wura, a power which subdues all evils. In other words, although they may perform religious activities to ward off *honhom fi*, peoples in traditional African societies direct these activities to a powerful being. The *honhom fi* should not be interpreted as the core of traditional religious behaviour.

The Practice of Magic and Medicine

The concerns of magic and medicine are as primordial as human societies themselves, because sufferings and illnesses and other misfortunes have always been part and parcel of human life. And in seeking solutions to and deliverance from them human beings have resorted to various means. Among them has been the practice of magic and medicine.

In the context of African societies, as in many other societies of the world, magic, like medicine, cannot be understood separately from religion. In fact, many thinkers have preoccupied themselves with the question whether or not religion and magic are the same; or whether they are related; and whether religion precedes magic or vice versa.[49] It is not necessary here to resolve these debates. It is sufficient to note that in the African context we can safely say that magic comes within the scope of the traditional religions. For there are cults of certain divinities which have definite practices of magic connected with them. Also, in their ritual performances Africans, like most ritual performers in other religious traditions, more often than not, intermingle religion and magic "in the fact that certain things *must* be done according to definite prescriptions or certain words said repetitively and in particular order."[50] Idowu makes an interesting observation concerning the intermingling of magic and religion and how in practice they are confused with each other. He says:

> For example, prayer often becomes so repetitive that efficacy comes to be attached to the correct repetition rather than to the spirit and content of prayer. It is also believed that certain elements of prayers must be repeated a stated number of times, . . .special divine names called a number of times in a certain order. There are Christian denominations which believe that certain rituals must be said in a particular language or in archaic or cryptic formulae. In Islam, all the main rituals must still be universally said in Arabic. In each of these

cases, it is believed that efficacy depends on the form rather than the spirit; and this is magic.[51]

While they acknowledge the practice of magic in their religions, African beliefs do, at the same time, "recognize a clear distinction between what is man-made and what is of the spirit." They also distinguish between licit (good) magic and illicit (bad) magic.

> There is . . . a definite practice of magic connected with the cults of certain divinities. The divinity Esu among the Yoruba, Agwu or Ekwensu of the Igbo, in Nigeria could be invoked as a tutelary divinity in connection with licit or illicit magic. . . . At the same time, most divinities do not regard magic in the sense of fetish favourably. One of the praise titles of Sopona, . . .is 'One who causes medicine or magic designed for wicked ends to be thrown away.' This is true of the Dahomean counterpart, Sagbata. Tano, the archdivinity in Ashanti, hates magic.[52]

As the above quotation indicates, among the Ashantis, thus the Akans, there is the practice of magic, but its practice (in the sense of fetishism or illicit magic or sorcery) is not generally regarded favourably. It is often associated with the dealings of witches and sorcerers and other evil beings. The Akan believes that the individual who possesses magic works the same way as the witch does, only that the magician uses visible objects in order mystically to attain his or her end. Despite the fact that magic employs technique, it also recognizes the transcendental power, a power beyond human beings. The individual who practices magic believes that the powers that are utilized "are spiritual, even if lower in the hierarchy of forces than are the gods."[53] The magician believes that "there are powers that are hidden, secrets that can be tapped; not necessarily that he can force these powers to a different purpose, but there are laws which may be set in motion by the knowledgeable, as an electrician uses the force of nature to light his house."[54]

Medicine is related to magic. In fact, it is difficult to speak of magic separately from medicine in the African context, because both terms are spoken of in the same way at times. Among the Akans the term *aduro* ('medicine') has come to be used for both the medicines ('charm' or 'amulet', which the Akan calls *suman*) whose usage suggests miracle-working or has magical connotations and those herbal and nutritional and chemical and mineral medicines understood in medical terms as medical means of healing. Therefore, it is important for us here to distinguish between them. So the term medicine, as I use it in this context, refers to a charm or amulet or what the Akan calls *suman,* but not to its other meaning as medical means of healing.

The *suman* is a manufactured object. The Akan believes that this charm or amulet contains a power, or breath of life. It may be the abode of a spiritual being or an impersonal force or spirits of an inferior status who generally belong to the vegetable kingdom. Its ingredients could be a single element of a root, a herb, a bark of a tree, a part (such as a piece of bone or a feather) of an animal or a bird; or it can be a mixture of these and other elements. It is believed that the power of the *suman* comes from the particular object or objects which it is made of, or sometimes, directly or indirectly, from a spiritual force like *sasabonsam* (forest monster), a witch, or *motia* (a fairy). They are usually worn by a person around the neck, the waist, the leg, on the arm; or they are hung on posts or trees or buried in the ground where the presence and the efficacy of the power is being sought. Good *suman* (though tolerated, and not encouraged by the Akan) are used as protective measures. They are used to mystically protect families, houses, cattle, fields and other property from thieves, evil and other harmful beings. Some are also "used in the treatment of diseases, in counteracting misfortunes, and in warding off or diluting evil 'power' or witchcraft."[55]

Bad or offensive or illicit *suman* are employed by witches, sorcerers, evil magicians and people who solicit their help to harm or destroy others and their property. They do this, it is believed, by sending "flies, bats, birds, animals, spirits and magical objects (like the 'magic snake' which does not bleed) to achieve their ends; they harm with the 'evil eye'; they dig medicine in the ground where the victim will pass; they put magic objects in the homes or fields of their victim; or send 'death' from a distance; they might change into animals in order to attack their victims; or they place harmful medicines where the victim would come into contact with it."[56] In short, most sicknesses, misfortunes, accidents, deaths, and other tragedies are believed to be caused by the use of bad 'medicine' or mystical power by sorcerers and witches on their victims.[57]

It is useful to clarify the distinction between the *suman* and the *obosom*. The *suman* is not the same as *obosom* nor does it derive its power from the latter. Although some *suman* are closely associated with *abosom*—it is taught that priests make *suman*, and the temples of some *abosom* contain *suman*—the power of the *suman* resides in itself and not in an *obosom*; and also the *suman* works magically while the *obosom* is believed to be an intercessor between the Supreme Being and the people.[58] The relationship that an Akan who possesses *suman* may have with the *suman* is a relationship of fear and not of reverence. While *suman* is believed to bring protection, it is also believed to bring harm to the individual who possesses it if it is not handled or used properly.

I have pointed out the difference between *aduro* as *suman* (a charm or an amulet) and *aduro* as medical means of healing; and I have also pointed out the difference between *suman* as a manufactured magical object and *obosom* as an intercessor. I have also shown how they are employed and who employs them. The lack of clarity of them often led to the colonial officials' and the missionaries' general condemnation of, and proscription against the practices of indigenous medical practitioners, and also, as I will show below, the condescending attitude of some Western educated Africans, particularly health professionals, towards indigenous practitioners.

The Religious Functionaries

As it has been pointed out by several authors, this is an area where terminology is also very disputed. One difficulty is that the duties of these religious functionaries heavily overlap, and for this reason one does not know whether to describe them individually or as a collectivity. Another difficulty is that every individual who plays a leadership role in traditional societies in Africa also plays a functionary role, directly or indirectly, in the traditional religion and, in most cases, also in the traditional medicine. This is much more evident in the Akan society, among others in Africa, where the king or queen is regarded as a divine or sacral ruler, with his or her authority being both human and spiritual. The fertility of the soil, peace in the land, and hence the material and spiritual well-

being of a predominantly farming people (of Akanland), depend upon his or her rule. Even in such societies, I think that
it is necessary and also appropriate to describe the religious
functionaries individually, bearing in mind, however, that in
most cases the "distinctions are convenient for general analysis," but "in practice they do not always apply."[59]

Another problem concerns the collective application of
terms such as sorcerer, witchdoctor, fetish-priest, for a variety
of priests and diviners in Africa. These terms are often used
derogatorily to imply that these people are disreputable, igno-
rant, or evil-working persons. In contrast, Parrinder refers to
them all as Sacred Specialists.[60] Among them it is possible to
distinguish different kinds of functionaries by using different
terms for them. The term priests, he says, may be used to signify "those who are attached to temples and offer sacrifice;
Devotees or Mediums, those connected with the temples and
who give messages from the gods; Diviners, those concerned
with oracles and divination; and Doctors or Medicine-men,
those concerned with healing the sick and preparing magical
medicines."[61] While calling them "'specialists', in virtue of their
specialized office, knowledge and skill in religious matters . . .",
Mbiti also distinguishes between them. He groups them under different terms: (a) The medicine-men; (b) Mediums and
diviners; (c) Rainmakers; (d) Kings, queens and rulers; and (e)
Priests, Prophets and Religious Founders.[62] Appiah-Kubi and
Fink also call these functionaries Priest-Healers and Healers
respectively. Generally, these functionaries have become popularly known in the literature as indigenous or traditional
healers.

According to Fink, the general term the Akans use "for healer
is *asofo (osofo,* sing., *asofo,* pl.)." She says there are two main
groups of *asofo.* These two groups are distinguished from one
another by the terms "*okomfo (okomfo,* sing., *akomfo,* pl., priest,
priestess, religious specialist, priest-healer; *akom,* obsession)
and *dunsini (dunsini,* sing., *nnunsifo,* pl., herbalist). The *abosomfo
(obosomfo,* sing., *abosomfo,* pl., state priest) form an important
subgroup within the group of *akomfo.*"[63] She includes
bonesetters and midwives in the category of herbalists. Fink,
however, is mistaken in one respect. She mistakenly claims that
the *okomfo* and the *dunsini* are *asofo.* The term *asofo* which Akans

use for healers may be translated into English as "priests", but the term is not used to include traditional, indigenous, religious functionaries. It is a term which is used to designate religious leaders who have been ordained, and the so called 'self-ordained' ministers of religious groups or sects or church communities of Christian origin. It is used only in church contexts. In other words, the term *asofo* is used specifically for male and female priests, prophets, healers, and others who are attached to churches, people who minister to others in church milieu. The term "priest" as understood in the English language may be used for the *okomfo* or the *dunsini* for the simple reason that their activities have religious dimensions, but "priest" used in this sense is not equivalent to the Akan term *osofo* used to designate church ministers, healers, prophets, etc. Perhaps the term Fink was looking for, and which is very close in pronunciation and spelling, to the term *osofo*, is *osafo*. *Osafo* means 'one who heals', healer. Another term is *oyaresafo or oyaresani*, which means 'one who heals or cures illnesses and pains.' In any case, the Akans, as Appiah-Kubi puts it, "use terms such as *Okomfo, Obosomfo*, and *Sumankwafo* to designate the various functions of the priest, diviner, and so-called medicine man."[64]

In the Akan situation, and also for the purposes of this study which specifically deals with medical practices, it is appropriate to use the terms as Appiah-Kubi has sketched them. In this sense, we shall exclude from the list the roles of kings and queens as healers in the broad sense of the word. According to Appiah-Kubi, in the traditional setting, the healers who are recognized as handling the various health needs of the people are: 1) the *doctor/physician* (popularly referred to as the *herbalist*); 2) the *diviner*, or the *diagnostician*; 3) the *traditional birth attendant*; 4) *Bone-setters*; and 5) the *exorcist*, known in the literature as the *witch doctor*.[65]

The *doctor/physician*, or the *herbalist*, is the person who "uses the traditional Akan herbal remedies." The *doctor/physician* has a wide knowledge of the medicinal properties of many roots, herbs, bark, leaves, minerals, and parts of birds and animals. Although his or her work may seem to be confined to healing of physical complaints and illnesses, the *doctor/physician's* work has religious dimensions, and therefore he or she has a position in the traditional religion. The *doctor/physician*, as well as his or her patients, share belief in the spiritual universe. They do not look at the treatment as only material or physical, but also as spiritual since illness has a spiritual dimension. Also the attitude of the practitioner towards the remedies he or she uses is spiritual: the herbalist "knows of the *sasa* (souls) of plants and animals and of the deities and spiritual beings that dwell in nature." Therefore, before a herbalist picks a plant that is believed to have a strong *sasa* for medical use, he or she will pray and make sacrifice (egg, fowl, schnapps) to the *sasa* of the plant. "This is to prevent the spiritual forces from turning against the *dunsini* and/or his patients by withholding the plant's curative power."[66]

The *diviner*, or *diagnostician*, has the duty to diagnose. Thus the individual's duty is of medical, priestly, and social nature. The *diviner* is the agent of unveiling mysteries of human life. His or her concerns in the society are to seek "to interpret the mysteries of life, to convey the messages of the gods, to give guidance in daily affairs, and settle disputes, to uncover the past and to look into the future. . . ,"[67] and also to heal. The *diviner* learns to observe well whatever goes on in the community and therefore is able to accumulate a vast store of knowledge concerning human nature. The *diviner's* careful observance and deep acquaintance with human nature helps him or her to operate on psychological levels. "Through special techniques, he tries to elicit the details of the illness in terms of cause and effect. His work is so delicate that he must be very careful both socially and religiously to avoid exaggeration, gossip, and slander."[68] People go to the *diviner* with all kinds of concerns ranging from "betrothals, marriages, before and at the birth of children, at the appointment of a chief or king, before a journey, in time of sickness, in time of loss or theft, and at any time for guidance and comfort."[69] Mbiti also describes the diviner as one who plays the role of a judge, counsellor, supplier "of assurance and confidence during people's crises," adviser, pastor and priest, solver of problems, and revealer of "secrets like . . . imminent danger or coming events."[70] Thus the diviner helps to confirm a sense of orderly, meaningful human existence. He or she is called on both to delimit the causes of physiological, psychological, spiritual, and social problems and to indicate the means of resolution. The nature of the *diviner's* profession demands that he or she lives a life that measures up to the dignity and respect the people in the community have for him or her.

The term *traditional birth attendant* has been used by the World Health Organization (WHO) to describe a traditional midwife in Africa, Asia, and elsewhere. The WHO defines the term "traditional birth attendant" as an individual "'who assists the mother at childbirth and who initially acquired her skills delivering babies by herself or by working with other traditional birth attendants' . . . whereas the term "midwife" is used to refer to a person with formal medical education who is officially registered or licensed."[71] But, as Cosminsky has rightly pointed out, birth attendant is inadequate for it is "too narrow and understates her actual functions."[72] The term "traditional midwife" is preferable for it describes better the work of the person. Among the Akans this profession is generally practised by middle aged and elderly women who have had no formal education. The traditional midwife is an expert in all maternity needs. She assists in childbirth and also provides prenatal and postnatal care. She has considerable knowledge of the medical needs of women and children. "She can prescribe medicines for childless couples after the necessary spiritual requirements have been met." Women in menopause and young girls with painful menstruation go to her for assistance. "She could, but normally would not, induce abortions. She combines the work of a gynaecologist and a pediatrician and is skilled in family medicine generally."[73] The traditional midwife occupies a field of great importance and, therefore, has great respect in her community.

Bone-setters. Although bone-setting is a specialized practice, it is common to many other healers. Among the Akans, it is mostly a family profession, passed from one member to another. The bone-setters "function as orthopaedic doctors. They specialize in repairing broken limbs." And most of them "are also skilled in handling rheumatism and arthritis", for most of the herbs, roots, and barks of some trees which are used in treating broken bones are also medicines for treating rheumatism and arthritis. Bonesetting is also regarded as a sacred profession because during the period of treatment, the healer and also the patient go through some spiritual exercises such as cleansing, libation pouring, divination, and abstention from sexual intercourse.[74]

The *exorcist* has been known in the literature as the *witch doctor* mainly because of the person's ability to exorcize. Among the Akans, the causes of illnesses and misfortunes are classified under physical/natural and spiritual/supernatural causes.[75] The main spiritual causes of illnesses, death and other misfortunes that come upon people are believed to be the mechanizations of witches and other evil spirits. And so, after an illness or a misfortune has been diagnosed by the *diagnostician* as the doing of a witch(es) or an evil spirit(s), it is the *exorcist*, the specialist in that area, who frees the individual from this influence. So the tag that has often been attached to the *witch doctor* as an evil person is not correct. Although this specialist has been frequently regarded by some European and also some African writers and "even by legislators as a witch, an evil man seeking to poison his neighbours, or a perverted priest, the witch-doctor is really none of these things."[76] The *exorcist* is an essential figure and a highly respected and recognized person in his or her society. The *exorcist* is able to point out those who are witches and are inflicting harm and other disasters on their neighbours and their properties. In this way the *exorcist*, the *witch doctor*, is said to be able to "catch the witch". This specialist is also able to ward off a spell or a curse that has been cast upon an individual. Thus, the function of the *exorcist* "is not to harm but to heal, and to release from their pains those who believe themselves to have been bewitched. It is against the evil activities of nocturnal witches that the doctor operates in the public interest."[77]

So among Akans and other Africans, for the religious functionary, i.e. a priest-healer, or the indigenous or traditional healer, to maintain his or her good reputation, "one must be good and honest, a good psychiatrist, a good psychologist, a gifted performer, and a sincere leader of the community."[78] In other words, the priest-healer must be knowledgeable and must also maintain high moral standard in his or her community.

This chapter has briefly described the Akan traditional society and religion. I have reconstructed the structure of the traditional religion and pointed to the misrepresentation and wrong interpretation of it and its elements by foreigners. For the purpose of this study which deals with medical practices, I have emphasized the political and religious leadership and particularly the people's cultural and religious beliefs which give meaning and relevance to the traditional medical practice. In other words, the purpose of this chapter has been to give a picture of the political, cultural, and religious systems of the Akans before their encounter with Western cultural, political, religious, and medical institutions.

The next chapter reviews colonial rule in Ghana and indicates how British officials and missionaries, acting upon their socio-natural surroundings, i.e., modes of political, religious, economic, and medical production, tried to destroy chieftaincy and, thus, all the traditional institutions which derive their function and prestige in relation to it. Also, the chapter points to how the Akans made reference to the principal form (traditional leadership and religion) on which they situate and orientate themselves, and resisted colonial and Christian encroachment. The chapter helps give a clearer picture of the concerns of this work. I believe that historical retrieval and reinterpretation are essential steps for gaining insight into the wide range of effects of capitalist expansion in Africa.

Chapter 5

Reconstructing the Colonial Era

A Short Overview of Colonial Expansion and Rule

The destiny of Akans, and African peoples generally, was to be directed into new and unfamiliar patterns of life when Europeans decided to expand their trading activities to other parts of the world. The familiar political, economic, social, religious, and medical patterns and values of Africans were to be changed. Traditional leadership was to lose its authority. History must be reconstructed, as I attempt to do in this study, to demonstrate the impact of the destruction of African political leadership on the traditional institutions, including traditional medical practices. In other words, history must be rewritten to show the bond, inherent values and spiritual qualities in relationships, between chieftaincy and medical and economic and other institutions of Africans. Again, history must be reconstructed to show further the methods employed by the colonial officials in establishing and administering colonial rule in Africa. These will help shed light on the constant reproduction of colonial and neo-colonial ideologies, institutions, and structures in independent Africa, and thus, the predicaments of African peoples today.

The first Europeans to come into contact with the people of the Gold Coast were the Portuguese. The European traders stumbled upon the yet unknown west coast of Africa when they were seeking new ways to reach the wealthy countries of South and Southeast Asia. Western Europe was trading with India and the Far East, for its gold, ivory, silk, precious stones, and other luxuries. But access to India was blocked to the European traders when the Turks, who were Muslims, took control of the lands of the Far East and monopolized the trade in those areas. Europeans desired to find new routes to India and the East, while avoiding passing through the Turkish country; this was one reason for contact between Western Europe and the west coast of Africa. But there were more. ". . . Europeans wanted to gain access to West African gold supplies, which were also a monopoly of the Muslims."[1] Another motivating factor was "missionary zeal: any African Kingdoms which they might convert to the Christian faith could be used to provide a counterbalance to Muslim power."[2] In other words, the motivation was threefold: to open a sea route to India; to accumulate wealth from the rich resources of Africa; and to convert Africans to Christianity, for the "sake of their souls" and as allies against the Muslims.

The first ship to undertake the exploration of the west coast of Africa was sent by Prince Henry of Portugal in 1418. In January 1471 the Portuguese, the first Europeans, reached the Gold Coast itself. They gave the name Gold Coast to the coastal area between Cape Three Points and Cabo Corsa, later Anglicized into Cape Coast, because the whole region was so rich in gold. Trading activities started immediately between the Portuguese and the Africans. In 1481, after some years of trading, the Portuguese decided, at the reluctant consent of Kwamina Ansa, the chief of Edinaa, a town popularly known today as Elmina, to establish a permanent post, in fact a fortress, of their own on the Gold Coast. The Portuguese decided to build the fortress so that they would "secure the trade against foreign competition or against interruption by hostile tribes."[3] The fortress was finally completed and, in 1486, was named St. George by the king of Portugal. Several smaller fortresses were built by the Portuguese at Accra, Shama and Axim.

The Portuguese monopoly of trade, including slave trading, in places on the west coast of Africa was broken when other European nations, including the French, the Dutch, the English, and the German, ventured along the coast. In the late part of the sixteenth century, the Dutch arrived. They visited what is modern Ghana; the presence of their ships on the coast of Ghana made the Portuguese uncomfortable. The Portuguese fought to drive them out but the Dutch were determined to settle. In 1598 they built a small fort on the coast at Mori, and soon after another at Kommenda. Eventually the balance of power shifted. With the help of some of the natives on the coast, the Dutch engaged in series of battles with the Portuguese and finally, in 1642, after 160 years of Portuguese settlement in Ghana, drove them out altogether.

For about a decade the Dutch took control of European trading activities with the natives. Their monopoly was broken in 1652 when Swedes arrived and settled at Cape Coast and later also at Osu, near Accra. About 1659 the Danes also arrived and took over the Swedes' fort at Osu, naming it Christianborg after Christian, the king of Denmark. In 1662 they were followed by the English[4] who eventually became the chief European power on the coast. Later, in 1685, the Germans also arrived.

After many long years of trade and intermittent battles in Ghana—battles between Europeans and Europeans, Europeans and Africans, Africans and Africans, and Africans allying with European group(s) and fighting other Africans and vice versa—and after many years of treaties, armistices, and bonds signing, the British became the colonial masters of Ghana. British officials appealed to the Bond of 1844 to legitimate their turning Ghana into a colony. That Bond, as Ward has indicated, "marks the beginning of real British rule."[5]

The Bond of 1844 was signed on March 6 by the British Governor in charge of the Coast, Commander Hill, and eight local chiefs, including the chiefs of Abora, Assin, Denkyira, Cape Coast, and Anomabu. The bond was signed by the chiefs for two main reasons: i) to seek protection from the British against one another and the powerful enemy in the northern hinterland, the Ashantis; and ii) to give authority to the British on the Coast to help settle disputes that might arise among the coastal people, as had the former Governor, Captain George Maclean.[6] Maclean's duties, in this regard, had been "to sit in court with the Fante chiefs and try cases where Africans alone were concerned, in accordance with Fante customary law and the principles of British equity."[7] Those areas in which lived the chiefs who signed the agreement came to be referred to as the 'Protectorate'. Ward has observed:

> The effect of the Bond was to legalize and define the jurisdiction which had grown up in the 'Protectorate' under Maclean's influence.

It will be observed that the language of the preamble clearly implies that the power and jurisdiction are to be exercised in the future as they have been in the past, and in no other way. There is no intention to grant to the Crown any territorial sovereignty and suzerainty, nor is there granted any authority beyond that of enforcing compliance with the orders of the court. Whatever may be said of the connection so often put forward on the Gold Coast today that the Bond of 1844 is still the only legal basis for British rule, it is certain that the Bond cannot be construed, and at the same time was not construed, as granting any authority beyond this.[8]

The protection entailed in the Bond of 1844 attracted many chiefs. In fact it seemed more reasonable and attractive at that time to adhere to the seemingly benign terms of the British than to stay outside the 'Protectorate' and to risk attack by the powerful Ashantis threatening invasion. With more and more chiefs agreeing to come under the terms of the Bond, British authority began to spread. And with this expansion the pressures for the Government to increase its activities, such as road building, educational and medical services, grew more pressing. However, the grant from the British Crown was inadequate for the provision of such services. Accordingly, a large assembly of chiefs and elders was convened by Hill, the Governor. The meeting, resolving "itself a legislative assembly 'with full powers to enact such laws as it shall deem fit'", decided that a reasonable and necessary tax of one shilling per head be paid by every man, woman, and child in the 'Protectorate', "in consideration of the advantages derived from 'the protection afforded them by Her Majesty's Government'. . ."[9] And this tax was to be collected, "not (as might have been expected) by the stool authorities", but by appointed officers of the Governor. The proceeds from the tax "were to be used in paying stipends to the chiefs, and in providing for 'the public good in the education of the people, in the general improvement and extension of the judicial system, in affording greater facilities of internal communication, increased medical aid' and other measures of improvement and utility."[10] These and other resolutions were approved by the Governor, becoming in 1852 a legal ordinance called the Poll Tax Ordinance.

The idea behind the Bond of 1844, to give protection to the people against invading enemies, and the idea behind paying taxes for the proper administration of the 'Protectorate' did

not seem harmful in themselves. But they came to be interpreted quite differently. The Bond, for example, was miscon-
strued by the British as the coastal natives' surrender of their
rights and authority, land and resources, and their independence to the Crown. Concerning the Poll Tax Ordinance, Ward
notes:

> On this matter the Governor, like so many other Governors, was mis-
> informed. The self-styled legislative assembly was an assembly of men
> who had no constitutional authority to levy on their people, even for
> the recognized purposes, without the express consent of their people.
> The poll tax was a novelty, and the people had not had enough op-
> portunity of discussing the proposal in their villages and giving their
> opinion on it. Moreover, the tax was not collected by the chiefs or
> stool authorities, but by specially appointed agents, who were not in
> any way under the control of the people. A poll tax could have been
> collected satisfactorily if several months had been allowed for discus-
> sion beforehand and if the collection had been left in the proper hands.
> Levied as it was it caused great dissatisfaction.

Ward continues:

> Not content with this, the Government committed another blunder in
> spending the money. The intention of the assembly had been that all
> the money collected, apart from the expenses of collection, should
> be directly spent on work in the country. The Government naturally
> regarded central administrative expenses as a necessary part of the
> cost of maintaining services in the country districts. This point of
> view, however, was not shared by the people, and when the Govern-
> ment spent part of the proceeds of the tax on salaries of headquar-
> ters' officials they regarded it as a breach of the agreement on which
> the Ordinance was based. The natural result was that more and more
> difficulty was encountered in collecting the tax, and very soon both
> the tax and the assembly which had decreed it vanished forever.[11]

Although the British had established a monopoly of trade
and also asserted some jurisdiction over the coastal people
through the Bond of 1844 and the abortive assembly of chiefs
and the Poll Tax Ordinance, their exercise of jurisdiction over
the entire country was far from complete. They knew that they
had the powerful Ashanti Union and their allies to reckon
with.[12] In retrospect, it is clear that the protection the British
offered for the 'Protectorate' was also, in a way, protection
they were seeking for themselves, their interests and power.
For example, their capacity to maintain the safety of their own

forts had been threatened by the successive invasions of the 'Protectorate' by the Ashantis.

So, for the British to have a peaceful atmosphere and complete jurisdiction over their 'Protectorate', in which some inhabitants were still subjects of the Ashantis, British officials concluded that the formidable Ashanti army should be brought under control. Most importantly, controlling the Ashantis would allow the British and many European and African merchants access to the wealth of the interior. On their side, the Ashantis also felt that the strengthened British position was a direct threat to their interests and freedom. Therefore, they determined to drive the strangers out of the Gold Coast. This conflict erupted in open warfare in 1873. According to Kimble, ". . . added to their long-standing ambition to subjugate the Fantis . . ." the war of 1873-1874 was the first, of all the wars fought by the Ashantis, "to be inspired largely by anti-European sentiment. . ."[13] With the help from the British allies[14] in Ghana and some troops from other British colonies in West Africa and East Africa, the British beat back the Ashantis and confined them within their own boundaries.

The war of 1873-1874 marked the real beginning of the disintegration of the Ashanti kingdom, and the spread of British power. After this success over the Ashantis, and at the demand of some colonial officials, especially those in Gold Coast, and the Gold Coast Chambers of Commerce and the British Chambers of Commerce, the Colonial Office in London decided to station consuls in Kumasi, the seat of the Ashanti kingdom, and in the various points in the interior. The reasons were twofold: (a) to break the unity and strength of the Ashanti Kingdom altogether by placing them under British domination "'in the interests of trade and of the gold mining concessions'";[15] and (b) to stop the competitive penetration of the French and the Germans into the interior and the northern parts of the country.

The proposal to station a British Resident in Kumasi was rejected by the natives. The current King of Ashanti, Agyemang Prempeh, refused Governor Brandford Griffith's offer firmly, but with some courtesy:

'The suggestion that Ashanti in its present state should come and enjoy the protection of Her Majesty the Queen and Empress of India,

I may say this is matter of a very serious consideration and which I am happy to say that we have arrived at this conclusion, that my Kingdom of Ashanti will never commit itself to any such policy; Ashanti must remain independent as of old, at the same time to be friendly with all white men. . ..Believe me, Governor, that I am happy to inform you, that the cause of Ashanti is progressing.'[16]

The King also sent a deputation to her Majesty the Queen in London, in April 1895, to explain his stance against the proposal for a British Resident in Kumasi. He and his people feared that placing a British consul in Kumasi would soon be followed by the conversion of Ashanti into a 'Protectorate'. The Colonial Office refused to receive the deputation.

With the refusal of the Ashantis to comply with the proposal, British officials decided it was time to demonstrate British supremacy. *The Gold Coast Chronicle*, reflecting a fighting mood, declared:

We have reason to believe that the King of Asantee [Ashanti] means nothing but mischief. He may pretend to be a friend; he may do a great deal to induce us to believe that he does not wish to fight. . .We must go straight to Kumasi this time. The King must be deposed and sent about his business. . . . A District Commissioner with a strong force of Haussas must be left in Kumasi. . . . When we have once annexed Asantee [Ashanti], the moral, intellectual and social elevation of the people in the interior of our part of the dark continent, will be thoroughly effected. . . .With Asantee [Ashanti] once conquered, we shall have the foundation for a West African Empire (12 December 1895).[17]

Similar sentiments had been expressed earlier. In December 1893, a document from the Colonial Office asserted:

As regards Ashanti the present moment seems more favourable than we may get again. The King is cowed & the bulk of his people wish for protection, so the time is ripe for a bold stroke such as tells with savages. The Colony is rich & can afford the outlay (say £10,000) which will be necessary for a few years.[18]

On November 30, 1894, *The Gold Coast Chronicle* proclaimed:

We must go straight to Kumasi and occupy or annex it, declaring Ashantee [Ashanti] a British protectorate . . . if there are 800 Hausas in this Colony, send them all to Ashantee [Ashanti] with the Union Jack, and let the whole of that country be declared once and for all a British protectorate in spite of all opposition. . .It is a reproach more-

over to the civilization of this country, that any savage King should be
suffered by the British Government to do what King Prempeh is daily
doing.[19]

Backed by such sentiments British troops entered Kumasi on
January 17, 1896, despite all the attempts made earlier by
Prempeh to resolve the issue amicably. The British troops "met
no opposition". Indeed, some analysts claim that the Kumasis
and their allies had miscalculated the intentions of the British,
believing their lack of resistance would result in the quick return of British troops "to the coast after a display of force."[20]
But Maxwell, the Governor, called a public meeting where he
asked Prempeh, among other things, "to produce immediately
50,000 oz. of gold (about £175,000) to help pay for the expedi-
tion." The 680 oz. of gold which Prempeh offered in return,
all he could pay, he said, was not regarded by the British officials as a serious offer.

> To the horror of the assembled Ashantis, Maxwell then took the
> Asantehene prisoner, together with his mother, father, brother, two
> other close relatives, two linguists, the Chiefs of Bantama and Asafu,
> and the Kings of Mampong, Offinsu, and Ejisu. The Ansah brothers
> [who led the deputation to London], too, who had reached Kumasi
> just before the expedition, were detained in custody and sent to the
> coast to stand trial for forgery. The mausoleum at Bantama was de-
> stroyed, and the sacred trees blown up. Valuable gold ornaments were
> sent to England, and the remaining content's of the Asantehene's pal-
> ace were sold by auction ('to check looting' by the carriers). The main
> body of troops was quickly ordered back to Cape Coast, escorting the
> political prisoners, who were then sent by sea to Elmina Castle.[21]

The Asantehene and his party, excluding the Ansah brothers,
were later sent into exile in Sierra Leone, and then to the
Seychelles Islands.

With this defeat, and the complete disintegration of the
Ashanti Kingdom, the road was paved for the total annexation
of the whole country by the British Crown. After the
Asantehene had been exiled, the British, as Adu Boahen succinctly summarizes in his "Politics in Ghana, 1800-1874", "then
went on to annex Asante and to declare a Protectorate over
Northern Ghana between 1900 and 1901. The British Colony
of the Gold Coast with its three separate but related territo-
ries of the Colony at the coast, Asante and the Northern Terri-
tories came into existence on 1 January 1902. . ."[22]

With the whole Colony of the Gold Coast now under the Crown, the British rulers searched for ways of consolidating their position. They did this through their administrative machinery. They sought to make the administrative apparatus more effective so that funds would be easily generated and control over local resources firmly secured. This requirement called for a suitable system or systems of government. "This requirement in turn raised the issue of whether, and in what way, existing African systems of government could be incorporated into, or attached to, the new quasi-state structure of colonial administration."[23]

Analysts have put forth two contrasting interpretations of British rule in Africa. The first approach, as Forbes Munro notes, claims that "under Indirect Rule the colonial officials permitted traditional authorities to exercise many customary powers under their jurisdiction." The second and contrasting line of approach claims that "under Direct Rule the colonial administration either ignored traditional authorities or reduced them to a subordinate position with derivative powers."[24]

There is a consensus among scholars that, in British West Africa, the colonial officials tended towards Indirect Rule. What is not clear among scholars, however, is the meaning of Indirect Rule. "Much of the argument", says Crowder, "really boils down to a question of semantics—what one scholar refers to as indirect rule is not what another one considers it to be."[25] Although this is not the place to decide this issue, one observation is in order. As Munro has observed:

In fact, the distinction between the two methods was far from clear on the ground, and a wide range of local government systems evolved across the continent within a spectrum of which ideals of Indirect or Direct Rule were the extremes. The development of British administration in Africa was highly empirical, at least in its initial stages. It was lack of funds, shortage of trained European officials, and the consequent need for local manpower, rather than preconceptions and theories about appropriate forms of colonial government that were paramount. In the establishment of local systems of government it was these which dictated British attitudes and opened the way for bargaining with African authorities and for African initiatives. Where indigenous authorities seemed suitable for colonial requirements, as in the case of existing systems, local settlements were quickly and easily reached, sometimes to the advantage of African negotiators.[26]

In other words, it is not simply that the British willingly employed Indirect Rule, allowing Africans to govern themselves through their own chiefs because the British felt unsuited to govern the institutions which Africans have devised for themselves;[27] rather it was lack of personnel and funds, and also the need for local manpower on the part of the British Government. For instance, around 1880 when Ussher, the administrator and governor of the Gold Coast, suggested that Europeans be brought into immediate contact with the inhabitants by appointing District Commissioners to live in the rural areas and rule in conjunction with the Chiefs, there was an outcry in London.

> What man of integrity and ability, unless imbued with the zeal for the secular welfare of the negro which animates the missionary for his religious conversion, would be willing, or could be tempted by any conceivable remuneration, to undertake such a duty? The horror of such a life is appalling to contemplate—the isolation and absence of society or companionship; the constant prospect of sickness and death far from friends or medical assistance; being ever surrounded by foul sights and fouler sounds and smells; the monotony and weariness! If, as we so often hear, officers stationed in coast towns take to drink to drown their cares and discomfort, what would be the temptation to such a course to the man in Akim or Wassaw[28]

Colonial Officials even felt compelled to strongly disclaim any intention of reforming native customs, or abolishing the power of the chiefs: "In some aspects, they should even be strengthened, since the Government was not in a position to substitute its own authority in 'the inaccessible wilds and impenetrable forests of the interior'."[29]

Also, it can be argued that the British employed chiefs instead of the Western-educated Africans in administering the colonies not because they wanted to maintain chieftaincy and traditions and to slow development in the colonies. The British took this approach so as to maintain their political, economic, and social interests. In fact this was a necessity. As indicated above, they employed the traditional elites for reasons of funds, forces, and personnel; and, ironically, they discarded the Western-educated elites, who "generally held most of the assumptions about the superiority of Western civilisation common among the British themselves . . .", for reasons of imperialism and racism: "with the development and spread of racism in the late nineteenth century, British officials came to prefer the former elite who accepted or tolerated them as rulers to the educated elite who claimed equality with them."[30] In fact, it is no exaggeration to say that the British set their eyes on the destruction of African nationalism. For instance, after the defeat of the Ashantis, "it was British policy as far as possible to break up the states and stamp out traditional nationalism by an attack upon the monarchy." Prempeh was exiled. And the people "were commanded to surrender the Golden Stool to prevent it becoming 'the rallying point of latent Ashanti nationalism.'"[31] Thus, it was the aim of the British to focus people's loyalties on the smallest possible political units to create avenues for possible political frictions among the people, so that they (British) could have opportunity to "pose as the only force capable of holding together the antagonisms inherent in the structure."[32]

The ultimate restoration of some monarchies which they had destroyed earlier in West Africa might be countered as British interest in maintaining African chieftaincy and other traditions. It may be noted, in the case of Ashanti for example, that in 1924 Prempeh was allowed to return to Kumasi and later restored as the Kumasihene and, in 1935, the Ashanti confederacy was also restored. But as Webster has pointed out, these gestures were "in response to the force of traditional nationalism", (which, of course, derived its force from the traditional religion), which they had tried to quench and the flames of which, unfortunately for the British, still lingered. Indeed, Prempeh was allowed to return but only as 'a private citizen'. It was the people's allegiance to the sacred stool which the king occupied, and also their desire and effort to maintain elements of their culture and religion that saved that aged and cherished Kingship tradition. In other words, the Golden Stool which derives its validity from the traditional religion and which the Asantehene occupies, was a force which rallied the people behind Prempeh.

While the British insisted he be called 'Mister' the Asante called him 'Asantehene'. In 1926, still bowing to the force of traditional nationalism, the British permitted Prempeh's installation as Kumasihene, a title previously unknown to the Asante. Fearful of a revived Asante

nation the British attempted to confine his authority to Kumasi division. But to the Asante he was, despite British officials, the Asantehene,
King of all Asante. Secret tributes were sent to him from other divisions which when discovered brought down the wrath of the British
on those concerned. Frankly admitting the failure of their administration in the other divisions the British finally decided it was easier
to support than fight Asante nationalism. In 1935 they officially restored the Asante confederacy and recognised Prempeh II as
Asantehene.[33]

It must be acknowledged that the 1920's saw revived interest in native institutions and customs and also favourable policies towards the chiefs. Guggisberg, the governor, even felt
the need to research native customs and traditions. So in 1921
he set up an Anthropological Department in Kumasi under
the directorship of Rattray. The new policy affirmed that "'an
accurate acquaintance with the nature, habits and customs of
alien populations is necessary to all who have to live and work
amongst them in any official capacity.'"[34] But it is clear that
this renewed interest in the natives and their "customs and
institutions fitted in well with the policy of indirect rule."
Guggisberg and Fraser said: "we must aim at the development
of the people along their own racial lines, and not at the whole-
sale replacement of their ancient civilizations by our own."[35]
"Yet it should be remembered", Kimble reminds us, "that
Rattray himself gave a warning against the contradictions inherent in the principle of indirect rule:

> we would therefore appear to be encouraging on the one hand an
> institution which draws its inspiration and validity from the indig-
> enous religious beliefs, while on the other we are systematically de-
> stroying the very foundation upon which the structure that we are
> striving to perpetuate stands. Its shell and outward form might re-
> main, but it would seem too much to expect that its vital energy could
> survive such a process.[36]

The administration of the Akan states, as briefly shown in
the previous chapter, centred on chiefs and their elders. The
chief, as leader, and his elders are the political, economic, religious, and social administrators of the community. Thus the
proper functioning of the administrative machinery in the
society is the responsibility of the chief. So, interference in
the affairs of the chief in his capacity as a leader of the com-

munity inevitably affects the general governance and stability of the society. The forcible manipulation of the chiefs by the British made them mere agents of colonial rule weakening their authority. Chieftaincy "was being looked down upon by the educated as being nothing more than an agency that did the 'dirty work' of the British for them."[37] They became aliens to the people they were supposed to rule. Inevitably, the prestige, power, and status of the chiefs were reduced. The appearance of chieftaincy was more or less maintained, but the source from which it derived its vitality and its functioning was severely weakened. And the morale of the chiefs themselves was broken, as evident in the ineffective leadership provided by the chiefs in the march towards emancipation. "The Chief, as the traditional leader of his people, might have been expected to be in the forefront of the Gold Coast national movement. This was to some extent true of King Aggrey, and later of the Fanti Confederation. But both these examples revealed inherent weaknesses in the structure of chieftaincy that prevented any similar movement developing on a national scale."[38]

Colonization dealt a slow but deadly blow to chieftaincy, and thus on all traditional institutions—medical, religious, legal and the rest—which derive their functions and prestige in relation to it. The underdevelopment of traditional medicine and medical practices, as well as other aspects of the cultures, and the economic and political conditions currently prevailing among African peoples, as I emphasize in this study, cannot be properly explained and resolved if they are not viewed from the proper historical context.

The Missionaries and the Christian Message

The many celebrations of centenaries and other anniversaries of Christian churches in Africa today are indications of the peoples' appreciative remembrance of the zeal, courage and selfless work of the missionaries in establishing the Gospel of Christ among them. Many of the missionaries put their lives on the line for winning Africans for Christ. Literary education and Western medicine in most parts of Africa have their roots in the missionary efforts. The spirit of African nationalism, and hence the various marches towards independence, was reinforced in missionary teachings of Christian ideals of personal dignity and freedom. Many agricultural products, both cash and food crops, were introduced to Africa by them. Their work in the field of language has been also immense. The missionaries laboured on dictionaries and produced books in local dialects. In some situations "it was they who, more than any other force, roused European feeling against the slave-trade and thus promoted colonialist intervention"[39] to stop it. It is acknowledged by analysts that the invasion of Africa by Europeans "would certainly have had different consequences—and from any humanitarian point of view they would probably have been less desirable consequences—if it had not included Christian missionaries along with the settlers and administrators."[40] Africans appreciation of missionaries and their services was summed up by the first President of Ghana, Dr. Kwame Nkrumah, in his address to delegates of the International Missionary Council in 1957:

> Ghana is glad and proud to pay its tribute to the great work of missionaries in West Africa. If you have time to visit more widely in this country, you will often find as you travel along the roads, little cemeteries lost in the bush where lie buried the brave men and women who, in bringing the Christian faith to this country, gave "the last full measure of their devotion". They knew that they faced the certainty of loneliness and imminent risk of death. Yellow fever decimated them and their families. But still they came. They belong to the martyrs of Christianity. . .[41]

Yet observing what is taking place in African countries and other developing societies today, one also cannot ignore the other side of missionary impact. However unconsciously, the missionaries were among the earliest bearers of alien culture in Africa.

Separating 'missionaries' from 'Europeans' is impossible. Any attempt to do so must involve an abstraction so ideal as to have little touch with African reality. "If it were possible, in the Western academic tradition, to see mission as one set of institutions acting parallel to those of government and commerce," as Welbourn puts it, "the task might be relatively simple. But this is not how it works out in practice, nor how it looks through African eyes; . . ."[42] The close similarity of fundamental attitudes of missionaries and commercialists made this identification objectively possible. Commenting on Christianity and the Ghanaian situation, Kimble observed:

> European influence in the Gold Coast can never in fact be entirely dissociated from the impact of Christianity, which has had a long and chequered history since 1471, when the first Portuguese Catholics to reach this part of the coast erected a wooden cross at Shama. Eleven years later [January 20, 1482], when a Portuguese fleet founded the settlement of A Mina, they 'assisted at the first mass that was celebrated in Guinea, and prayed for the conversion of the natives from idolatry'.[43]

Kimble again points to the evidence that a mass baptism of the people of Efutu in 1503 "owned something to a lucrative commercial offer made to the local Chief."[44] Reindorf also has alleged that before they shipped off their slaves, the Portuguese catechized and baptized them.[45]

As indicated above, the first Europeans to arrive on Ghana's coast had in their company Christian missionaries. But the first organized missionary work, taking the Christian faith beyond the trading settlements, was begun in 1752 by the Anglicans through their Society for the Propagation of the Gospel in Foreign Parts. Before this organized work, however, there had been other short-lived attempts by the Augustinians in the sixteenth century, the Capuchins in the seventeenth century, and the Moravians in the eighteenth century. This first organized attempt also did not last long. It ended in 1816 with the death of Philip Quaque, (the first Ghanaian and also "the first man of any non-European race to receive Holy Orders in this [Anglican] church since the Reformation").[46] Philip Quaque succeeded Thomas Thompson, the first Anglican missionary in all of Africa, who had returned to England because of ill-health. So properly speaking, it was only from 1828 onwards that Christianity began to take roots in Ghanaian soil. In 1828, the Basel missions arrived, followed by the Wesleyan Methodist in 1835; then the Bremen in 1847; the Lyons Fathers arrived in 1880; in 1898, the African Methodist Episcopal Zion; and only in 1904 did the Society for the Propagation of the Gospel in Foreign Parts return.

The short-life span of the missions begun earlier by the Portuguese Augustinians and the French Capuchins and the Moravian Brethren in Ghana has been blamed by scholars on the Dutch Calvinists who ousted the Portuguese. They did not exert any effort for the survival of the missions. An eyewitness account of 1680 reported that the Dutch, as well as all other Europeans, settled or trading in Ghana, were greatly concerned with the gold, and not the welfare of those souls.[47] According to Mobley, the major reason for Christianity's failure in Ghana may well have been the "failure of these first missionaries to dissociate themselves and their services from the political and economic concerns of their governments. . ."[48] For example, at the time of Azambuja, the chaplain ranked next to the governor.

Mobley refutes the contention that the second attempt made by the Anglicans to bring Christianity to Ghana failed because of opposition and hostility of Ghanaians to Christianity; the futility, he says, was rather the result of European apathy and susceptibility to disease.[49] Even if we grant that Ghanaians were opposed and hostile to Christianity, could they be blamed for rejecting doctrines and practices that were foreign and which were being imposed on them, which uprooted them from their traditional mode of worship and practices? Casely Hayford writes: "When he comes to examine the teaching of the missionary he finds there is a good deal in it that is unsuitable to his condition and that he is required to give up practices which to the unscientific mind seem barbarous, but which, when critically examined, cover a mine of truth and inspiration."[50] Christianity and colonialism seemed indistinguishable. As Welbourn puts it: "Christianity was simply the ritual aspect of European colonialism".[51] The embrace of European manners and customs and the physical and spiritual rejection of anything African were too often prerequisites for admission and fellowship to Christianity. Kofi A. Opoku confirms this judgment: "The main trust of European missionary activity was to 'Christianise' Africa in the manner and fashion of the European appropriation of the evangel; and much of missionary endeavour was based on the presupposition that African ways were necessarily pagan and had to be done away with." Opoku continues further: "Thus an uncompromising attitude towards African culture became synonymous with the propagation of the Gospel, and the salvation in the missionary sense became a rescue operation from the bondage of African culture",[52] and, it should be added, religion. It was a rescue from the jaws of perdition, inhumanity, barbarism to civilization and humane living. Examples of these abound when we look at missionary Christianity—teachings and actual practices—as it was presented to Africans.

We have already discussed in the previous chapter some elements in Akan traditional society and religion, concerning especially how the society operates and how the people understand the spirit world and organize their lives in relation to it. With the coming of Christianity, however, these elements and attitudes—the concept of God, the idea and the attitudes of Akans to the ancestors, the practices of the traditional medical practitioners (priest-healers), etc.—were attacked as idolatry, fetish, and superstition. They were branded as evil. People who accepted such ideas and resorted to the benefits of such practices were regarded 'heathens' and they were considered lost, eternally doomed to hell.

There are several examples which have been cited by both theologians and social scientists concerning the assaults on African customs and religious practices by colonial governments in co-operation with missionaries. For example, in 1923, in Kisangani, formerly Stanleyville, the Superiors of the Belgian Congo Mission listed customs they considered harmful to public order, and asked the colonial government to act against them: hunting and dancing ceremonies, religious rites on the occasions of birth, circumcision, the appearance of a child's teeth, girls' puberty, marriage, and illness; offering to ancestors and spirits; co-operation in rituals in honour of ancestors; carvings representing the spirits of the dead, etc.[53] Massive attacks on funeral rites, bridewealth, widow rites, and polygamy by administrators and missionaries have been witnessed in many parts of Africa.

Among the greatest demands that Christianity has made on its converts in Africa has been the forcible acceptance (by converts) of monogamy as the only pattern of marriage. It was made, and is still is in some mission churches in Africa, a requirement for the reception of baptism and holy communion. Indeed, even the first wife in a marriage, who is not responsible for her husband's taking another wife or wives after her,[54] is also not allowed, in some mission churches, to receive baptism on conversion to the Christian faith. She is asked to divorce the husband before baptism can be administered to her.

Western Christian ideas of marriage forced on African converts have radically altered the structure of the family, and hence the support they usually offer one other. The demand for monogamy by missionaries has caused conflict between families and communities, and given rise to secret conflict in the minds and lives of many Christians. Kwesi Dickson points to other incongruities in the Christian theology and rite of marriage. For example, the ceremony affirms that the husband and wife have "become one flesh". But, Dickson points out, there are "unresolved incompatibilities here", for "there is the matrilineal custom which prevents a child from inheriting the father's property; also, with the children issuing from the union belonging to the mother's family, it is less than meaningful for the Church Order to note simply that the bride and the bridegroom are one."[55] Moreover, among Akans, I will add, family and marriage go beyond the relationship among husband, wife and children. They are communal affairs. The welfare of the members involved, and also the survival or the disintegration of the marriage, do not depend on the husband or wife or children alone, but on the whole community. Indeed, Dickson observes that the Church fails to observe and comment on incompatible situations which sometimes arise because of its alien theological orientation. He gives an illustration.

> The Methodist Church of Ghana, like all the historic Churches in Ghana and elsewhere in Africa frowns upon polygamy and does not admit those involved in polygamous marriages to the Lord's Table. A few years ago a member of the Methodist Church of Ghana who had been a polygamist died. In accordance with the Church's policy the body of the deceased was not taken to the church for the pre-burial service; it was taken direct to the cemetery, and at the graveside the story of his life was read by one of the five ministers present, though the account contained no mention of his having had two wives. Among the prayers read was one which featured the words, '. . . we have joy at this time in all who have faithfully lived, and all who have faithfully died. . .' It may be wondered why the deceased's body was not taken to the church if he had 'faithfully lived' and 'faithfully died'![56]

"It cannot be right", indeed, "to brutalize human beings in the name of some so-called Christian law, nor to present catechumens with an undignified choice between 'baptism or wives' which seems to have precious little to do with the love of Christ."[57]

The issues of polygamy, drumming and dancing, puberty and nubility rites and the rest border on questions of morality. The missionaries called for the cessation of these customs because they believed them unChristian, obscene and promiscuous. In short, such practices and customs were regarded as things which were incompatible with the Christian faith and its moral teachings. And the African who stood in dire need of taming, a human being in the making, should be protected from them. I remember when I was a child being instructed as a Catholic not to eat the *eto* (mash plantain or yam, mixed with red oil) and the eggs which had been used at a nubility rite or any other traditional rite, and the meat of the cow or goat, or chicken which had been used for any sacrifice, for they had been contaminated with evil spirits through those evil practices. Such an instruction deeply affected me so that I felt extreme nausea and guilt whenever I was told that the food or meat I had eaten was from one of these ceremonies. In fact, even today I react in the same way. Another thing that pupils were punished for was watching the so-called "fetish" or "pagan" dancing! One could receive six to twelve strokes of the cane at the back or lower bottom and/or heavy manual work either on the school compound or farm which could take days to finish. Before our own school days it was reported that frequent attendance at such ceremonies could result in the pupil's expulsion from the Church denominational schools. All of this was done in the name of missionary teachings and observances, and preservation of Christian sanctity (or sanity?)!

Another missionary factor, in addition to Western marriage and missionary schooling, which contributed to the disintegration of family and community life was the setting up of "salems", popularly known to Akans as *Oburoni kurom* ("White man's town"). The "salems" were European residences developed on the finest and most elevated areas of towns far removed from areas occupied by the natives. These European quarters were built initially supposedly to protect Europeans from transmission of diseases such as yellow fever and malaria from the native inhabitants. But these quarters continued to exist long after the discovery of prophylaxis for yellow fever

and malaria.[58] In a deeper sense, the "salems" were developed
by the Europeans to separate their lives from African lives.

In the nineteenth century, when they properly settled in
Ghana, the missionaries adopted the residential patterns of
other Europeans. They built their "mission houses" on ridges.
This practice of building missions, and also governmental resi-
dencies, away from townspeople still remains in Ghana. And
the practice was taken over by the African churches and governmental institutions which are successors to the European
missionaries and the colonial institutions.

The "salems" did not remain only "white man's towns" but
later included Christian converts as well. The missionaries built
salems for their converts, setting them apart from the non-
Christians. This policy had detrimental effects on both Christianity and the communities from which converts were taken.
J. B. Danquah observed that the Basel missionaries' insistence
on building their mission stations separate and apart from the
towns tended to create a gulf between the Christians and non-
Christians.[59] The Christians regarded the townspeople as heathens and had nothing to do with them.

The creation of "salems" also gave the impression that becoming a Christian meant becoming physically attached to
Oburoni kurom and all that it offered—Western medicine, worship, laws, morality, and customs. According to Danquah:

> The effect of the separateness of the two towns was to make the people
> look upon becoming a Christian as a physical act of embracing the
> bodily removal of one's person from the heathen to the Christian
> town, the sending away of all but one of the convert's wives, and the
> normal upkeep of one's attendance at prayers and at services of the
> Church. From the earliest times it became a fad to be a Christian.
> Christians were those who were free of the restraints and taboos of
> the heathen town, and as they thought, of the authority and rule of
> princes of this earth.[60]

The establishment of "salems" for converts was strongly
encouraged by the colonial Government, because "it lessened
daily bickering". The truth is that the Government encouraged
it because it helped to set the people against themselves (di-
vide and rule) and helped to undermine the leadership role
and the authority of the chiefs. According to Busia, Ashanti
converts alienated themselves and "formed communities apart

from the heathens" not only because they did not want "to participate in fetish observances", but more importantly, because the missionaries insisted on it:

> When Christians in the village are asked why they refuse these services they usually reply: "I now go to Church, I am not under the chief", or "The Priest (Father or Sofo) says we must not do them" or "It is against the law of the Church". They see the question in terms of regulations issued by the priest or minister. By becoming Christians they have put themselves under a new authority. Their disputes are settled by the catechist, the leaders of the congregation, or the priest or minister. . . . They regard themselves as a separate community under the authority of the European missionary who is the head of the church. This is how most Ashanti Christians think of their new status. This is how the chiefs see it too.[61]

The undermining of the position of the chief in Akan society, and therefore the other traditional institutions and practices, then, cannot be regarded as the work only of the colonial administrators, traders, and soldiers; the missionaries, as part of the machinery for the propagation of colonial expansion,[62] contributed to this process. Thus F. M. Deng, considering the impact of the West among his own people, the Buganda, concluded that "alien religions have stripped (the chief) of his divine powers".[63] In other words, foreign religions have contributed immensely to weakening the foundation on which traditional chieftaincy and social order in general stood. In their concern for efficient administrators who would promote Christian teachings and demands among the people, missionaries were reluctant to accept even secular criticisms brought against their favourite chiefs. In Kikuyu, as in many societies in Africa, people who were not members of ruling families were elected senior chiefs by colonial administrators and missionaries and imposed "onto a social system which had never previously known them; and in general chiefs found themselves in the most impossible position of having to mediate the instructions of central government to tribesmen who denied their right to rule and despised them for their ignorance, or neglect, of custom."[64]

Although chieftaincy, cultural and traditional religious beliefs and practices, and other things "native" were sought to be destroyed, they survived. For example, traditional medical

practice, pouring of libation, and funeral rites which were condemned and banned by the Europeans still persist. In short,
despite European-oriented education and massive cultural and
religious imposition, the core of African cultures and religions
exist. This confirms modes of production analysis that alien
religions and cultures do not completely destroy or replace
indigenous ones. Although there has not been, as far as I know,
any documentation of "religious" expressions of economic and
political resistance, the persistence of traditional institutions
and elements, which derive their validity and function from
the traditional religion, in the face of massive colonial and
Christian encroachment are indications that dimensions of the
old modes of production were adopted and continued on the
margins as part of indigenous strategies of resistance and
survival.

This chapter has reviewed colonial rule and missionary activities in Ghana. Its primary objective has been to provide us
the historical basis for analyzing and understanding properly
the medical, economic, and political conditions prevailing in
Ghana and other African countries today. The chapter has indicated the impact of cultural and religious changes which were
introduced into the Akan society during the colonial era. It
has described briefly how the British, capitalizing on internal
political conflicts made Ghana a colony. The chapter has also
described how British officials, in their effort to control the
political, religious, and medical fields, tried to destroy chieftaincy, and thus all the traditional institutions which derive
their function and prestige in relation to it. They tried to replace the traditional religious beliefs which give inspiration
and validity to indigenous institutions with Christian beliefs
and practices. The persistence of cultural and religious beliefs
and practices are indications of the viability of indigenous institutions and practices. It is an indication that Akans resisted
European encroachment.

The next chapter is concerned with the dichotomy that has
often been created between medicine and religion. It is also
concerned with the inadequacy of the narrow and limited
Western understanding of health, illness, and healing which
replaced the broad and integrating understanding of illness,

health, and healing of the Akans. The chapter shows that Africans' understanding of health, illness, and healing which the Europeans refused as nonsense is the one which the Western world is appropriating today. It points to the dominant attitude of the colonizers towards Africans and, thus, their refusal to learn and know and appreciate anything "native".

Chapter 6

Concepts of Health and Healing

The Concept of Health

It is certainly difficult and highly controversial to say precisely what health is, as health itself is a complex of processes instead of a single and unified entity. As something dynamic and complex, "health . . . probably cannot be rigorously defined in a manner that will be appropriate to all people, places, and times."[1] In other words, "what counts as 'healthy' at a particular time in a particular society changes considerably in the history of civilization. It reflects the system of received values in the society in question, and serves the adaptation of the human body to the demands of that society."[2] It may seem to be a futile search, then, for the formulation of a homogenous and suitable concept of health. In their search for the meaning of health, however, experts in various disciplines developed various concepts of health which have seemed useful for their particular concerns and purposes. Some of the definitions have been restricted to the degree or state of health of individuals, while others have social connotations, taking into consideration the health of society in general. Now there is a welter of conflicting views, both narrow and broad conceptions of health, and of healing.

In an attempt to show the application of planning theory to health concerns, Henrik Blum developed a typology of definitions of health. The definitions, as he suggests, are "the mainstreams of social concerns that contribute to our present-day confused views about health."[3] The following are the main approaches as he presented them.[4]

The first is the *medical view* (i.e. modern medical model). According to Blum, the Renaissance era made it irresistible for some physicians to apply their new found knowledge, "the dwindling handful of empirically satisfying health-restoring procedures which had survived from the Graeco-Roman golden era . . .",[5] to the ills of human beings. Science that accompanied the Renaissance provided evidence that disease or illness was either a superimposition of some malignant force upon human beings or, on occasion, was a deprivation of a necessary item of intake. In this sense cure for an afflicted person should consist of the "removal or neutralizing of some superimposed noxious substance or parasite or the addition of certain required life-maintaining substances."[6] Health is, then, in this perspective, the "freedom from superimposed or unnatural influences." According to Blum, one failure of this model is its emphasis on medical technology. In other words, the concern of the proponents of this view may come to focus on technological achievement *per se* rather than on whether the technology is beneficial and suitable to the recipients of health care, and society. Also, with the exception of the encouragement it has offered medicine in seeking causes of disease, this model has little interest in the prevention of disease occurrence or reoccurrence.

The second approach he listed is the *prevention or public health view*. This model concerned itself with prevention, early detection and, thus, the avoidance of disease, illness, and premature death. Like the medical model, it views illness and disease "as resulting when man is pitted against the various elements of the environment about him or is deprived of certain essential nutrients." In this sense, health is viewed here also as the freedom from superimposed disease and illness. The accomplishments of this model are that it has contributed to the control of many plagues, great deficiency diseases, etc. Its failure lies in the fact of its emphasis on mechanical and biologic forces and avoidance of "the forces at work beyond the interactions of man and some disease vector in the immediate environment." Because it has ignored "overpowering background or ecologic forces, few of even the well understood deficiency diseases are really under control, and similarly, many preventable contagions remain unprevented."[7] Public health has not taken sufficient consideration of the social factors of illness and disease.

The third is the *humanitarian or well-being view*. By placing emphasis on the survival of infants and their mothers, freedom from hunger and also from inhumane treatment or punishment, ready availability of care or succour for those in illness, pain or distress of any kind, and a safe and pleasurable environment, this view makes human beings the centre of society. That is to say, for a society to be regarded as suitably wise and healthy, human beings must be at its centre. Thus, the survival of human beings is made to depend solely on human beings without the consideration of impacts of other social and environmental (physical) forces. Blum sees the successes of this model in terms of the impetus it has given to various movements, the social welfare movement, the education movement, the clean and sanitary environment movement, the maternal and infant welfare movement, and the city beautiful concerns, which have had broad effects on society. One of the failures of the humanitarian view is that "it has substituted charity for justice, and has tended to obscure issues of equity by use of philanthropy."[8]

The fourth approach is the *economic view*. The economic view of the meaning of health is well expressed in terms of freedom from incapacity, disability, and premature death. In other words, illness or disease is viewed in terms of factors that might: i) prevent education, and entry into the work force; ii) cause the loss of effective workers and homemakers, and partial losses resulting from sick workers' low productive capabilities; iii) affect cost-benefit ratios of health or social interactions due to their productivity and, thereby, lower a country's gross national product; and iv) divert resources to the care of the sick and the unproductive. This concept has led to concern for the proper care of the health of workers and future workers, their protection, and their education. Its failure, however, has been that the well-being of human beings was overlooked in favour of how much they could produce. In other words, being human was dependent on one's aggregate production. Thus, human beings have been made to ignore their well-being in their pursuit of survival. Also, "this view opens the way to extermination (calculated neglect) of poor risks and poor producers."[9]

The fifth is the *super-biologic systems view of health and disease*. This model sees disease as a phenomenon that is natural, and health as the individual's adaptation to the environment to the degree to which he or she is capable. It calls for the ideal of an individual's normal growth and development, his or her normal anatomic achievement, and normal physiological, psychological, and sociological functionings. The model "acknowledges that from the beginning of life *in utero* there are genetic "short-changes" and that there are harmful environmental impacts on the infant from the mother and from the environment, even if mediated by her life processes." Thus, from this viewpoint, man and woman "clearly remain at the center of the universe of concerns." They radiate and receive impingements which shape them and which shape their world. The model, being largely technological, has influenced scientific research. It has also helped to make scientists accountable to society for their activities. The failure of this model is that its "overwhelming scientific commitment. . .to the control of diseases of advancing age reduces the means to conquer diseases of childhood and young adulthood. . . ."[10]

The sixth approach is the *philosophical view of health*. This view is synonymous with the *mental health view*. Health is regarded here as the "pursuit of the maximal capacity for self-realization or self-fulfilment." Thus, this view calls for the alteration of the environment to suit the individual's capacities to cope with the challenges of life as he or she strives for self-realization or self-fulfilment. The advantages of the model are that it has led to the realization that man and woman are goal-seeking, self-fulfilling beings, and that the labours of man and woman are to bring them joy and not to enslave them. Also, the notions of "social justice have reinforced the ideal that man must be given reasonable equality of opportunity if he is ever to be more than an animal seeking to exist from day to day."[11] This philosophical view has also led to "many formulations about the purposes of life, to opportunities for self-fulfilment, and to a more ecological or overall environmental focus, with the expectation that man may be able to reach new levels of self-realization." In other words, healthful living has been encouraged. The disadvantage of this model is that it has led people to interpret their individualism and selfishness as proof of self-fulfilment and self-realization. Also, it opens up opportunities for the wealthy and the educated to aggrandizement at the expense and neglect of the "incompetents".

The seventh approach Blum listed is the *ecological view (survival of our species)*. Here, man and woman are not seen as the centre or the *raison d'etre* of the universe, because the changes that an activity of an individual may induce are regarded as great improvements by some people while to others they are disasters. Ecology, according to Blum, "refers to the interrelationships of all things. These interrelationships continue to shift with man's interference as well as with natural changes, such as earthquakes, lightning-set forest fires, floods, or volcanic eruptions." Thus, the ability of human beings to maintain the ecological balance would determine human health: "As man learns the significance of his own strength, he finds that he can move the world toward the extinction of a bearable life, even to the extinction of most life. Alternatively, he can change his activities so that his environment becomes safer and more pleasant."[12] According to Blum, although this view has not been operative long enough for us to know its strengths and weaknesses, some can be anticipated. The model has the advantage of supporting the mobilization of support for the preservation and protection of great natural resources and areas. However, it has the disadvantage of lending itself to exploitation as many questionable ventures will be urged in the name of ecology. Some industries will, in the name of ecology, develop and, through well-promoted advertising campaigns, sell "antidotes to control environmentally poisonous influences . . . without reasonable prior ecological study. Moreover, such campaigns create a magnificent diversion away from the real issue, which is whether ecologic mischief should be permitted to continue."[13]

The last model on the list is the *third world view (survival of "victims")*. This model views health as "the natural state, God-given and neutral to enhancement by the human element." This viewpoint on health brings into focus three major themes, *productivity, reproduction, and mysticism*, which bear on health outlooks and practices among third world populations. According to this model, *productivity* is very important in the third world. The survival of the family and of individual is dependent on it. The inability of an individual to reproduce (the absence of health) is shameful. In order to keep on producing, people quite often completely deny the existence of health problems and avoid treatment until the conditions are very serious and too late for corrective procedures. "Motivated by the basic need to be productive and reinforced by the fear of being unable to—death is the only solution." Ironically, there is tolerance and compassion for the apparent lack of health in others.

In the third world *reproductivity* is also very important. It is viewed as a way to guarantee a future. Children are viewed as the extension of the family. The welfare of children becomes, therefore, a major community concern.

Mysticism is the last major theme which bears on health outlooks and practices of third world populations. Third world peoples place much emphasis on metaphysical elements. All health matters are viewed as "God's will be done." There is a strong reliance on folk medicine in solving health problems of the peoples.[14]

The strengths of the model are its concern for strong community concerns, solidarity, commitment to survival, as well as for the survival of social and religious values. Inherent in this view is the call for equity and universal social justice. Among its weaknesses, according to Blum, is its reliance on mysticism, interpreting circumstances in terms of the supernatural, which sometimes "augur poorly for concern about habits or practices which pertain to or protect health, or to the use of relevant health care early or late."[15]

According to Blum, each of the preceding "major value-belief systems" contains essential ingredients of a definition of health that can be brought together and reconciled into a working definition. After quoting Romano's definition of health, (as consisting in "the capacity of the organism to maintain a balance in which it may be free of undue pain, discomfort, disability or limitation of action including social capacity"), Blum offers his own definition of health:

> health consists of (1) the capacity of the organism to maintain a balance appropriate to its age and social needs, in which it is reasonably free of gross dissatisfaction, discomfort, disease, or disability; and (2) to behave in ways which promote the survival of the species as well as the self-fulfilment or enjoyment of the individual. If this concept were harshly condensed it might conclude that: health is a state of being in which the individual does the best with the capacities he has, and acts in ways that maximize his capacities.[16]

While acknowledging the fact that the concept of health can be properly understood when it is related to a host of others, for example, ecology, economics, religion, biology, and medicine, Blum, unfortunately, still formulates a concept which falls into the same category as the preceding concepts he has discussed. In characterizing health briefly as "the state of being in which an individual does the best with the capacities he has, and acts in ways that maximize his capacities", Blum formulates a definition which "is appropriate to his immediate practical purpose, but it does not provide a fundamental concept that might unify all these diverse aspects."[17] Thus, the problem with Blum's definition is its failure to recognize other aspects that contribute to human well-being. In this sense, the definition he has proposed is equally narrow as those models he has discussed. The narrow definitions of the concept of health are no longer tenable because the factors that contribute to making peoples' conception of an individual as a 'healthy' person are complex and many. Moreover, the causes of illness and disease are also complex and diverse, and, therefore, their treatments take various forms.

Many broad definitions of health have also been proposed. The most popular and also the most criticized broad definition of health has been the one formulated by the World Health Organization (WHO). In an International Health Conference held in New York from June 19 to July 22, 1946, with the representatives of sixty states in attendance, WHO came out with its definition of health.

> Health is a state of complete physical, mental and social well-being and not merely the absence of disease or infirmity.[18]

The World Health Organization's definition has been criticized for being not only excessively broad (identifying health with human welfare in general)[19] but also making medicine the antidote for "such states of non-well-being as poverty and ignorance."[20]

Among the strong critics of the WHO's definition is Daniel Callahan. According to Callahan, the very generality of the WHO definition "and particularly its association of health and general well-being as a positive ideal . . . [make] it. . . simply a bad one."[21] The definition, he says, has given rise to a variety of evils. There is the tendency to define all social problems, "from war to crime on the streets", as "health" problems. Thus, according to Callahan, by defining every problem in the world as "sickness", the World Health Organization seems to imply that science would be sufficient to deal with the causes of physical disease.[22]

Thus, Callahan argues that the definition, by implication, "makes the medical profession the gate-keeper of happiness and social well-being." In other words, the definition gives too much power and authority to the medical profession. Medicine, thus, becomes the norm of everything, including morality: "medical judgment" becomes moral judgment, and to be healthy is to be righteous. Thus, human beings must and ought to have health "if they are to live in peace with themselves and others. Health is no longer an optimal matter, but the golden key to the relief of human misery. We *must* be well or we will all perish."[23] The World Health Organization's definition fails to distinguish the different roles of different professions. The role of medicine, therefore, should be "limited to those domains of life where the contribution of medicine is appropriate. Medicine can save lives; it cannot save the life of society."[24]

Callahan raises some significant issues here. In defining health as "a state of complete physical, mental and social well-being and not merely the absence of disease or infirmity", the World Health Organization's definition takes an excessively wide sweep. The definition is utopian in that it is impossible, in my view, to conceive of the health of many individuals as "complete", for a high level of health in some people is compatible with some level of impairment, disease, and injury. It is too wide because it makes health synonymous with every social ideal. And more importantly, the definition implies that all elements of social well-being such as political power, social prestige, wealth, legal capacity, which contribute immensely to health can, if they are deficient in an individual's situation, be ameliorated by the medical profession. This conclusion is reinforced, in real life terms, in complaints about the health and medical system in the United States. For example,

At present, the health and medical care of this country is overwhelmed by the responsibility for dealing with a host of social, political, and

economic ills that do not belong to it. . . . We are continually broad-
ening instead of limiting our definition of illness and then telling the
medical care institutions that they must deal with the growing number of symptoms displayed by Survivors and the life-defying and life-
denying attitudes displayed by the ill. Alcoholism, criminality, antiso-
cial behaviours, drug abuse, mental retardation, anomie, fright,
loneliness, stress, and all kinds of thwarted developmental issues are
placed within the medical system.[25]

Approaching the issue of defining health positively, Callahan
says that however inchoately the World Health Organization
might have looked at "health", it certainly recognized the difficulty in talking solely in terms of "the absence of disease or
infirmity." The World Health Organization's definition tried
to place health in the broadest human context.

In place of the World Health Organization's definition,
Callahan suggests his own. In his view, health is a state of "physical well-being." "That state", he says, "need not be "complete,"
but it must be at least adequate, i.e. without significant impairment of function." That state also need not cover the area of
"mental" well-being because one can be healthy yet anxious,
and one can be well yet depressed. And that state "surely ought
not to encompass 'social well-being,' except insofar as that well-
being will be impaired by the presence of large-scale, serious
physical infirmities."[26]

This definition is, however, narrow, and worse, very closed.
He seems, in my view, to fall into the same pit as predecessors
who advocated narrow concepts of health. Also, Callahan seems
to advocate dualism of the human being, the mind independent of the body and vice versa. And worse still, he seems to
strip the human being of his or her social, cultural, as well as
religious beingness. Thus, one's health or well-being is seen
independent of the social, economic, religious, cultural, and
environmental forces at work everyday. In this sense, the cure
of sickness or disease must be restricted and should be the
sole responsibility of the medical profession—here specifically
the physician (and not the social worker, the priest or chaplain, the counsellor, and so on). In this sense too, the physician is to regard his or her patient as a symptom bearer of
disease, and, therefore, his or her responsibility is solely to
treat the disease within the sick person. By implication, the
problems of human well-being such as those related to poli-

tics, economics, religion, law, and so on, are also not to be the
concern of the medical profession.[27] Here, Callahan advocates
physical reductionism, for he seems to exclude the psychological, social and behavioral dimensions of sickness and illness.
Instead of calling for the close collaboration or the bridging
of the institutions—political, economic, religious, health, educational, etc.—Callahan seems to be advocating for continuing
divisiveness, ("professionalism"), which has been destroying
our societies for centuries. In short, this definition of health,
like its counterparts, is severely limited: it disregards the fact
that health is the result of many factors, and that health, conceived as a human phenomenon, is organic and sociocultural.
This concept of health does not go far enough; it does not
augur well for the kind of integrative and less conflictual society we are all working hard now to achieve.

While also regarding the World Health Organization's definition of health as too general, Talcott Parsons preferred the
broad notion of health. In "Health and Disease: A Sociological and Action Perspective",[28] Parsons described health and
illness as central aspects of human condition. In his view, just
as the human being "is both living organism and human actor,
who is personality and social cultural being at the same time,
so health and illness are conceived, as human phenomena, to
be organic and sociocultural."[29] He distinguishes health (which
at its organic level "is conceived to be highly generalized underlying capacity") from agility, strength, or intelligence. In
the same way, the meaning of health, at the action level, "is to
be carefully distinguished from the relevant aspect of intelligence, from knowledge, from ethical integrity, and from other
qualities of the individual."

> At the same time it cannot be confined to the organic level, to say
> nothing of the still more narrowly conceived "physical." It must be
> conceived as bridging both organic and "social" or, more generally
> still, "action" in the sense of symbolic involvements. . . . It concerns
> the underlying conditions of the organic life of human beings, their
> biological births, and their ultimate deaths, and levels of functioning
> in between, but at the same time it concerns the problem of the mean-
> ing of life and its vicissitudes. To squeeze out either aspect would be
> to vitiate the significance of the concept as a whole.[30]

Jürgen Moltmann has also criticized WHO's definition of health. Unlike Callahan and others, however, Moltmann criticizes not so much the broadness of the definition, but its idealism. According to Moltmann, defining health as a condition of complete physical, social and mental well being, and not merely the absence of disease, is a maximum definition.[31] Health is presented here as an ideal which can only be achieved by the society and not the individual. From this ideal point, then, there will be only a few people who will call themselves 'healthy'. From the point of view of this ideal, no society can guarantee their members the state of general well-being because there are no healthy societies. So for Moltmann, it is utopian to regard health as "an ideal of the undisturbed functioning of the physical organ, an existence free of conflict, and a state of general well-being. . . . It is the utopia of a life without suffering, happiness without pain, and a community without conflicts." If this condition is what we want to call 'health', according to Moltmann, "then to be a person in the fullest sense of the word is to be healthy."[32] This 'state' of general well-being, he contends, disregards "the strength to be human itself; it merely ties that strength down to an unattainable condition." And if we are to adhere to this definition of health, then psychotherapy and social therapy would have to form part of the therapy for the body. "Not least, a political therapy would have to be developed in order to make this state of well-being possible." He says, the proposals to expand clinical medicine do in fact move toward this direction. But such proposals evoke contradiction, in that human beings would eventually have no rights[33] over their own health: "If someone makes over to the medical system of his society his rights to his own health, he is reverting to the state of serfdom—for which the German word *Leibeigenschaft* (property rights over a person's 'body') is a precise definition."[34] So Moltmann questions if a counter-movement must not be initiated to rescue the humanity of people concerned; and he questions if there must not be "a personalization of health which has been socially expropriated, so that human beings can be called 'healthy' in a human sense?"

Recognizing that health can be viewed as the state of the human being's physical, mental and social well-being, Moltmann suggests that:

> . . . health can also be viewed as a subjectively ascertainable *attitude* on the part of the person concerned to his fluctuating condition. . . . 'Health is the term for the process of adaptation. . .the capacity to adapt to a changing milieu, to become older, to recover one's health, to suffer, to wait death in peace.' Health is 'the ability to cope with pain, sickness and death autonomously'.[35]

Moltmann argues also that health is not the absence of malfunctionings, rather the strength to live with them. He insists that "health is not . . . a state of general well-being; it is 'the strength to be human'" which "is displayed in the person's capacity for happiness *and* suffering, in his acceptance of life's joy *and* the grief of death."[36]

In Moltmann's view, it would be unacceptable to make health (as the state of general well-being) the supreme value in human life and in society, for it will imply a morbid attitude to health, and the equation of being human with being healthy. In this sense, illness is no longer a part of the individual life; it must be suppressed. This also means that the sick are to be "pushed out of the life of society and kept out of the public eye." To look at health this way, he says, robs the human being of the true strength of his or her humanity. And if the person is to suffer any serious illness, "it robs him of his confidence in life, and destroys the sense of his own value." According to him, then, being human is more important than being healthy; "a person has to prove the meaning he has found in his own life in conditions of health *and* sickness. Only what can stand up to both health *and* sickness, and ultimately to living *and* dying, can count as a valid definition of what it means to be human."[37] In other words, we must discover the strength to be human still more in sickness and in dying, rather than basing it on the illusory notions of the modern cult of health.

> The modern cult of health produces precisely what it wants to overcome: fear of illness. Instead of overcoming illness and infirmity, it projects a state of well-being which excludes the sick, the handicapped, and the old who are close to death.[38]

The modern cult of health turns away from the sick, the handicapped, and the old, and in so doing condemns them to social death. What is supposed to support healthy life becomes death for people who are excluded. According to Moltmann, then, the WHO definition of health is "open to such misunderstanding because it talks only about illness and infirmity, but not about death. But without the remembrance of dying, every definition of health is illusory."[39]

Health is a dynamic process, so it is "a process of continual adjustment, including the final adjustment to death"[40]; illness, disease, and pain are aspects of human existence; dying is inevitably the final stage of human (physical) life here on earth, and to live without the fear of suffering and also dying must be part of human strength for living, for we are created for "transformation through and beyond" suffering and death. It seems to me absurd, however, if human beings are to think that there is some dignity in sickness, pain, and suffering, and that we are to embrace them stoically without seriously working to alleviate them from our societies, where and when it is possible to do so. Dying, as Moltmann rightly puts it, "is not an end, and death is . . . a transition to a different kind of being, . . ." But must we allow its premature occurrence when it is possible to prevent it? Must we merely look on while people suffer poverty, disease, illness, pain, discrimination, and injustices in various forms because we know those (conditions) would eventually lead them to death after which they would be metamorphosized *"into a different Gestalt"*?

Although the World Health Organization's definition of health is too ideal, it is my view that the definition does not essentially disregard "the sick, the handicapped, and the old who are close to death." The World Health Organization's definition, I think, is one that can be seen to call for the involvement of all peoples (and the utilization of all other available resources) to making the societies bearable places for all, including the sick, the handicapped, and the old. One can be sick, or handicapped, or old and close to death, one needs the support, love and concern of family, friends, church, and society in general in his or her situation. The sick, or handicapped, or old individuals need help to make the best out of the situation. In other words, the World Health Organization is calling upon human beings who form society to work to help bring about the 'mental and social well-being' of all—the sick, the handicapped, and the 'healthy' individuals—even here on earth before they finally behold what they have always hoped for, the face of God. According to Moltmann, being human is more important than being healthy. It is true that health is not a precondition for being human; neither is it synonymous with "humanness". But the question is: How can we live true human lives if we are not healthy (in the broad usage of the word)? Let us face it: Does a person who has grown extremely weak and is dying due to starvation, a condition in which he or she lives because of the greed, selfishness, and exploitation of others in a system of injustice and domination, as the modes of production analysis points to, any dignity or self esteem in his or her own self as human being? It would not be fair on our part to tell an exploited mine worker at Obuasi, Ghana or Johannesburg, South Africa, for example, who, because of poor working and living conditions, inadequate food and medical care, is dying of tuberculosis, to embrace death with all his strength because it is "*a metamorphosis into a different Gestalt*", when we (society in general) can help to prevent or alleviate the cause(s) of such a condition. As suggested by The World Council of Churches, it is important for us always to remember to "make a distinction between preventable, untimely death and death which is our home-coming forever—the great hour destined by God."[41] In fact, we, the society in general, can help prevent untimely death by being just, respectful of the dignity and life of others, and by helping to lift the chains of domination and oppression, as the inculturation approach insists.

Reporting on a recent research conducted among white, middle-class men and women, ages 35-55, Saltonstall argues that ". . . the experience of 'being healthy' is another-instance in which the phenomenological body is explicitly salient."[42] According to him, the body can no longer be "considered theoretically as an abstract universal concept, but must be considered in its concreteness as lived experience of socially and historically situated men and women."[43] Saltonstall implies that health cannot be conceived independently from the social, historical, cultural situations of human beings. The definition of health must not be limited to the 'physical'. In Saltonstall's

research, asked to define 'health', many defined it "comprehensively, referring to it as state or condition of being. . . ."
And, he observes, the "cosmos of health depicted in [their]
definitions included most aspects of being human: physical-
ity, consciousness, emotions, spirituality, and social situation
(family, work, and income level.)" Saltonstall supplies some
examples:

> My definition of health would be physical, mental and emotional well-
> being (male).
> (Health is) being balanced in the things you do (female).
> A really healthy person is a well person, they take care of themselves
> and their family and friends, . . .
> Its [sic] also being loved and being able to love.[44]

Saltonstall concludes, therefore, that despite the fact that
"health is seen as an organic and inherent reality independent
of selves, it is a creation of those selves." Thus, health is a
social reality, and not an abstract condition or state of being.
It is a constructed reality through "the medium of the body
using the raw materials of social meaning and symbol." And it
is social, constructed in interaction with others on the terrain
of the body. This view, as he points out, contrasts with other
views which regard health as a material issue, or an objective
state in policy analysis, or the absence of illness.[45] If health is a
social reality, as Saltonstall argues, then it must be defined in
terms of the broad social context. It must also be seen as something complex and dynamic, and not a single, static entity. It
must be conceived to involve all the elements that contribute
to human well-being.

Our discussion so far has pointed to some problems and
difficulties we encounter in talking about health. Both the
narrow and broad definitions suffer. So do we discard both
concepts? In discussing the nursing conception of health,
Bandman and Bandman offer a promising way forward. After
pointing to some difficulties of both narrow and broad views,
Bandman and Bandman say that we can resolve this dilemma
by making a distinction between the scope and the core of
"health". Using the body of a person as an analogy, they say
"the scope of a person, for example, includes all his or her
limbs, but if a person has to lose a limb or if a person is even a
quadriplegic, we will still identify him or her as a person whose

core (or essential) features are nevertheless intact."[46] In the same way we can imagine two concentric circles, and identify the inner circle as the core of health and the outer circle as the scope of health. The two concepts, they say, are complementary and not mutually exclusive. "An adequate concept of health calls for both the narrow and broad views of health and disease." Thus the core of "health" becomes "the narrow physiological circle with the larger one being social and cultural." According to them, then, the broad, more dynamic concept of health is preferable. It takes into account all aspects of society and its institutions that contribute to health.

> In this view, the social, economic, political, moral, and religious conditions of health and illness . . . are given greater emphasis than that given by defenders of the traditional core of "health" and "illness.". . . The broad concept of health, for example, directs more attention to health-promoting and disease-promoting conditions than the narrow, traditional concept of health, and thereby reveals aspects of health previously ignored.[47]

It is the position of this work that the narrow concept of health is inadequate and unacceptable. The broad concept of health is comprehensive and dynamic. This concept, as Bandman and Bandman have pointed out, is the scope of health and therefore embodies the core of health. It *reveals aspects of health* which have been long ignored, the result of which, as I will contend, has been the blurring of our understanding of the health conditions of peoples in Africa, Latin America, and Asia.

The Concept of Healing

The definition of health as the 'absence of disease' is no longer acceptable. As our discussions have shown, health requires more than the "removal or neutralizing of some superimposed noxious substance or parasite or the addition of certain required life-maintaining substances". In other words, the concept of health can no longer be understood on the basis of disease alone; it goes beyond it. In this sense, then, the concept of healing too must not be seen in terms of disease alone as has been popularly done. The concept of healing goes beyond the popular (bio-medical) conception "based upon the model of the doctor and his patient, conceived as the relation of subject to object. The patient has a physical defect and the physician does something to it which removes it."[48] And thus, the meaning of the word to 'heal' goes beyond the meaning of 'cure' as commonly understood.

It may be helpful to look at some dictionary definitions of the word 'heal'. According to *The Shorter Oxford English Dictionary*, to heal means "(1) to make whole or sound; to cure (of disease or wound); (2) to cure (a disease); to restore to soundness (a wound); (3) (figuratively) to save, purify, cleanse, repair, amend; (4) to become whole or sound; to recover from sickness or wound; to get well."[49] *The New Lexicon Webster's Encyclopedic Dictionary of the English Language* defines heal as "to become well or whole again; to restore (someone) to health; to restore (a diseased or damaged bone tissue or a wound) to its normal condition; to cause (painful emotions) to be no longer grievous **to heal a breach** to bring about a reconciliation."[50]

As the foregoing dictionary definitions show there are several infinitives which regularly appear: "to make whole or sound", "to restore". It is interesting to note that *The New Lexicon Webster's Encyclopedic Dictionary of the English Language* uses the word "restore" several times but does not use the word "cure" at all as a meaning contained in the word 'heal'. Also, in defining the word "cure", it avoids using the word "heal" but uses the word "restore" again. It defines "to cure" as "to restore to health; to remedy; to preserve by smoking, salting, pickling etc.; to treat (hides) with salt or chemicals so as to stop decomposition. . . ."[51] By implication, this encyclopedic dictionary does not regard the words "heal" and "cure" as synonymous, although each of them contains the meaning of 'restoring' something.

In explaining healing, Michael Wilson points out that the ordinary meaning is to "cure". Ordinarily, a general practitioner would not use the word "heal" in his or her practice. Neither would the word normally be used to describe the work that goes on in a hospital. As he puts it: "a doctor 'cures'; a cut on my finger 'heals'."[52] When a person who is afflicted with boils, for instance, comes to a physician, the physician cures him or her. A physician who has the expertise at restoring his

or her "patients to full activity is doing his job well, as a tech-
nician." However, being human and not a robot, the doctor
cannot escape the implications of a personal relationship with
his patients. More often than not, personal concerns are involved in the healing situation.

According to Wilson, the human being should be recognized
as a social being, in relationship to other human beings. Therefore, a definition of "cure" as "restoration to function" is inadequate. It lacks social content. Illness or disease has its roots
in the life and relationships of the patient, "if not causally,
certainly as an event which affects the lives of others." For it is
common knowledge, to both the biblical writers and some
modern doctors, that sickness is a situation involving the whole
family and other significant relationships. It requires social
rehabilitation in family, church, club, and work situations to
cure an individual who is suffering from mental sickness, for
example. So, according to Wilson, "cure" can be defined as
"'restoration to function *in society*'." The meaning of the word
"heal", as used by Christians, goes much deeper. The word
"heal" contains an additional reference to the purpose of life,
the purpose of life of this particular patient envisioned by God.
"The surgeon may restore an injured hand to function: 'healing' looks at the hand as part of a person-in-relationship, and
is concerned for the purpose, loving or hating, to which the
restored hand is put."[53]

It becomes evident, therefore, in Wilson's view, that any
model of sickness (or health) which views "it in terms of static
pathology, rather than as a dynamic process, is *now out of date*."[54]
To be hospitalized for a period of time "is an unusual event in
a long sequence from life before it to life afterwards." A sick
person, he says, must not be approached as if he or she were a
still photograph, but rather as a picture in motion. Life is a
process; it is continuous, and sickness is not just a pause in it,
"but a creative or destructive period of life." It is in the middle
of this living process that we meet the sick person; it is incum-
bent upon us to try to understand what went before, and to
help the individual to respond creatively. Sickness, like any
event in human life, such as earthquake, bereavement, impris-
onment, traffic accident, "is a learning situation, a crisis event,
and an opportunity for progress or regress." No one emerges

from it as the same person, and the way he or she will handle future crises will be influenced by what he or she has come to learn in this one. Healing, according to Wilson, then, means *"restoration to purposeful living in society."* He says this meaning of healing is given not as an alternative to the definition given by Dr. Lambourne, to which we will turn below, "but as a further description of what we mean by 'satisfactory response'. . ."[55] And since he has defined the word "cure" as "restoration to function *in society*" and healing as *"restoration to purposeful living in society"*, Wilson sees any conception of 'curing' as, "therefore, embraced within the word 'heal', and given purpose."

A distinction between healing and curing has also been proposed by Appiah-Kubi.[56] Basing himself on an African community's understanding of curing and healing, Appiah-Kubi points to a fundamental difference between the two terms. Like Wilson, he sees the term healing as more encompassing than the term curing. Although in modern medical discussions the terms healing and curing seem to be used interchangeably, there is a world of difference between the two terms. According to him,

> A closer look at the terms reveals that curing is an event. For example, a doctor who cures a cut on a toe repairs a physically broken or afflicted part of the body. Curing is normally the work of humans, whether scientific physician, surgeon, or traditional healer. Healing, on the other hand, is a process entailing a long, complicated interaction of other human beings and of the community, and entailing, above all, the intervention of God. Thus, one can be cured of a disease but still remain unhealed. Healing implies the restoring of equilibrium in the otherwise strained relationship between a person, fellow human beings, the environment, and God. This process includes physical, emotional, social, and spiritual dimensions.[57]

Basing himself on the current medical thinking and theological understanding of healing, Lambourne suggests a new definition of healing.[58] According to him, as we have indicated above, healing must no longer be conceived as doctor (subject) and patient (object) relationship whereby the "patient has a physical defect and the physician does something to it which removes it." The new concept of healing, which is a modification of the old model, takes into account the healing of the whole person—body, mind, and soul. The old model, he says, is individualistic. It fails to do two things: Firstly, it "does not meet the new concepts of healing which are the result of the impact of the social and psychological sciences upon medicine. . . ." Secondly, it does not "meet the needs of a theology of healing which takes account of recent emphasis in New Testament studies upon the historical and corporate aspects of Christ's work."[59] In this sense, then, the old individualistic model is inadequate. "A new model is required which will take account of the old, but be deeper and wider." Lambourne suggests a new definition:

> Healing is a satisfactory response to a crisis, made by a group of people, both individually and corporately.[60]

A crisis, according to Lambourne, may be of many kinds. And with a quotation from Professor Caplan, Lambourne explains what he means:

> 'A crisis is provoked when a person faces an obstacle to important life goals that is, for a time, insurmountable through the utilization of customary methods of problem solving. A period of disorganisation ensues, a period of upset, during which many different abortive attempts at solutions are made. Eventually some kind of adaptation is achieved which may or may not be in the best interests of that person and his fellows.'[61]

The crisis, Lambourne says, is an opportunity. It is an opportunity for both the individual and the group, and it is psychological and also cultural and political. "If it is grasped, it results in a new balance at a higher level: both the individual and the group find a fresh external relation and a fresh and satisfying life within themselves." On the other hand, "if it is not grasped, both individual and group go back and find a balance [or death] which is inherently unstable; in fact a neurosis, or something akin to it."[62]

According to Lambourne, then, it is important to see situations in perspective in assessing cases of healing. The cure of a sick individual may lead to a different situation later. Lambourne gives two illustrations. The first instance is the case of the couple whose permanent separation was a result of the strain that they went through after their child, who had been ill for a long time, had been cured. The second instance is the case of a child whose death brought the parents into a much closer relationship. Which of these two cases, he questions, is to be considered the best "cure"? Lambourne says the choice may seem easy at first sight. "But follow the events of years and it may become difficult, as the broken home produces its psycho-pathology, perhaps alcoholism or suicide."[63]

Lambourne identifies seven advantages of his proposed definition of healing. 1) Since the study and practice of healing arts are no longer confined to the National Health Service and medical schools, the definition, he says, has the advantage of avoiding the usage of a specifically medical word. Healing is now a concern "shared by other university departments and various educational, welfare, and legal authorities. Priest, social worker, psychiatrist, and other persons can all play a part in the response of people to a crisis." 2) The definition encourages recognition of all people, both those who are involved in and those who refuse to concern themselves with the crisis; it does not restrict itself to only the sick person and the one who does something to him or her. 3) The definition does away with the dichotomy in pastoral ministry between a ministry of healing (based on Christ's healing ministry) and a ministry to the dying (based on Christ's suffering ministry). It thus makes possible one theology for both. The definition "also makes possible one medical philosophy for both care of the curable and care of the dying." 4) While the definition allows for the particular roles of professionals and specialists (such as doctors, priests trained in pastoral care of the sick, and probation officers) in healing, it places emphasis on the role of "the group or team in the healing work, rather than the work of skilled professionals who keep free of personal involvement." 5) Learning is the ability to adapt. And the human being, an intelligent and learning creature, is able to adapt himself or herself to new situations. Crisis of all kinds, "including the crisis of sickness, is an opportunity for adjustment to a higher quality of life. . . ." Unlike the older model of healing, it is not "a mere return to the previous situation. It is an advance." This model "gives their proper place to the crises of youth and the contributions of the educational psychologist, and it is true to the New Testament record of life of him who used every crisis as a stepping stone to higher things."[64] 6) Although the definition does not give a solution to "the problem of the nature of the relation between faith, goodness, and health," it suggests "that the relation may be seen more clearly in the history of a community than in the life-span of one individual." 7) The definition also allows for the employment of any process that would bring about healing. This seventh advantage which Lambourne gives is very crucial for this study:

> It also leaves open the nature of the processes employed by those who do the work. Everything, including penicillin, prayer, public water and sanitation arrangements, psychotherapy, sacrament, and surgery, is allowed, and the quality of work is measured not by its analysis into spiritual, psychological, and material factors, but by the quality of its fruits.[65]

Although he does not suggest a new definition, Jean Comaroff expresses a similar approach to healing. According to Comaroff, healing in all cultures is about the "human intervention in disorder".[66] It is the specific attempt of a group "to mend the physical, conceptual and social breaches entailed in illness."[67] In contrast, illness, according to him, is "a particular expression of a universal feature of human experience, that of threat to the normal state of being, or to survival."[68] This means an overshadowing of the *social* nature of the human being by his or her *natural* state, which results in frequent challenges posed to existing order. In this sense, illness "touches upon universal paradoxes of human existence, and their symbolic expression in particular cultural schemes." The main issues which these paradoxes center upon are the problems of "the unity and, at the same time, the duality of body and mind, the ambiguity of self as subject and object, and the opposition of natural and social being." It is not only the historical resolution of these dilemmas that illness or sickness calls into question, but also "and often the entire system of social relations and values which encompass the sufferer." In other words, illness touches on the lives of both the individual and the society in general; and healing too, in this sense, as Lambourne and Wilson have argued, involves both the individual and the society.

According to Comaroff, human selfhood finds its tangibility in the physical body. The physical body is the symbolic frame through which the paradoxes of human existence are most strongly expressed. This is so because

> . . . the perception of the body is culturally ordered, and everyday social action serves to reinforce or transform the mutual interdependence of physical and social being. But the body . . . is not merely a convenient source of symbols which provides a functional image of social form. It is a scheme through which universal contradictions are shaped by historically specific values, but it also permits such values to be 'naturalized'—i.e. to achieve the status of transcendent truths, or realities which are above temporal interests.[69]

Comaroff also points out that the dysfunction of the body, i.e. the illness of a person, is an indication of the disruption of the harmony which exists among the physical, social and moral aspects of being. And such a disruption, he says, "sets in motion the search for reconstitution." The experience of such a disharmony shakes the person's existing conceptions and may lead to "anxiety and heightened self-consciousness." More often than not, the contradictions that are deeply embedded in the entire socio-cultural order are more clearly perceived when illness sets in. Illness or disease calls for healing. And the healing process, at the minimum, "mobilizes potent symbolic resources. . ." This is because in their attempts to rectify the breaches caused by illness, healers in all cultures "manipulate symbolic media which address a mutually entailed physical and social order."[70]

> In the face of the doubt and anxiety which often accompanies illness, healing processes powerfully reinforce the validity of meanings drawn from the dominant forms of knowledge in the wider culture. Healing affirms the hegemony of established images of self and context. It touches upon deep seated paradoxes of the human condition, addressing them through definitions of reality which imply specific interests. Explicit medical knowledge provides the rationale for the process, presenting as 'natural' what is actually a culturally constituted and socially motivated image of man.

Comaroff continues:

> But illness cuts across everyday accommodations and the reflex patterns of action which seem to reinforce them, and often heightens awareness of more fundamental dilemmas in the healing process and the social order it represents. Affliction may thus lead to more thoroughgoing self-consciousness and 'disease' within the social system

itself. It follows that the context of healing affords privileged insight into the relationship between individual experience and the socio-cultural order, a relationship which lies at the heart of social transformation generally. And the evolution of therapeutic systems themselves cannot be considered adequately without taking account of these more encompassing processes.[71]

The concepts of health and healing we have discussed so far can be said to represent the current health and healing models of the Western world, though with many insights gained, I must emphasize, concerning the extended views, from other non-Western cultures. In other words, these concepts (bio-medical and social science constructs) of health and healing represent, to some extent, both the traditional, i.e., "modern" (classical antiquarian model, which still dominates) and recent modified views of health and healing. The traditional Western concepts of health were narrow and severely limited. They reflect the individualistic and materialistic worldview of Western philosophy and science. Such concepts were those which, though contrary to the communal and spiritual sensibilities of Africans, and other third world populations, were imposed upon them through colonization. The modified approaches, however, move away from that individualistic and materialistic outlook in promoting awareness of many other aspects of human life which can affect human health and well-being. The broad concept of health, and thus the WHO's definition of health is, therefore, good not only because it is broader, but because it moves towards a comprehensive outlook: it resonates with the worldviews of health and healing of many other societies of the world, particularly, in Africa, Asia, and Latin America. Also it promises to help promote better understanding of many illnesses and healing processes and, therefore, to contribute to the eradication of many health problems plaguing our societies today.

Health, Illness, and Healing in Akan Tradition

Conceptions of health, healing, and illness are aspects of all cultures. People everywhere experience illness or disease;[72] they experience healing; and they experience also well-being, and so know how it feels to be healthy. In fact, the concepts of illness or disease, health, and healing constitute important components of the worldview of a people. And being important components of a worldview, they are moulded or shaped by that particular worldview and its relationship to a particular mode of production. The traditional (narrow) Western views of health and healing, as discussed above, have been determined by the Western (capitalist) worldview of which they form a part. They are rooted in a worldview which is limited by its individualistic, rationalistic, and materialistic approach to things. Institutions exist independent of one another. Medicine, for example, has become divorced from religion, law, morality, etc. The human being, also for example, has been split into body, mind, and soul, whereby healing is undertaken by the physician, the psychiatrist, and the priest, respectively, each of whom is independent of the other. Health, healing, and illness are, therefore, viewed independently from other factors.

Unlike the Western worldview, the worldview of the Akans in particular, and Africans in general, is holistic. Health, healing, and illness are components of the broad and integrated worldview of the Akans. Health, illness, and healing are deeply rooted in the Akan traditional religion which is a major determinant of the people's worldview. It is no exaggeration, therefore, when Mbiti says of Africans:

> Because traditional religions permeate all the departments of life, there is no formal distinction between the sacred and the secular, between the religious and the non-religious, between the spiritual and the material areas of life. Wherever the African is, there is his religion: he carries it to the fields where he is sowing seeds or harvesting a new crop; he takes it with him to the beer party or to attend a funeral ceremony; if he is educated he takes religion with him to the examination room at school or in the university; if he is a politician he takes it to the house of parliament.[73]

And speaking specifically of the Akans, John Pobee writes:

> The first thing that strikes one about Akan society's world view is the fact that 'homo Akanus' has religious ontology. Religion is all-pervasive in Akan society. Thus a good deal of communal activities of the Akan and other societal institutions are extricably bound up with religion. . .[74]

So unlike the Western models, in the Akan tradition, it is impossible to view the concepts of healing, health and illness apart from traditional religion.[75] "Health", as Appiah-Kubi says, "is not an isolated phenomenon, not merely the absence of disease, but part of the magico-religious fabric of existence."[76] Among the Akans, health is considered a gift from the supernatural powers, particularly from the supreme being and the ancestral spirits. The themes of health and healing particularly dominate the traditional religion.[77] The Akan, therefore, does not separate health, healing, disease and religion. As Mbiti has emphasized, "in African villages, disease and misfortune are religious experiences and it requires a religious approach to deal with them."[78]

Among the Akans health is very important in many ways. Health is viewed in terms of the ability of an individual to fulfil his or her responsibilities in the community. The Akans regard an individual who is not disabled in any way and does not suffer any incurable disease or illness, achieves great success in farming or business, and is not impotent or barren and able to reproduce many children, as a "complete" and "perfect" individual.[79] Permanent disabilities such as blindness, barrenness, impotence, etc. are considered as dreadful misfortunes. So in his or her prayers, the Akan prays: *Mma mennwu awia; Mma mennwu anadwo; Mma mennwu koraa*—"Do not let me die in the day (Do not make me blind); Do not let me die at night (Do not make me impotent); Do not let me die at all (Make me fruitful and not barren or childless)."[80] While a person who is blind may be seen by the community as handicapped and, therefore, deserving sympathy, an impotent man or a barren woman may not be treated the same way. The reasons for such a view lead us to the discussion of the three major themes of *productivity, reproduction,* and *mysticism,* referred to above.

Productivity has a very important place in African conceptions of health. The survival or the well-being of a group depends upon the ability of each of its members to produce. The inability of an individual to produce, because of permanent disability or ill-health, causes the individual to feel irresponsible. Permanent disabilities are considered dreadful and ill-health is shameful because it incapacitates the individual in his or her responsibility to himself or herself, to the offspring if there are any, to the extended family, and to society in general. Each individual's productive activities are very essential to the survival of the group. The group is dependent on the individual and the individual, in turn, is dependent on the group. That is also to say, the well-being of a person depends upon his or her fellow men and women in the group. In short, there is a reciprocal relationship between individuals in society, and between the individual and the society. This, however, does not mean that an individual who is unable to produce at all because of permanent disability or ill-health is rejected and not cared for by the community. Traditionally, it is the responsibility of the community to care for its members.

For the Akan, while production is an individual's own responsibility in some respects, consumption is mostly a communal affair. One produces not for oneself and one's family alone, but for the entire community. The support for communal life does not mean, however, that individual achievement is not encouraged.[81] Individual achievement is encouraged because the Akan believes that human beings have to account to the Creator for each one's earthly accomplishments and failures. While individual achievement is encouraged, the communal life is given the stronger place, for as some Akan proverbs have it:

> One finger cannot lift up a thing.
> If one man scrapes the bark of a tree for medicine, the pieces fall down.
> The left arm washes the right arm and the right arm washes the left arm.[82]

Thus, in the Akan framework, "the idea of the individual would be meaningless without the total idea of the community." As Appiah-Kubi puts it:

> The Akan maintain that the phrase "it is for me" is meaningless unless it is linked with the idea "it is for us." The individual *is* because his or her family, kinship ties, extended family, and clan *are.* . . . The communal life ensures physical security and comfort, economic cooperation, and social life for the individual and the community.[83]

Reproductivity is also very important to the African conception of health. Like productivity, reproductivity is essential for survival and well-being of Africans. Children are viewed by Africans and other third world peoples "as the extension of self" and reproductivity as a "way to guarantee a future." This idea can be explained in many different ways. It can be taken to mean the extension or survival of clan or lineage or family names, or the extension and strengthening of social relations among different families, clans, kinships, and social groups through the bonds arising out of marriages, or as a means to curtail extinction. But for our concerns we will understand "the extension of self" and the guarantee for "a future" here as the extension of health and the insurance for a better to-morrow. In other words, for Africans, reproductivity or child-bearing is the extension of health of parents, so to say, and therefore a guarantee for the future. Among Akans and other African peoples, it is customary that a man may marry more than one woman. The idea behind such a custom is that the man and the wives will have more children, a larger nuclear family, so that their productivity in economic terms will in-crease. Thus, to Africans, children are wealth and strength. The well-being of children, therefore, becomes a major com-munity concern. In traditional Akan societies, the provision of food and shelter for children is the responsibility of par-ents. However, other members of the community do concern themselves with the general upbringing and welfare of all the children in the community. An Akan proverb reinforces this concern in terms of a warning: *Wotan wo yonko ba a, wo ba wu aperepere* (If you hate your fellow's child, your own child dies a sudden death). Today parents invest a lot of their resources in their children's education and trade so that the children in turn become the extension of the strength of their parents in the future. Again, the Akans have a saying which is often used to remind grown-up children of the responsibility they have to their old parents and old people in general: *Obi hwe wo ma wo se fifiri a, wo nso hwe no ma ne se ntutu* (When somebody takes care of you while you are a child (growing teeth), it behooves you to take care of the person in his or her old age (loosing teeth)). In their old age when old people are no longer able to produce, and where there is no income for them, they still need food and shelter to survive; and young people become the logical extension of the strength (i.e. health) of the old people in the community. They work to provide for their own needs as well as the needs of the old and the weak in the community.

The importance of reproductivity in the African conception of health can also be seen in terms of the anxiety, shame, and low self-esteem a childless woman or man endures, and on the other hand, the joy, dignity, high self-esteem, and honour a mother or father of many children enjoys. Speaking about the Ashantis, Radcliffe-Brown and Daryll Forde have indicated this:

> Childlessness is felt by both men and women as the greatest of all personal tragedies and humiliations. Prolific child-bearing is honoured. A mother of ten boasts of her achievement and is given a public ceremony of congratulation.[84]

They quote T. E. Kyei, who was Principal Research Assistant to the Ashanti Social Survey:

> A barren woman (*obonin*) is looked upon with pity not unmixed with scorn. She feels an outcast. And the lot of the childless man (*okrawa*) is equally hard. However rich he may be he feels that there is something seriously lacking about him if he is sterile.[85]

Writing about the concept of health of the Yoruba of Nigeria, one of the largest ethnic units in West Africa, Ademuwagun says, *Alafia*, which literally means peace, is the people's generic concept for health.[86] It is a word which embraces the totality of the individual—his or her physical, emotional, social, spiritual, and psychological well-being in his or her total environmental setting. This means that the word means more than physical health. It is the belief of the Yoruba that to be healthy, to possess Alafia, "is a result of the dynamic interaction of all these variables." The absence of any of these variables is an indication that the individual is not well. The Yorubas, like the Akans and most other African cultures, view health as wealth: *Alafia l'ogun oro* (Health is wealth), and *Eni ba l'Alafia l'ohun gbogbo* (Whoever has health has all things). In fact the Hausa people of West Africa go even further in saying that *Lafiya ta fi dukiya* (Health is better than wealth). And so for the Hausa *"Zama lafiya ya fi zama sarki,* "being well is better than being chief"—physical, emotional, spiritual, and domestic tranquillity are far superior to material goods or politi-

cal power."[87] The salutation methods of Africans are particularly indicative of their concern for health. The Akan, for example, say in a greeting to another: *Wo ho te sen?* (How are
you? or: How is your body?). The Yoruba, for example, greet
each other with the common greeting: *Se Alafia ni?* (Hope you
have Alafia? or: How are you?). These greetings, as
Ademuwagun has indicated for the Yoruba, are intended to
inquire about the total well-being of an individual. The Akan
or the Yoruba who is being greeted responds, if his or her
health condition is positive, *Nyame adaworoma, me ho ye* (By
God's grace, I am well), and *A dupe* (Thanks to God, I have
Alafia), respectively. "This kind of greeting and response is
reminiscent of the diagnostic process involving a patient and
a doctor."[88]

Good health, among the Akans and other Africans, is also
"symptomatic of correct relationships between persons and
their natural environment, the supernatural environment, and
their fellow men and women."[89] Thus, good health is not only
a state of wellness in the human body, but also a state of domestic tranquillity, environmental balance, social order, and
moral propriety. As stated above, the Akan culture is communal and cohesive. Individuals depend on one another, on the
community, and on the spirit world. Therefore, deviant
behaviour (e.g., disrespect for parents and other adults and
ancestors, incest, theft) on the part of a member affects the
other members, the ancestral spirits who also form part of the
community, and thus the harmony of the community in general. For that reason, the Akan believes that deviant behaviour
does not go unpunished; it is subjected to sanctions from the
elders of the community and particularly from the ancestral
spirits, the custodians of traditional morality and values.
Among the punishments which may be inflicted on the deviant is ill-health. So in the Akan culture, good health and prosperity are enjoyed when one is in good standing with the other
members of the community and also the spirit world. "Litiga-
tion, for example, among lineage members is a taboo strongly
disapproved of by the gods and the ancestors."[90] Anything that
causes disharmony among members is disapproved of because
it does not augur well for the well-being and the survival of
the entire community.

It is the belief of the Akan that to achieve, and to maintain wholeness and total health, one has to be in harmony with nature. For this reason, much stress is placed on the interdependence of human beings and their natural environment. The relationship that exists between the individual and nature is expressed in Akan tradition in terms of kinship, identity, and mutual respect. "As human beings, the Akan consider themselves part of creation and intimately bound to nature. Thus, our well-being in all spheres of life is dependent on how we treat nature, our fellow human beings, Mother Earth, and God our Creator."[91] The natural environment is there for the use of human beings, but it must be treated with respect; it is to be nurtured, and not to be raped, exploited and destroyed. The Akan sees health in terms of the proper balance between human beings and nature. The tilting of the balance in favour of one or the other causes disharmony. As the human being needs rest from time to time so does nature. "Nature is a living thing; a river is not just a river; it is the repository of the divine spirit."[92] In Ghana and among many other African peoples, days are set aside in the week when some aspects of nature are not to be "disturbed". For instance, in Ghana the sea is not to be fished or "disturbed" in any way on Tuesdays. Among the Akans, there are some days in the week when some lands are not to be tilled, and also days when some rivers are not to be visited or fished. And in fact, there are certain feast days when all lands are not to be cultivated, except one's home surroundings. Nature is sacred and human beings, whose health is strongly dependent on it, must treat it as such. The sacredness of nature, and human dependence on it, can also be seen in the way Africans relate to the earth. The Igbo of Nigeria and the Akans regard the Earth as Mother. She is the Queen of the underworld who is responsible for human survival and also public morality. Among some Africans, the Earth "forbids, among other things, wanton spilling of human blood on her, incestuous practices, burying a dead pregnant woman without an autopsy to extract the unborn baby from her womb, and above all, sexual relation in the bush."[93] Among Ghanaians, as Bishop Sarpong writes:

> there is . . . a general sense of dependence upon the earth. A drum language puts it better than I can: "Earth, whether I am alive or dead,

I depend upon you". I hazard the opinion that this is not merely because our corporeal elements, whether alive or dead, rest on the earth,
but also because the earth provides food, water, trees, on which we
survive. She is not simply the symbol of fecundity but she is the fer-
tile woman *par excellence*; among some Ghanaian peoples she is described as God's own wife. She is impersonal, but alive, a controlling
agency in the lives of men. Incalculable like all mystical agencies, the
cause of prosperity, fertility, and health as well as of drastic retribution for sin or sacrilege, witting or unwitting, she is regarded with
great awe.[94]

The concept of health for the Akan, then, is comprehensive
and broad.

Health is seen in terms of fulfilling one's social, moral, and biological obligations. Thus, to be healthy implies health of mind, body, and
spirit, and it calls for living in harmony with one's neighbors, with
the environment, and with oneself—a total harmony that encompasses
physical, social, spiritual, natural, and supernatural realities.[95]

This broad and comprehensive Akan concept of health common among many African peoples, renders it incorrect, strictly
speaking, to speak of ill-health as "disease"—as understood in
modern medicine—in African cultures. If we want to apply the
word "disease" to the ill-health of a person in terms of African
culture, then we need to return to its original but now obsolete meaning. According to L. Lewis Wall, the *Oxford English
Dictionary* gives the meaning of "disease" as "absence of ease;
uneasiness, discomfort, inconvenience, annoyance; disquiet,
disturbance, trouble." Wall argues that this is the way the term
"disease" is understood by the Hausa of West Africa: "In Hausa
this is the state produced by the absence of *lafiya* [health], a
state of "dis-*lafiya*," if one may coin such a term."[96] Thus the
word disease can be used in the African sense if it is understood in its now obsolete but broad meaning. The narrow
meaning of the term disease, now operative due to the development of Western technological medicine, is inadequate for
communicating the African sense of ill-health. In fact Africans speak of a person as ill or unwell, and not as having "a
disease". "Disease in terms of the background to illness is not
before the observer or the sick. The picture that appears is
that of a person who is not well, who lacks *alaafia*. . . ."[97] Diseases are said to be abstractions, while illnesses are processes

in individuals. Pointing to the distinction between disease and illness, Reading indicates that the term *disease* tends to be used to refer to what is wrong with the patient's body, and *illness* to what is wrong with the patient.

> Illness is what the patient suffers from, what troubles him, what he complains of, and what prompts him to seek medical attention. Illness refers to the patient's *experience* of ill-health. It comprises his impaired sense of well being, his perception that something is wrong with his body, and his various symptoms of pain, distress, and disablement. *Disease*, on the other hand, refers to various structural disorders of the individual's tissues and organs that give rise to the signs of ill-health.[98]

So, one may say that Hausa medical thought fully recognizes illnesses (signs and symptoms), but has no concepts of disease in the Western bio-medical sense. "Hausa medicine sees only medical "problems" or "ailments," each of which requires its own "medicine" or "remedy," (*magani*)."[99] This lack is due to the cohesiveness of the peoples' worldview and their broad understanding of health and illness.

As we have noted above, the Akan conception of health is broad. It denotes stability, spiritual balance, domestic tranquillity, moral propriety, good neighbourliness, social order, peacefulness, environmental balance, as well as wellness in the human body. In other words, health denotes an entire network of interrelations: correct (balanced) relationships among human beings and between human beings and their natural and supernatural environments. For this reason the Akan sees illness as a departure from this delicate balance. It is the absence of equilibrium in the human body itself as well as in society. Thus, illness is not limited only to a particular destructive process in an organism. In Akan the term for illness is *yadee*. *Ya* in Akan means pain; *Adee* means thing, or something. Thus *yadee* literally means a thing or something that is painful or causes pain.[100] However, the Akan knows that not everything that is painful or causes pain is illness. For example, the experience of a severe famine or a drought is painful but a famine or a drought is not illness or sickness; the tragic death of a relative or a friend is painful, but death is not illness or sickness *per se*. And the destructive process in an organ in the human being is not the only thing which is painful or causes

pain; anything that may cause human beings to suffer disturbance, anxiety, disharmony, discomfort, etc. may also cause
them to suffer pain. In this sense, anything that may cause
pain may also cause disequilibrium, disharmony, chaos in the
society and in and among individuals. In fact, because his or
her view of the focus of illness is cosmic, the Akan views illness as resulting from a sick or broken society. The Akan believes that the condition of the society is a major determinant
of the health or ill-health of its members. The point here is
that, although the Akan word *yadee* may not refer to all that
causes pain, death, insults, separation, starvation, and so forth,
it is a perfect example of a term which suggests a broad conno-
tation of the term illness. It is a term which is illustrative of
what most illnesses are: they cause pain. Illness cuts across the
ordered, energized, and balanced universe of which human
beings form part. And like any other misfortune or chaos, it
shakes the very foundation of the pivot of the life of the individual, and in so doing, causes disorder (pain or 'sickness') in
all other aspects of nature and society close to the individual.

Among Akans, as indicated above, health is not just the absence of disease, and illness or disease is also not just the presence of an organismic pathology in the human body or merely
a pathological change. Illness is an imbalance, a disequilibrium in the order of the nature of the person's existence. Illness is believed to affect the whole person—body, mind, and
soul—and not just part of the person. The causes of illness fall
into two categories, naturally caused illnesses and supernaturally or spiritually caused illnesses. Naturally caused illnesses
are those whose causes are empirically known and which are
easily treatable. For example, illnesses which are caused by a
symptom, worms, insect bites (fever and malaria, for instance),
poorly prepared food, poor sanitation, impure drinking water, etc. are traced to nature. Under the naturally caused illnesses are also illnesses which are of a socio-psychological nature. For example, illnesses which are caused by poverty,
joblessness, unjust treatment (at home, at work, etc.), inability
to get along with others (in the community, in an association,
at home, at the place of work), strained human relations, separation, lack of husband or wife, lack of children, unsettled home
or family, experience of exploitation and/or abuse, etc.[101] It

must be pointed out here that some illnesses of a socio-psychological nature may also be regarded by the Akan as human-caused illnesses. Human-caused illnesses can be grouped under spiritually caused illnesses. They are illnesses that are caused (mystically) to bear upon the sufferers through the mechanizations of evil persons or individuals in the community who do not wish them well. So for the Akan and other African peoples, when a person falls ill, the first thing the person does, with the support of kinsfolk, is to seek treatment. But when an illness continues to persist, when it fails to respond to treatment, there is cause for serious concern. People begin to question if there is not more to it than the "natural" cause they identified. At this point people begin to talk about supernaturally or spiritually caused illnesses and their causal agents, ancestors, witches and wizards, sorcerers, medicine men and women, and other alien spirit beings. So it is not that Akans, and other Africans, although existentially very religious, see in all illnesses the hands of supernatural beings. After his eight years of experience with the ethnomedical system of the Techiman-Bono people, Warren makes this clear.

> Spiritually caused diseases are less numerous in terms of disease names; they are also relatively infrequent in terms of actual cases taken for treatment. Some diseases can be classified as either naturally or spiritually caused depending upon the circumstances surrounding the onset or development of the disease. Gonorrhoea contracted after a visit to a prostitute would be classified as a naturally caused disease. If, on the other hand, the patient has broken the social norm against adultery and contracted the disease, it would more likely be classified as spiritually caused by medicine placed upon the sufferer by the offended spouse. . .[102]

Segun Gbadegesin and also Appiah-Kubi[103] confirm this insight that spiritual explanations which include sorcery, witchcraft are sought only when an illness fails to respond to medical care. In some cases when it is feared that a person's illness has been effected by an action at a distance, for instance when the illness is a result of poison, a combination of spiritual and empirical causes is appealed to.[104]

Among Akans, the logical explanations for the persistence of an illness despite medical care are founded on two principles, immorality and the malevolence of an evil spirit. It is the belief of the Akan that people who suffer spiritually-caused illnesses are people who, either themselves or through closely related family members, have offended or been disrespectful to God, the ancestral spirits, elders, and the community at large by breaking a taboo. Or they are ill due to the malevolence of evil spirits or evil eyes. In both cases, the diagnoses and treatments are performed by appealing to the spirits involved and by re-establishing social relationships.

The comprehensive approach of the Akan to health and illness makes the elimination of illness or disease, or the reinstatement of health of the sick person, also comprehensive and whole. In other words, the people's approach to healing is holistic. Despite the fact that an illness may be seen as either spiritually caused or naturally caused, treatment for it is not restricted to the psychological or psychical or physical; rather it is human-centered. It is the whole person—in his or her physical, psychological, psychical and social nature—who is ill and therefore needs to be treated. Healing, therefore, among Africans, is a combination of what in Western terms are referred to as biochemical medication, psychology, religion, and psychotherapy. "The healing ceremonies involve confession, atonement, and forgiveness. The healing rituals elicit the confession of specific mistakes based on detailed reviews of the patient's history with special reference to the events surrounding the patient's illness."[105] Any approach to healing that does not take cognizance of the whole human person, his or her social, emotional, spiritual, psychological, political, economic, and intellectual realities, that is, any one sided therapeutic approach, is regarded by the African as incomplete and, therefore, inadequate.

In my view the holistic approach of Africans to healing is the basis of the erroneous impression that peoples in Africa do not make a distinction between a supernaturally caused illness and a naturally caused illness. Africans do, indeed, make this distinction. In fact it is the healing (therapeutic) methods employed in combating the two categories of illness which are not often distinguished by Africans. As indicated above, the methods of healing are more often than not combinations of both the natural (biochemical—herbs, roots, seeds, parts of animals and birds and insects, charcoal, etc.) and the supernatural (ritual, divination, etc.). And the reason for this is due to the way Africans look at illness. Illness affects the whole person—mind, body, and soul—and also the entire community and environment in which the individual lives. Writing about the Bantu-speaking people of Central and Southern Africa, Janzen confirms this.

> The fact that African disease etiology acknowledges the place of emotions, communications, interpersonal relations, and symbols in causing and alleviating affliction leads to the use of rather different measures in dealing with what Westerners might regard as "mere" physical affliction. Indeed, the distinction of physical and psychological and psychical and social diseases is not drawn. The concept behind the term *muntu* (person) is that of an individual linked integrally to lineage and thus to those who passed ahead and those who will follow, as well as to those in the immediate surroundings of life and work. Thus the attribution of an affliction to human or mystical causes requires both "empiric" and "symbolic" attention. This may mean, for example, that a man who has fallen from a palm tree and broken a leg requires routine bonesetting, splints and massaging, and rest, as well as ritual protection from the individuals who may have wished his accident and calming from hallucinations he may have had about his having offended the ancestors.[106]

So it is the person, in his or her religious, physical, psychological and social nature, who is healed. The distinction Africans make between natural and supernatural illnesses does not mean, however, that illness, healing, and religion are not separated from one another. In African cultures, healing, illness, and religion are aspects of the same process. One cannot think of healing without illness or affliction, and one cannot think of illness and healing without religious sanctions, rituals, and practices. Similarly, the experience of good health cannot be thought of without the involvement of God, the ancestors and the other spiritual entities. Healing, as well as illness, embraces the whole human person and the society, and religion is the index or the determinant of the peoples' beliefs, conceptions and practices. The peoples' conceptions of health and illness and their methods of healing are integral parts of cultures (worldviews) which have religious dimensions.

These discussions of the concepts of illness, health, and healing in both Western and Akan traditions are relevant to our concerns for several reasons. They point to the different views of Westerners and Africans and, thus, to the different approaches to medical practices. But, as indicated above, the traditional Western views of health, healing, and illness, which did not resonate with those of the Akans, were imposed on them through colonization. Their own views were condemned. Western medical practice, as the next chapter indicates, has remained unsuitable and inadequate to the health care needs of Akans because of its materialistic approach to healing. Western medical practice is geared towards treating diseases (physical) and not human beings (who are composites of physical and spiritual). As indicated above, medicine has been separated from religion. Akans are resisting Western medical practice which does not take their own understanding into consideration. This resistance is explained by the dynamics the modes of production approach points to: people resist innovations which have been imposed on them and which drastically change their mode of life for the worse.

The discussions also indicate the importance of economic, religious, political, and social issues on human well-being. Exploitation of human beings by other human beings, social injustices, selfishness, disrespect, intolerance, greed, as the Akan concept of health indicates, have great impact on human well-being. The asymmetric economic and political relationships between the developed and underdeveloped nations produce poverty and insecurity for third world peoples. In Ghana, the rate of unemployment is high. Many people have no jobs and so they cannot produce and care for their families. These failures undermine their dignity, integrity, and self-esteem which do not augur well for well-being. In short, if Africans and peoples of other developing societies are to enjoy good health and general well-being, then cultural, economic, religious, political, ethical, and ecological exploitation, domination and oppression should be stopped by the nations which perpetuate them.

The discussions are also relevant for the understanding of the growth of the healing churches (AICs) in Africa. Both social scientists and theologians would better understand and appreciate the healing practices of the now fast growing new religious movements in Africa if the healing theologies and practices of those churches were viewed in terms of Africans' holistic approach to healing.

In this chapter, the narrow and broad definitions of health and healing have been reviewed. The traditional as well as more recent Western views on health and healing have been discussed. Also, Akans' views on health, healing, and illness have been discussed. The traditional narrow Western views of health and healing have been rejected as inadequate; more recent views which move towards holistic views, like those of Africans, have been seen as adequate and acceptable. The social, economic, political implications of the imposition of narrow Western views of health and healing on other societies have been indicated.

The next chapter examines the current situations of Akan traditional medicine, Western medical practice, and the Christian religion vis-a-vis Akan traditional religion. This will shed light on postcolonial developments up to today. The purpose here is to show the conflicts—political, medical, and economic—resulting from the contacts between the Western worldview and the Akan worldview. For the resolution of the conflicts the chapter insists on dialogue, equity, and social justice. Some weaknesses of both Western and indigenous approaches to health and healing will be shown.

Chapter 7

Emerging Picture

Current Traditional Medical Practice

The colonial penetration of Akanland with its assault on traditional institutions and customs, as shown above, has had a profound impact on the nation. Colonialism did not only bring
the people into contact with Western economic, medical, religious and legal institutions, but also placed them under those
institutions. The encroachment of traditional institutions by
those of the West led to suppression and stripping away of
rich resources in the development of traditional beliefs and
practices. In other words, the development of traditional institutions was disturbed. Attention and interest turned away
from the relevance and importance of the traditional institutions in the indigenous context. Indigenous medicine, for instance, was no longer given official recognition at the national
level and its practice was circumscribed.

Western medical practice was introduced into Ghana and
other African societies by colonial officials and missionaries
in order to displace indigenous medical practitioners and to
eliminate them as political and medical authorities, and advi-
sors to the political leadership. The strategy included infil-
trating into the political leadership and massively injecting
Western ideological interests. Fako emphasizes this in pointing to the conflict between missionaries and traditional healers in Botswana. In his view Tswana medicine was crushed by
the missionaries, not primarily because the traditional medicine was fundamentally at odds with the presumably more
enlightened systems of health care of the West, "but mainly
because, as a system, it competed as a major ideological, moral

and political force, capable of inducing collective rejection of the missionary and his ways."[1] To supplant them and their positions, the missionaries "downgraded" the indigenous healers and their practices. It is worth mentioning here how some Orthodox Church missionaries, like their Western counterparts, exerted pressure on traditional rulers to persecute practitioners of traditional medicine and outlaw their practices. In Ethiopia the emperors, under pressures from the Ethiopian Orthodox Church leaders, even decreed to banish or punish "by the unceremonious excision of their 'lips and noses'" people who 'chewed, smoked, or sniffed' tobacco, because tobacco was considered sacrilegious because it was often used by the traditional healers and their followers.[2] Western curative medicine was introduced to oust traditional medicine. However, despite the fact that traditional medical practice was circumscribed, it was not destroyed altogether. It persisted.

In Ghana, as indicated above, the practice of traditional medicine was banned in and around urban centres by the colonial administration. The practitioners had to practice their trade in obscurity. It was only after independence of the country that President Kwame Nkrumah, in his Africanization policies and programs, attempted to revive, develop and encourage traditional medicine. He directed that traditional healers come together and form an association whereby their practices could be improved and advanced, and their dignity and status in the society be restored. This association, known today as the Ghana Psychic and Traditional Healers' Association, has spread throughout the country. Nkrumah also directed that the Faculty of Pharmacology of the University of Science and Technology (U.S.T.) in Kumasi undertake research on traditional herbal medicines. Another institute, the National Institute and Research Centre, was established at Nsawam to study the efficacy of herbal medicine and to train people who are interested in traditional medicine. Today, the institute offers, in its herbal clinic, daily consultations and treatment to the public. There is also the Danfa Rural Health Project, a joint project of University of Ghana (Legon) and the University of California, Los Angeles (UCLA). The project was established to train traditional midwives and also to gather further information on their knowledge and practices.

Today, practitioners of traditional medicine are better organized. Under the auspices of the Ghana Psychic and Traditional Healers' Association, healers are licensed. The localities where they operate and their specialities are documented and they can be contacted through offices which are established in all the regional districts. The National Institute and Research Centre is operating well and is contributing to the restoration of the prestige of herbalism in Ghana today. However, its future has been uncertain, for it has not been easy for the Centre to recruit a physician, i.e., an M.D., who is experienced and interested in indigenous medicine, to take up the directorship of the Centre when it is vacant.[3] Also, as is frequently the case in Ghana and other African countries, an overthrow of a government by the military means a cessation of the programs and projects initiated by previous governments; the project begun at U.S.T. in Kumasi collapsed when Nkrumah was overthrown by the military in 1966. In fact the governments which came after Nkrumah did not pursue the program of reestablishing an indigenous medical institution. It was only in 1972 that the military government of Acheampong showed renewed interest in indigenous medicine. In 1973 the government established a Centre for Scientific Research into Plant Medicine at Mampong Akwapim. Among the objectives of the Centre are: to improve plant medicine through promoting and conducting scientific research; to ensure that drugs that are extracted from plants maintain their purity; to help in the dissemination of useful technical information and research results; to act in co-operation with the Ghana Psychic and Traditional Healers' Association and other organizations; and to promote and encourage global exchange of ideas in matters of plant medicine.[4]

There have been remarkable achievements of the indigenous medical establishments. For instance, the Centre for Scientific Research into Plant Medicine has already conducted clinical research into the following diseases: arthritis, epilepsy, hypertension, sickle-cell and related diseases, anaemia, rheumatic diseases, asthma, infective hepatitis, piles, diabetes mellitus, skin diseases, malaria and peptic ulcer.[5] The efficacy of traditional medicine in treating ailments, even some with which bio-medicine has been unsuccessful, has been documented. In

other words, the traditional healers (herbalists, midwives, ex-
orcists, bone-setters, and the diviners) have made many significant contributions to health care delivery in Ghana and
elsewhere. For millions of people in Ghana, (both rural and
urban dwellers), traditional practitioners are the major source
of medical care. These accomplishments should not surprise
us, because long before the introduction of bio-medicine into
Ghana by Europeans, the indigenous healers provided health
care to the people. What is astonishing today is that, despite
the emphases the various regimes of Ghana have placed on
the inadequacy of the resources of modern medicine, the importance of indigenous medicine,[6] and the need "to create a
system of medical care tailored to the specific socio-economic
and cultural realities in Ghana",[7] no steps have been taken in
developing indigenous medicine. As Anyinam has observed,

> no formal training programme has been instituted to upgrade, im-
> prove upon, and develop healers' medical skills on any appreciable
> scale. *No budgetary allocations have been made for the promotion and de-*
> *velopment of ethno-medicine since independence.*[8]

For the above reasons, I argue that in Ghana, as yet, there
has been little development of indigenous medical practice or
its integration with the Western medical practice on a national
level. It is not enough, I think, for governmental regimes to
endorse the importance of indigenous medicine without actu-
ally supporting its development. The levels of support by local
and foreign governments, organizations, churches and other
institutions for the development of modern medicine in Ghana,
though comparatively small in relation to funds that are made
available for other sectors of economy and programs, keep
indigenous medicine in a secondary position. This, I argue,
stems from colonialism and neo-colonialism. (i) Through its
education and religious teachings, colonialism displaced indigenous medicine and its practitioners. Ghanaians were encouraged to look down on indigenous medicine as ineffective,
even as the work of the devil. Western medicine was supposed
to take its place. The curriculum for studies in medicine for
medical students in Ghana, like their counterparts in other
disciplines and fields, was and still is Western. Generally, the
physicians who are produced by the system become doctors in

and for the perpetuation of Western medical interests. (ii) The demise of colonialism did not end the imperialist pattern of thinking in which they had been educated. Many Ghanaians, like their counterparts in other third world societies, have become neo-colonialists. Many of the modern doctors have become professional elites who situate and orientate themselves[9] through their former colonial masters. And, as has been said of African doctors, and of other professionals and government officials in their various work milieux, they become helpless "outside a technology-based urban hospital."[10] The doctors' reliance on Western medical technology also helps to explain why post-colonial African and other third world nations have developed into major purchasers of the products of the world's largest pharmaceutical companies.

> It has been estimated that poor countries have taken about 30 percent of the total exports of the world's pharmaceutical industries owned mostly by Americans, Germans, and Swiss. The health professionals and the political elite see importation of pharmaceutical products and medical technology as the most authentic way of promoting health. Fundamentally it accumulates wealth for the neocolonial bourgeoisie as well as the giant corporations at the expense of the health of the people.[11]

It is even not uncommon to hear reports of some corporations and companies, in collaboration with health planners and government officials of third world countries dumping pharmaceutical products which have been banned or have expired in the Western world.

Governments in Ghana so far have failed to allocate sufficient funds for the development of indigenous medicine, even though they proclaim its importance. Among the reasons for this failure are that the overseas donors or lenders often give directives as to how funds are to be distributed or used. In other words, the Ghanaian government has programs and projects tailored for it, whether or not they are suitable and relevant for its people. This often happens, I must add, because African and other third world leaders are often anxious to negotiate contracts, however unfavourable they might be, with Western corporations and companies, because the leader gets his "cut" of the deal. Thus, on the homefront, the politicians and the planners of health services align themselves with

their former colonial masters, Western politicians and health
planners, and perpetuate significant features of the latter's
ideological interests, specifically Western medical, political,
and economic interests. They become, consciously or unconsciously, neocolonialists. Like their former colonial masters,
they uphold Western medicine and overlook the important
contributions indigenous therapy can make to health care delivery. In other words, we see here the impact of Western political, socio-economic and religious forces on the attitudes of
politicians and health planners in Ghana.

From his field research work on ethno-medicine conducted
among the Akans, Anyinam has concluded that the practice of
indigenous healing not only persists but is generally increasing. Although he groups faith-healers[12] under practitioners of
indigenous medicine—and that considerably increases the percentage of the overall number of practitioners today compared
with previous years, a proportional increase in traditional healers has been registered. However, a look at the numbers and
the different types of practitioners from the urban-rural perspectives indicates a different trend. While in the urban areas
there is an increase in herbalists and faith-healers but marginal increases in *akomfo* (priest-healers) and *abosomfo* (cult-
healers), in the rural areas there is an extremely slow increase
in the number of herbalists compared with priest-healers.

Several factors explain the decline in the numbers of re-
cruits for the practice of herbalism in the rural areas. Many
herbalists see the slow decline in interest in herbalism as a
career. It is no longer lucrative or financially rewarding for
people to enter into the practice, for the patronage of herbal
treatment is small. People now have easy access to drug stores
and drug peddlers, and rely on self-medication. The use of
patent medicines is considerably increasing, for "when there
is no spiritual content to healing, herbs and pills are essentially equivalent."[13] In other words, people increasingly see less
need for going to the herbalist whose practice today seems to
have very little religious significance. (Because of the pressures
from Christian teachings which regard their practice as evil,
and in the effort to attract more clientele including Christian
converts, some present day herbalists are trying to dissociate
their practice from the traditional religious understanding of
disease and illness. They are trying to do something which is,

however, impossible since among Akans religion and medicine are intimately bound together.) Many people prefer to patronize the healing churches (African Independent Churches) where treatment for their diseases and illnesses will be spiritually based rather than patronizing the traditional "religious"-turned-"secular" healer.

The introduction of Western education is another factor contributing to the decline in herbalism. The children or family members who would have been in training under the family expert are in schools. With their acquired knowledge through Western education, herbal practice becomes no longer attractive; they move into the urban areas[14] in search of lucrative jobs. Adding to the pressures against herbalism is the slur often cast on the practice by many educators. The herbalist is still portrayed as one who practices evil. Because of the picture created of the traditional healer and the low remuneration practitioners in the rural areas receive, children shun the practice. An exception to this tendency is where the practice is a renowned 'family speciality'. In that case patronage is high and the practice is financially rewarding. Examples of such specialities are bone-setting, midwifery, cure for blindness, and cure for some boils (*mpompo bone*) which are regarded as deadly.

Practitioners in the urban areas confront a different reality. The practice of herbalism in the urban areas is more attractive and lucrative than in the rural areas: "About 50% of the herbalists . . . in Kumasi are full-time practitioners compared with about 20% in the rural setting."[15] This difference may be explained in part by the high patronage and financial remuneration urban practitioners receive for their practice as an alternative to the high cost of bio-medical services in the urban areas. Unlike practitioners in rural areas, urban practitioners are able to practice full-time; they also have more opportunities to supplement their incomes than those in rural areas where the only alternative is farming. Also, the familiarity of rural practitioners with the people in the villages and towns where they practice may help to account for the low patronage and, therefore, the low income they receive. As one rural herbalist complained:

> Many patients fail to honour financial pledges (*aboade*) which they make prior to treatment. Many fail to report back when they get

well. . . . What worries me is that many of the patients are known to
us, and very often, it is difficult to charge them fees. You only hope
that when they get well, they will come back to show their appreciation; but many don't come.[16]

So when they finally decide to learn and follow the practice of
a parent or a relative, young practitioners seek better opportunities of their practice in urban centres.[17] The irony of the
situation is that medical services (bio-medical and alternate),
as I will show below, are becoming increasingly available for
urban dwellers while declining in rural areas.

To summarize, then, although official attitudes towards traditional medicine have been more positive recently, traditional
medical practice is still not adequately supported. It has no
strong official backing and, therefore, it is not well promoted.
Thus, it does not attract the youth as a career worth pursuing.
The wealth of medical knowledge that Ghana has is being lost
with deaths of practitioners, because the children of traditional
practitioners, the youth in general, and governments show no
interest in preserving and developing it. As one renowned
naturopath in Accra told me in conversation:

I am praying to God to give me many more years so that I can continue to help more and more people. I have not had the opportunity
to pass on my practice to anybody. My son is not interested. Who can
blame him? He has come to know that this practice requires a lot of
discipline but very little financial reward. When I die, this practice
dies with me.[18]

Much emphasis has been placed on the activities of the
colonialists, the Christian Churches, and the officials and planners and promoters of health care in the underdevelopment
of traditional medicine. However, the current low status and
patronage of traditional medicine in Ghana is also due to attitudes of some of the traditional practitioners themselves. As
indicated above, traditional medicine of Akans, as of other
African societies, is intrinsically bound up with religion—it
treats both the physical and spiritual aspects of the sick person. However, sometimes some traditional healers tend to place
undue emphasis on "ritualistic" performances and elaboration
in diagnosing and treating diseases and this sometimes dis-
courages subscribers from going to them. Rather than accepting their failures or limits in treating some diseases and ill-

nesses, some traditional healers make patients believe that their diseases and ailments persist because of a spirit being—an ancestral spirit, an evil-eye or witchcraft. In other words, too much stress on mysticism and rituals by some of the healers taints their otherwise comprehensive medical practice.

The kind of aura with which some healers try to surround their practice contributes to the secretive and closed nature of their profession. Like their modern physician counterparts and almost all other professionals, they jealously guard and monopolize their trade. Thus, the loss of traditional medical knowledge with the deaths of healers can be blamed in part on the healers too. Traditional healers generally hide, even from their own children and close relatives, the herbs and the ingredients they use in preparing their medicines. Some healers go to the forest to collect their herbs very early in the morning or very late in the evening lest their collections be exposed for others to see. Until recently, practitioners refused to have their *materia medica* documented. Their recent cooperation in the documentation of traditional medical know-how may affirm Fako's contention that the colonial persecution of Tswana medicine forced traditional doctors "to adopt rugged protectionism."[19] As a way of defending their credibility and positions as healers against penetration by both local and foreign hostile elements, Tswana traditional doctors "became secretive and mystified their practice"[20] Latter day doctors continued mystifying and being secretive of their practice. Fako's thesis notwithstanding, I suspect that even before colonialism in Africa, traditional healers were secretive of and mystified their practice. In pre-colonial Africa elites and professionals jealously guarded their social and religious positions and professions too.

The Ghana Psychic and Traditional Healers' Association has not been very successful.[21] The Association was established to restore the respect healers lost in colonial times. However, despite the good intentions with which the Association was established, and the benefits that might be accrued by becoming a member, only few healers have joined.

> More than 70% of the rural and 60% of the urban practitioners have never joined the Association while only 24% rural and 28% urban healers had previously joined the organization. For a total of 321 ru-

ral and urban practitioners, only 8% responded that they are members of the Association.[22]

Lack of success of the Association has been blamed on the poor organization and administration of the Association, and on internal wrangles and divisions among the different groups of healers. The internal problems are of ideological and professional nature. There is a power struggle among the healers. Competition for offices as a means to achieve fame and reputation on a national level is evident among members. There is also intolerance of belief systems of other healers in the Association. The result is that there is little cooperation and solidarity among members.

Concerning the low level of membership of the Association, some healers report that generally traditional practitioners want to work privately, to be independent of any association or organization, so that they will be able to maintain their individual autonomy. Many of them do not want to be controlled by or subordinated to their peers (other traditional healers), bio-medical doctors, or health planners and the government.[23] This desire for autonomy of individual healers contributes to the poor official and public recognition that indigenous healers enjoy today. This desire also contributes to the poor integration of traditional medicine and bio-medicine. Many of the traditional healers do not want to work in hospitals or clinics, in modern and better established institutions where their activities would be scrutinized, where they would be under supervision of other persons, and where the government will be in the better position to properly monitor their incomes and tax them accordingly. Traditional practitioners have been even blamed for being neo-colonialists themselves.

> Face-to-face with the enemy, the white colonial master, one could argue the necessity for the return to African traditional healing culture, especially since the colonial medicine was primarily for the colonial expatriates. But, now face-to-face with his own free Black Brother and Sister, it would appear that the Black Traditional Healer has the same compulsion to exploit, as even his colonial master did.[24]

There is the need for more hygienic equipment and environment in traditional practice. There have been arguments by some health officials and researchers that some healers expose patients to infections and prescribe medicines without proper dosage to patients. These arguments, according to Ityavyar, are plausible. But the plausibility of the arguments, he emphasizes, is that they suggest that it is not the medication prescribed and the methods employed by traditional healers which are inadequate, but the instruments which they use and the environment in which they work.[25] The proper usage and sterilization of instruments by traditional practitioners are more urgent when infectious diseases—AIDS, hepatitis, etc.—abound. More efficiency, respect, discipline and order, will be brought into the practice if traditional practitioners properly organize themselves into an association, as the Ghana Psychic and Traditional Healers' Association is trying to do, and if they avail themselves of training in other therapeutic methods, as in the 1970s programs established by the Danfa Project and by the Brong Ahafo Regional Integrated Development Programme. Traditional healers need to upgrade or develop their practice further, for the traditional medical practice, like other aspects of the culture, can never be static.

Current Western Medical Practice

Western medical practice was introduced to Ghana during the colonial period. Like the chaplains on the ships, medical practitioners accompanied the merchants, colonial officials, and the military to look after their health care needs. For many years, however, these doctors restricted their services to Europeans on the ships and in the forts. It was only after the bond of 1844, when colonial rule was formally established over the country by the British, that Western medical practice was institutionalized in Ghana. Specifically, formal medical work started in Ghana in 1878. Western medical practice was begun in Accra and spread slowly to the other parts of the country. The few hospitals and clinics which were initially established by the colonial government were built to serve the needs of the Europeans. They were built in administrative centres, mining and coastal areas where the British had their forts and ports.

When the various missions established themselves in the country, they also brought their medical officers to cater to

the health needs of their personnel and converts. They established clinics and dispensaries which were scattered throughout their areas of influence.

No significant attempts were made by the colonial government to make the services of Western medical practitioners
available to Ghanaians in general until the establishment of
the Korle Bu Hospital (now a teaching hospital) in Accra in
1924, during the time of Governor Gordon Guggisberg. The
Governor's concern to make available to Ghanaians Western
health care services was evident in his efforts to increase the
number of doctors and hospitals. By the end of 1927, the Governor had established the Kumasi Central Hospital (known
today as Okomfo Anokye Teaching Hospital), the Accra Mental Hospital, and the Sunyani Hospital.

Although the mission churches established their dispensaries and clinics to win converts[26] and also influence people
against the therapeutic practices of traditional healers, their
interests and intentions were more of service. While the missionaries built their medical establishments for the purpose
of evangelization, the colonial administration established medical services in the country "for the expressed purpose of keep-
ing labour "usable" and "productive". . ."[27] The hospitals which
were built by the colonial government were situated in 'productive' and commercial centres—such as cash crop, mining
and harbour areas. For example, at the time of Governor
Guggisberg, almost all the hospitals were located in the southern half of the country where economic gains were comparatively higher and where almost all the colonial administrators
and European commercialists resided. In 1927/28, out of the
39 hospitals existing in the country, only 2 (i.e., 13%) of the
hospitals were in the "dry" north while 34 (i.e., 87%) were in
the "green" south where minerals, gold, diamond, manganese—
and forest products, and the cash crops of timber, cocoa, coffee—abound. In 1953, about 90% of all hospital beds were located in the south. By the end of 1954, population-bed ratio
ranged between 35,000:1 in the north and 478:1 in the south.[28]

These data indicate the woeful maldistribution and inadequacy of health facilities and services in colonial Ghana. The
prevailing health problems during the colonial period were
mainly due to environmental factors which contributed to the
high prevalence of tropical diseases such as yellow fever, ma-

laria, sleeping sickness, yaws, worm infestation.[29] These diseases were largely preventable. But the measures which the colonial government provided were directed mainly towards the improvement of the health environment of colonial officials. Preventive as well as curative medicines were not available for the natives. Even in those areas where modern medical services were available, as indicated above, they benefited only a handful of the natives. The very few natives who benefited from the services of clinics and hospitals (i.e. curative medicine) were made to benefit

> only for the expressed purpose of keeping labour "usable" and "productive", since debility and disability resulting from diseases impair physical capabilities of labour, lower efficiency, and productivity of work performance and disrupt production process with the consequent losses of output and increases in production costs.[30]

In other words, in the cases where medical services were available for some of the natives they tended to be oriented to the cure of individual workers rather than to the prevention of diseases among whole groups. This was evident, for example, in mining areas where native workers lived (and still live) in slums with high prevalence of infectious diseases, particularly tuberculosis. The colonial government's attitude towards the health care needs of the people and its emphasis on curative medicine combined with the missionaries' attack on indigenous medical practice undermined the indigenous system without replacing it.

The inadequate health care services in colonial Ghana pushed the first post-colonial government to act quickly. In addition to its policy of reviving traditional medical practice, Nkrumah's government quickly set out to correct the maldistribution of bio-medical services in the country. Besides expanding existing hospitals and adding more to their numbers and training more medical personnel, Nkrumah initiated the project of building health centres throughout the country. The first health centres were built in 1957. By the end of 1963, eight years after Ghana's independence, Nkrumah's administration had built a total of 41 health centres throughout Ghana;[31] government hospitals totalled 37; mission hospitals totalled 27; and institutions for training nurses numbered 21.[32]

Although Nkrumah's government made efforts to improve health care services in Ghana, his accomplishments were limited. The rural-urban disparity of health care services continued. As characteristic of newly independent nations in Africa, Ghana was left economically raped by the colonial administration. And so financial constraint, coupled with poor planning and execution on the part of Nkrumah's government, resulted in inadequate and continued poor distribution of health care services. Subsequent governments also did not try to effect much change. For instance, the military government which overthrew Nkrumah in 1966 achieved little in terms of improving rural health care delivery, although it had planned to give priority to the intensification of health care needs of rural dwellers through public health education, and maternal and child health care activities. "The location of health care facilities was influenced by factors such as a locality's allegiance to the military government, the whims and caprices of those at the helm of affairs, financial burdens, and mis-management."[33] The localities which were in the greatest need of simple health care services were neglected. This approach to the provision of health care facilities, like economic and social facilities and services, was no different from that of previous colonial administrations. The colonial government provided health care services for the purposes of economic gains, while the military administration provided health care facilities in areas where it was supported. The rural-urban disparity of health care services continued.

Provision of basic health services in Ghana has improved over the years. Hospitals, health centres and posts, clinics (including mobile clinics), maternity homes, and dispensaries have multiplied along with health personnel, physicians (1,200 in 1990), trained nurses and midwives, para-medical staff, dentists, pharmacists. In 1991, there were 18,477 beds in health service institutions.[34] Programs in health education, sanitation, environmental health, maternal and child health care, nutrition, and communicable diseases control have also been launched. The mortality rates of adults and children have fallen. However, the overall conditions of health of Ghanaians and health care services in the country (with a population of 16,500,000 in 1993) still do not reach acceptable standards.

Health care facilities and services are concentrated in urban areas. Many people do not have access to modern health facilities, and even where hospitals, clinics, and health posts are available, they are often without medical supplies, equipment, proper sanitation, and the rest. Infant mortality is high, 84 per 1,000 infants. A high percentage of children is suffering from malnutrition: 27% of children under age five are underweight; 15% of children between 12 and 13 months are wasting,[35] 39% of those between 24 and 59 months are stunting,[36] and the mortality rate of children under five years is 140 per 1,000 live births. (Table 1). In fact, it is estimated that 8% of all Ghanaian children are wasted, compared to only 2% of children internationally.[37] And 30% of children in the country "aged 3-36 months are chronically malnourished, as measured against international standards. . ."[38] The rate of maternal mortality is also high—700 per 100,000 live births. An estimated 70% of the population has no access to sanitation, 44% has no access to safe drinking water; the ratios of population to doctors and nurses are high. (Table 2). Malaria, measles, tuberculosis, infective hepatitis, diarrhoea, whooping cough, and other communicable diseases are widespread. In 1990, life expectancy at birth of a Ghanaian was 55 years. This indicates that the provision of both preventive and curative medicines, and thus the provision of adequate health care facilities, has not reached any acceptable standards. The health conditions of the people are still poor.

Table 1 Child Survival and Development

Infant mortality rate (per 1,000 live births) 1991	Children Suffering from malnutrition % 1980–91			Under-five mortality (per 1,000 live births) 1990
	Underweight (under five)	Wasting (12-13 months)	Stunting (24-59 months)	
84	27	15	39	140

Source: Human Development Report 1993, New York and Oxford: Oxford University Press, 1993, p.157.

Table 2   Health Profile—Population with Access To

Health services (%)	Safe water (%)	Sanita- tion (%)	Pop. per doctor	Pop. per nurse	Nurses per doctor	Maternal mortality rate (per 100,000 live births)	Public exp. on health (as % of GNP)	
'87-90	'88-90	'88-90	'84-89	'84-89	'84-89	'88	'60	'88-89
76	56	30	20460	1670	12.3	700	1.1	1.2

Source: Human Development Report 1993, New York and Oxford: Oxford University Press, 1993, p.159.
Legend: Pop. = population exp. = expenditure

As indicated above, the health problems of Ghana during the colonial period were mainly malnutrition and lack of sanitation. Today, the health problems of Ghana are the same. A large percentage of the people has no access to good food, sanitation and biomedical services. The living standard of the population is low. And this reflects the impact of colonialism and neo-colonialism. It reflects the asymmetric distribution of wealth between the poor nations and the rich nations because of the continued exploitation of the former by the latter. Thus, it reflects the impact of foreign political and socio-economic policies on the country. Also, it is a reflection of the impact of Ghana government's socio-economic policies which benefit the very few who are rich. People who go to hospitals have to buy the cards on which their histories will be taken, those who are to go in for surgery have to buy their own materials such as intravenous infusion, cotton wool, bandages, gloves for the doctor(s) and nurses, adhesive dressings, gauze, etc. There are no medical and food supplies in the hospitals. For instance, a recent report indicates that because of a directive from the Ministry of Health, over "eighty in-patients of the Korle-Bu Teaching Hospital in Accra may die of hunger if the benevolence of the hospital administration which has been feeding them free of charge since the last ten days runs out."[39] These patients were among those on admission at the Department of Chest Diseases, Children's Ward, Department of Child Health, Chenard Ward, Fevers Unit, refugees and paupers. The ministry's directive was that with the exception of Accra, Pantang, and Ankaful psychiatric hospitals, as well as Ho, Kokofu, Kpando and Ankaful leprosaria, "feeding of in-patients at all the country's hospitals has ceased to be the responsibility of the government." In-patients who want to be fed by the hospitals will pay fees. A medical officer is quoted as having "described the situation as 'a murdering one.'"[40] It is not only the in-patients in the hospitals whose situation is a "murdering one", but that of the whole country, as in Ghana today even eating decent food is becoming a luxury, not only receiving hospital services. In fact, the quality and supply of health services for the health care needs of the people has been poor. The payment of high hospital fees, hitherto unknown, has been introduced by the government. There are no more free or subsidized health care services for the general population. And the poor, who are becoming poorer everyday, have no access to health services at all. In other words, socio-economic class differences are more strongly evident than before in the patterns of health care delivery and reception in Ghana.

In the field of health service, as in almost all the other fields of service, Ghanaians are experiencing a new colonialism. Ghana's socio-economic programs, like those of most developing countries, are not dictated by its own cultural and socio-economic needs, but by the policies of international donors and loan agencies such as the International Monetary Funds (IMF) and the World Bank. In its "Structural Adjustment Programmes" (SAPs), the IMF has obliged Ghana and other developing countries to remove, for example, subsidies and cut services, to impose fees in education and health sectors, to fire workers in order to increase efficiencies, to devalue money, to promote exports in order to earn foreign exchange.[41] These policies have contributed to the high rates of hunger and malnutrition in Ghana, for the government has to encourage private and state producers to export the little food that the country is able to produce to countries which already have much to eat and plenty of money to spend in order to earn foreign exchange while its own people are starving. Rates of illiteracy, ill-health, infant mortality, unemployment are increasing because the government has to remove subsidies on services like sanitation, health care, education and cut back its own work force so that it can save money to pay its foreign debts.

The colonial legacy and the neo-colonial approach to socio-economic problems of Ghana, particularly nutritional and sanitational problems, are also clearly reflected in the country's rural-urban disparities in access to services. In 1991, the rural population stood at 67% of the total population of Ghana. In 1988/90, only 39% of the rural dwellers had access to water, and as few as 15% had access to sanitation services. In the same period, rural-urban disparity regarding access to water was 42%, and sanitation services was 24%. In 1980/90, rural-urban disparity in child nutrition was 89%. (Table 3). A 1988 demographic and health survey showed that children "in the [more rural] Central and three northernmost regions of the country are more likely to show signs of chronic malnutrition than children in other areas."[42]

In sum, the health of the people and the conditions of modern health care services in Ghana are deplorable; the current grossly inadequate condition of health care in Ghana is partly the result of the attitudes of governments and the Church towards traditional medical practice. Like the state, the Church in Ghana continues to perpetuate the colonial mentality concerning health care. In their teachings, Church officials and pastoral workers in Africa have not substantially altered their attitudes towards the practice of traditional medicine, although some stress the importance of inculturation in the life of the Church today. Church officials emphasize rural health care in their programs; they build more hospitals, clinics and maternity centres in the rural areas, (a larger percentage of the over

Table 3   Rural-Urban Gaps—Population with Access to Services (%)

Rural pop. (as % of total)	Health		Water		Sanitation		Rural-Urban Disparity (100= urban parity: see note)			
	urban	rural	urban	rural	urban	rural	health	water	sanita-tion	child nutri-tion
'91	'87-90	'87-90	'88-90	'88-90	'88-90	'88-90	'87-90	'80-90	'88-90	'80-90
67	–	–	93	39	63	15	–	42	24	89

Note: The figures in the last four columns are expressed in relation to the urban average, which is indexed to equal 100. The smaller the figure the better the gap, the closer the figure to 100 the smaller the gap, and a figure above 100 indicates that the rural average is higher than the urban.
Source: Human Development Report 1993, New York and Oxford: Oxford University Press, 1993, p.155.
Legend: Pop. = population

90 mission hospitals are in rural areas); and they offer training programs for their workers in rural health care delivery. They do not, however, offer any training for indigenous practitioners or incorporate them in their hospitals and clinics. The official Church's attitude toward indigenous practitioners places Church members in situations of conflict with regard to receiving medical treatment for their ailments and diseases. Although they realize that Western-type medical practice often does not suit their health care needs, and is very costly, they are inhibited in seeking treatment, which may be more efficacious and cheaper, from indigenous healers because their official Church teachings prohibit them. Those Christians who do visit the indigenous practitioners, and many do, do so secretly, or risk being branded pagans and traitors by Church leaders and other Church members.

The Western-trained medical practitioners in Ghana are also antagonistic to traditional practitioners. In order to perpetuate their dominant position in society and, of course, in the field of health care which they have inherited from the colonial administration, many modern physicians oppose the therapeutic methods of the traditional practitioners on public health grounds. Many modern physicians, as Edward Green has observed, "regard the traditional healers as economic and prestige threats, and as a result, the former often oppose measures—including proposed educational programs—that would result in sharing power and medical prerogatives with the latter."[43] In other words, they do not wish to see the traditional practitioners achieve the same kind of status or power they enjoy.

But health officials, the government, and Church leaders should realize that cultural and religious beliefs of a people are never completely destroyed by foreign cultural and religious beliefs. Rather, as the mode of production analysis points out, they exist alongside each other even though the old cultural and religious elements are dominated. Western medical practice dominates in Ghana, but Ghanaians are ambivalent to it. So, while they are receiving medical treatment for their diseases and ailments from bio-medical practitioners, many Ghanaians also visit the traditional practitioners for treatment. As indicated above, it is the general belief of Africans that certain diseases and ailments are of spiritual and communal origins which Western medicine (with its "materialism" and "individualism") cannot treat.

The need for acceptance, respect, beneficial coexistence, and indeed, integration, as the inculturation approach insists, between bio-medical practice and indigenous healing is great. Apart from the spiritual or metaphysical background of the practices of traditional physicians, Africans regard the herbal medicines the practitioners prepare and prescribe as having more therapeutic potency in treating some ailments and diseases than bio-medicine. Edward Green has shown (Table 4) that the Swazi categorize diseases and ailments in terms of

Table 4   Conditions Believed Better Dealt with by Traditional vs. Biomedical Practitioners: A Comparison Between Swaziland and Nigeria[44]

African treatment better (Ranked in order)	Biomedical treatment better (Ranked in order)
Swaziland (Swazi)	
Madness	Chorela
Child diarrhoea	TB
Gonorrhoea	Syphilis or genital sores
Migraine headache	Bilharzia
Various bewitchments	Heart disease (anything requiring modern surgery or other technology doctors)
Nigeria (Yoruba, Tiv, Igala Idoma)	
Madness	
Childbirth	
Fractures and bone setting	(Whenever traditional treatment
Bewitchment	fails)
Gonorrhoea and other STDs	
Sterility and impotence	(When patient needs operation,
Snake bite	IV drip, blood transfusion,
Malaria and other fevers	sutures, etc.)
Diarrhoea	

Source: Reprinted from *Social Science and Medicine*, Vol.35, No.2, Edward C. Green, "Sexually Transmitted Disease, Ethnomedicine and Health Policy in Africa", page 124, Copyright 1992, with kind permission from Elsevier Science Ltd, The Boulevard, Langford Lane, Kidlington OX5 1GB, UK.

which treatment (ethnomedical practice or bio-medical practice) is better; also in Nigeria, people see bio-medical treatment as ranking higher than ethnomedical treatment only when the latter fails, and only in situations where a patient needs surgery, intravenous infusion, blood transfusion, sutures, etc. In other words, even though bio-medical practice dominates in Africa because of the support it enjoys from the government and the Church, traditional medicine persists. In Ghana, a survey has shown that of the 4089 births that were delivered during one period, only 7% of the births were assisted by doctors, 33% by trained nurses/midwives, 28% by traditional midwives, 24% by relatives, and 6% without assistance. While 40% of the births were delivered in bio-medical settings, over 58% were delivered in traditional settings.

For health care services to be suitable, relevant, available to, and also affordable by all Ghanaians, the government, the Church, and the Western-trained medical practitioners in Ghana need to alter their attitudes towards traditional practitioners, and support and work in collaboration with them so that health care services in Ghana would reflect the cultural, religious, and socio-economic needs of the people.

Current Religious Situation

Traditionally Ghana has been a culturally and religiously pluralistic nation. Different cultures and different traditional beliefs and worship have existed (and still exist) alongside each other. However, today the religious situation, as well as the cultural situation, is more pluralistic than before. In addition to the traditional religions, and the Christian religion which accompanied colonization, there are Islam, Hinduism, Buddhism, Taoism, in the country. Today 60% of the population in Ghana are listed as Christians, 23% are African Traditional Religionists, 13% are Muslims, and 4% others. Yet Christianity, which partly as a result of the colonial history of Ghana had a head start on other foreign religions, is the fastest growing religion in Ghana, and in Africa south of the Sahara in general.

Among the major factors for the growth of Christianity in Africa in recent years is the role of the new indigenous reli-

gious movements (African Independent Churches). It is estimated that over 7,000 of such churches are spread all over
Africa, claiming millions of people as their followers and members. In addition, thousands of Christians who are members
of the Roman Catholic and Protestant Churches are also great
sympathizers with the African Independent Churches.

African Independent Churches are emerging at a phenom-
enal rate. Scholars have expressed different views regarding
the emergence of these churches. Some have attributed it to
political and racial factors,[45] others to socio-economic factors,[46]
and others to spiritual hunger.[47] I suggest that the factors behind the rise of the AICs in Africa are diverse, and that in
Ghana particularly it is a combination of the above factors.

One of the most frequently cited reasons for the growth of
the indigenous religious movements in Ghana, often called
spiritual healing churches, is their healing activities (faith healing). The theologies and healing practices of the AICs are based
on the Christian and African conceptual frames. Although the
AICs have different approaches and theologies concerning illness and disease, they generally recognize African etiology of
disease and illness and healing practices. They seek to diagnose the illnesses, diseases and other social and economic problems of their patients through prophecies, divination, the interpretation of dreams, analysis of behaviours and life-styles
of patients and family members, and so forth, in the style of
the African diviner and the Old Testament prophet. Healing
also takes the same form. As I have indicated in Chapter 5, the
Akan concept of healing is holistic. It takes account of the whole
person—physical and spiritual—in community. Thus, it is spiritual and communitarian in outlook. Sickness and healing are
seen as affairs involving not only the individual who is the
sufferer, but the whole community. The AICs approach healing and sickness similarly. They do not see illness and healing
as affairs of the individuals who are involved alone, but the
affairs of whole church communities. In other words, the entire congregation of a church shares in the illnesses and problems of their afflicted members and take part in the healing
processes. The AICs' approach to healing which integrates
African traditional elements with Christian approaches is very
attractive to many Akans.

The spiritual healing churches in Ghana have influenced the theology and pastoral approaches of the mission churches, and the indigenous and Western medical practices in Ghana. With regard to mission churches, in the first place, the practices of the AICs question the former's position in relation to Akan culture and religion. The AICs study the Scriptures and place the teachings of the Old and New Testaments alongside the tenets of Akan traditional religion and culture. By analyzing the Scriptures and accepting the Old Testament (the religious and cultural experiences of the Israelites) as a necessary and indispensable base for the understanding of the New Testament, they have shown the relevance of the Gospel message to their own religious and cultural situations. As indicated above, they have integrated cultural and religious sensibilities into Christianity. In other words, they have shown that the Gospel message can be better understood and practised by Akans if it is linked with their own experiences of the divine through their cultural elements and religious practices and beliefs. By integrating African traditional elements with Christian approaches, they have practised what the Catholic Church has only preached—that "the doctrine and redemption of Christ fulfils, renews and perfects whatever good is found in all human traditions."[48] The AICs challenge the Catholic Church, particularly, to follow its own teaching in the Declaration of Vatican II on Missions:

> The Church must insert herself into the communities of people as part of the same drive by which Christ himself, through his incarnation, allowed himself to be bound by the social and cultural conditions of the people with whom he lived. (*Ad Gentes*, p.10)

By regarding moral and religious values of African traditions as providential and most fruitful foundations on which the Gospel can be based, the AICs are truly contributing to new societies centred on Christ.

Secondly, by their belief in and emphasis on healing, the AICs question the mission churches' position as regards the power of God over disease, illnesses, misfortunes, and evil spirits. In their teachings, the mission churches acknowledge the power of Christ over everything, including illness, disease, and demons. The Catholic Church, particularly, professes that the Sacraments of the church, baptism, reconciliation, anointing of the sick, holy communion, are efficacious for healing. The belief of the mission churches in the efficacy of prayers for healing is also evident in the recent rapid growth of charismatic movement all over North America, Europe and other continents. However, officials of mission churches do not give much attention to healing and to the religious sensibilities of populations of Africa. For instance, exorcism is a practice found in the Catholic Church and Anglican Church; it is also a practice found in the African traditional religions. But because they have rejected the belief in evil spirits and witchcraft as nonsense, ministers of the mission churches in Africa rarely perform exorcisms. In contrast, the AICs exercise the power of Jesus and the Holy Spirit over illness, the Devil and his agents. The attention that they give to African sensibilities makes the churches more attractive to the people.

The emergence of the AICs has affected the practice of traditional medicine in Ghana to some extent. Like their parent (mission) churches, and sometimes much more aggressively than the mission churches, the AICs condemn (particularly through their preachings) the practice of traditional medicine. They regard the practice as evil and the indigenous practitioners as evil incarnate. The verbal attacks on traditional practitioners by the leaders (usually called faith-healers) of the AICs may be explained in terms of the latter's "religious" zeal, and more importantly the competition the former offers.

As indicated above, in their healing activities the AICs have integrated African traditional elements with Christianity; they operate in the style of the traditional healer. The faith-healer and the traditional healer use similar approaches and *materia medica* in their healing activities. Also, they both observe similar taboos such as the avoidance of pork, alcoholic drinks, snails, etc.

Moreover, the faith-healer claims his or her healing power as coming from the Holy Spirit, and emphasizes the life, teachings, and healing activities of Jesus Christ. (This emphasis on Jesus Christ and on the Holy Spirit is one of the major differences between the faith-healer and the traditional healer.) But, as indicated above, the traditional healers too see healing or medical practice as inseparable from religion. Indeed, when they give medicines to their patients, traditional healers say to them: "If it is the will of God, you will be healed." In other words, they also believe in the power of God to heal.

So, because they use similar approaches and *materia medica* in healing, traditional healers are seen by faith-healers as rivals who compete with them for clients. Traditional healers, thus, are economic and prestige threats to the faith-healers. In some circumstances, however, there appears to be cooperation between some of their members. In fact, in Ghana, it is not uncommon to hear people saying that some faith-healers secretly solicit the aid of traditional healers in their healing activities.

The AICs' condemnation of the practices of the traditional healers has not only made traditional healers lose clientele but has also contributed to their declining vocations. First, the effects of Christian teachings and literary education upon traditional medical practice have rendered it unattractive to many prospective healers; many of the youth who acquire the indigenous medical knowledge tend to practice it by way of becoming faith-healers. In other words, those who decide to become healers choose to become healers in church milieux (faith-healing) rather than healers in the traditional setting. Such healers prescribe patent medicines and also herbs and other ingredients used in traditional medicine to their patients "when directed by the Spirit to do so."[49] In other words, they turn the practice into a "Christian" practice. They base their healing activities on the Bible. They do so to attract a wide range of clientele and also to avoid being labelled "pagans". This preference for practising their trade via faith-healing has contributed to an increase in the number of faith-healers in Ghana. In fact, faith-healers have been classified under the category of traditional or indigenous healers by some analysts.[50] However, I prefer to place faith-healers, in this case leaders of the AICs, in the category of leaders of Christian Churches since, as I have argued elsewhere,[51] many of the AICs are genuinely Christian churches which are trying to place the Gospel message in the African context by integrating African traditional elements with Christianity.

Although they are generally less emphatic in their condemnation of Western medicine than of indigenous medicine, some of the AICs also question the efficacy and the therapeutic methods of Western medicine. There are some churches which utterly reject the use of any type of medicine, and others which are ambivalent toward the use of Western medicine.

Speaking about one of the churches which rejects the use of medicine, Sundkler says that the Zionists' aversion to medicine derives from, among other things, their belief that the Bible is opposed to the use of medicine. They refuse to have anything to do with hospitals because they believe that people who seek help from "hospitals and European doctors 'get demons', i.e., will be possessed just as the *indki*-possessed people are when doctored by a Zulu *inyanga* [traditional doctor]."[52] The Nazarites also announce emphatically in their Sabbath liturgy: "For you, who are a Christian, it is a sin to touch medicines with your hands; [if you do] you will verily die."[53] Members of the Faith Tabernacle Church also believe that the use of medicine is the human way that goes against the ways of God. God is the only one who has healing powers for those who believe in him; medicine, they claim, is 'the way of the Devil and the unbelievers'. It is their belief that the use of medicine is wrong because it shows lack of faith and foolish because it relies on a human person rather than on God who is the Creator and the Healer.[54] A pastor of the Church of the Lord, who rejects all medicines for the cure of all illnesses, emphasizing the use solely of water, says medicines are to be rejected because they are "manufactured by human wisdom, and administered by expensive doctors."[55] No support, the pastor claims, can be given to the practice and use of medicine in the Bible, since there is no evidence that Luke the physician practised the profession after conversion, nor is the wine which Paul prescribed for Timothy's stomach to be regarded as "medicinal wine commercially obtained, but the freely given wine of God in Isaiah 55:1."[56]

Even those of the churches which accept the use of medicines insist that the reception of medical treatment must necessarily be accompanied by prayers, for the human body is both physical and spiritual; medicine can cure only the physical part of the body, and prayers can heal the spiritual part of the body. Thus, no medical treatment can be complete without spiritual healing, for illness or disease is an 'existential' issue, as well as a spiritual, personal, and communitarian crisis.

Such beliefs and teachings of the AICs undermine the confidence, trust, credibility, and patronage of Western medical practice. Also, they point to the weakness of the Western approach to medical practice where medicine has been dichotomized from religion and treatment of the sick person concentrates on the "physical" to the exclusion of the spiritual, and where too much reliance is placed on human capabilities. Such beliefs, coupled with the inadequate health care facilities and provision of services in Ghana and other African countries, further undermine the credibility of the work of physicians, nurses and midwives. On the other hand, the continued hostility to traditional culture and religion by mission churches' officials and Western educated health personnel, in the context of grossly inadequate services, make the AICs' approach attractive.

In their efforts to make Christianity more relevant for the people, African Independent Churches make mistakes. The activities of some of the AICs have been so deplorable that they have been classified in Ghana and elsewhere as 'mushroom' churches. Some of the leaders are out to make money and also to seek recognition and popularity. Some have commercialized the Christian message and their activities by charging exorbitant fees for the services they render. Some have been accused of idolatrous practices and neo-paganism by Christians from the mission churches. They have been regarded as "the back-door through which 'paganism' re-enters African Christendom."[57]

In their healing activities, some of the AICs deceive their followers and sometimes contribute to the death of patients. They diagnose illnesses and diseases through false visions, dreams, possessions, and prophecies. Some of the churches make their patients fast, pray, and keep vigils for weeks irrespective of condition of the patients. It has been reported that initially some Zionists did not even allow for vaccination—they regarded it as "the mark of the Beast". . . , and in highly malaria infected districts they refused to take quinine, leading to the death of many of the people of malaria.[58] Some of the prophets prescribe false 'medicines' for their desperate but innocent patients. And out of pride and over-enthusiasm, some of them continue to keep patients in their 'sanctuaries', 'hospitals', and 'healing grounds' although they know well that they will not be able to help. The environment in which they worship and "work", and the 'medicines' they give are sometimes unhygienic. In short, some of the AICs are death 'sanctuaries' for their patients. Some of the prophets of the AICs are "religious neo-colonialists" who see their activities and practices as superior to all others.

These criticisms of the AICs notwithstanding, it must be emphasized that the AICs are carving a path which holds a vision of hope for Africans. They are not only making Christianity more relevant to the needs and sensibilities of Africans by integrating African traditional elements with Christianity, but they are also telling the mission churches that inculturation is possible and it is relevant for the Church in Africa. They are, thus, challenging the Church in Africa to liberate itself from the dominant Western version of Christianity.

Equally important, their endeavours in establishing churches which cater for the religious and cultural sensibilities of Africans are indications that economic and political liberation are necessary and possible for Africans and peoples in other developing societies. Africans must draw their own political and economic agendas and carve their own trends of development instead of having their political, cultural and socio-economic needs dictated by foreign agencies such as the International Monetary Funds (IMF) and the World Bank.

Also important, the activities of AICs are indications that elements of a culture are not destroyed altogether by elements of a new culture however dominant the latter might be. The AICs have shown that the cultural and religious elements which the colonial officials and the missionaries tried to destroy persist today. The activities of the AICs are a reflection of the clash of different modes of production and the resulting resistance and adaptation.

Chapter 8

Challenges for the Future

Overview and Conclusions

This study has been concerned with the impact of cultural and religious teachings and practices on patterns of illness and medical responses. It has affirmed that serious conflicts ensued in the wake of European colonial and neo-colonial policies. These conflicts are reflected in the poverty, malnutrition, unemployment, and infant and maternal mortality and morbidity in Ghana.

Through the integrating lens of the modes of production theory, the study has shown that understanding the devastating conditions in Ghana and other developing countries requires setting them within a broad contextual framework of the development of a people's political, religious, economic, cultural, and social systems from precolonial times to the present. In other words, grasping the wide range of effects of capitalist expansion in developing countries requires attention to the relations of production which previously existed in those societies, to the disruptive effects of European policies, and to subsequent efforts by indigenous groups to adapt elements of both in their struggles to survive.

It has been a claim of this study that religious beliefs and practices play significant roles in shaping a determinate worldview. Religion constitutes a fundamental element of a people's consciousness and identity. It also plays a twofold role as a conservative force and a dynamic force. With regard to the Akans, religion's role as a dynamic force has been seen in terms of the references they make to their religious beliefs,

values, and practices. It has been evident in this study that the
Akan ideological-religious influences have persisted as forces
seeking to integrate the various institutions in the culture. The
Akan traditional medicine, for example, persists not only because of the effectiveness of the plant medicines used by traditional practitioners, but also because of the traditional religion which infuses the treatment with dynamism, and meaning.
Religion's role as dynamic force is also evident, however im-
plicitly, in the indigenous religious movements' (African Independent Churches') resistance to mainstream churches' theological teachings and practices. These movements have
reappropriated some traditional religious beliefs and practices
into Christianity (although they also resist other elements).

A unifying theme of this study is the illumination the theology of inculturation gives to the modes of production theory.
This study has shown that inculturation points to the same
dynamics as the concept of modes of production, from a different perspective, and helps to clarify the cultural and religious dimensions of the process.

The key concern of the theology of inculturation is the dialogue between a particular missionary version of the Gospel
and particular local expression(s) of another culture in a specific situation. Against the background of imperial Christianity and its legacy, proponents of inculturation call for reci-
procity and critical interaction of religious traditions and
cultures. They insist on dialogue, respect and peaceful and
beneficial co-existence among different cultures and traditions.

The importance, adequacy, and suitability of inculturation
as a theological approach in addressing the issues of dominance, conflicts, resistance, and sufferings which the modes
of production approach raises cannot be overemphasized.
Inculturation calls for a theological "praxis"—practical theology. Thus, it restates the important fact that theological thinking should lead to practical involvement with the poor and the
oppressed. Also, it restates the importance of and the need
for reconciliation, acceptance, and forgiveness—virtues which
the Gospel message preaches.

The concern for health care has been a major issue in this
work. This study has indicated that in the development of the
theology of inculturation, theologians have not, so far, devel-

oped this approach in relation to political economy generally or health in particular. In other words, the approach has not yet been developed to illumine the political and economic effects which result when different cultures meet.

This study has demonstrated particularly the need and relevance of inculturation in the area of medical practice or healing, specifically the inculturation (in this sense, "integration") of aspects of the Church's theology and approach to healing, bio-medical practice, and the indigenous understanding and methods of healing. Such an integration will not only make medical practice meaningful, beneficial and relevant to Africans, but will also enrich the practices of medicine or healing for the well-being of humanity.

The major cause of disease in the world, particularly developing societies, is poverty. There is so much disease in third world societies because such a high percentage of the populations live in abject poverty, which is magnified injustice, exploitation and oppression. Thus, health, healing, and disease or illness centrally involve issues of justice and peace, as well as of spirituality.

The role of the Church and theology, therefore, in human health and well-being is significant. In their proclamation, deliberations, pastoral and social actions, Church leaders and theologians must speak more strongly against foreign and domestic oppression and exploitation which result in poverty if they are truly to continue the salvific ministry of Jesus, and their own roles in the world as 'pastors', 'healers', and 'doctors' of the sick, the weak, and the oppressed. In other words, Church leaders and theologians have to be actively in solidarity with the poor and the oppressed in their struggles against distorted modes of production producing poverty, alienation and pathologies.

The responsibility of Church leaders and theologians in the fight for human freedom from all that stands in the way of life, human dignity, and respect cannot be overstated. Historically, the Old Testament prophets in announcing God's salvific plan for humanity cried out loudly against the exploitation and oppression of the poor. Jesus inaugurated his salvific ministry by quoting Isaiah's prophecy of liberation for captives, freedom for the oppressed, sight for the blind, and good news for the poor (Lk. 4:16-18). Thus, Jesus saw human salvation as beginning from the physical and the spiritual needs of human beings here and now, even if it is only finally achieved at the end of time. Indeed, theology has to begin with liberation from cultural, political, economic, social, religious, medical, legal, and ethnic forces of oppression if the ultimate aim of doing theology, and the preaching and pastoral activities of the Church, is human salvation, expressions of which are health and healing, and human well-being generally.

Some Implications for Social and Pastoral Ministries

Modern health care, as it was introduced to Ghana, did not take, nor does it take today, the peoples' own approaches to health care into consideration. Colonial approaches to health, illness and healing remain dominant today in Ghana. The medical field which is dominated by bio-medical trained personnel still perpetuates the colonial legacy of health care. The irony of the situation is that, while the Western world is moving away from the narrow concept of health, illness and healing towards more holistic approaches like those of the indigenous traditions, Western-trained medical practitioners and health planners in Africa are still clinging to the old approaches. In the University of Toronto, for example, the medical curriculum has been reformed and given a holistic focus. Medical students are introduced to traditional native (Indian) healing. Student pharmacists are taught the holistic model of healing and how to mix traditional medicines. In contrast in Ghana medical curriculum is still dominated by colonial approaches to health and healing. The colonial legacy of education still persists in Africa. Curricula for education at all levels of schools in Ghana must emphasize indigenous thoughts, approaches and models.

The need for the reinforcement and/or the development of the indigenous traditions by the government in its educational programs and the Church in its social teachings and pastoral ministries in Ghana is great. Such a development will help the indigenous people to accept the worth, dignity and nobility of their indigenous cultural elements and practices and, thus, assist them to acknowledge their own identity. It will also help them as individuals and as communities to adapt to new developments and new social circumstances. For example, bio-medical practitioners will be helped in this way to recognize and appreciate the worth of indigenous medicine and be open to and also integrate into their own practice some of the techniques employed in indigenous medical practice. Likewise, indigenous medical practitioners will also be helped to see more the worth, importance, and efficacy of many of their practices. In this way, they will be encouraged to perform their duties with more dignity, self-respect, and accountability, while at the same time, accepting and appreciating the weaknesses and limits of their practice and, thus, being open to training programs and new insights into medical practice.

Modern medical practice has tended to separate religion from medicine, with the result that there is growing dissatisfaction among peoples concerning modern health care delivery. The pastor's job is viewed to end with the Bible and the physician's begins with his or her prescriptions. Health care personnel see their work solely in terms of the physical, and even then, only the "diseased part" of the sick person; and the pastor also sees his or her responsibility towards the sick person as solely "spiritual", and not economic, political, social, and psychological. Even in some hospitals where pastoral care teams have been set up, some health care personnel seem to approach situations as if the pastoral care team does not count much, or at worst, as if it does not exist. In such a situation, the pastoral team seems to perform its duties alongside the medical personnel with feelings of "timidity" and "inferiority". "The Church", as Wilson puts it, "has been seduced by the specializers, so that often clergy fight shy of 'the ministry of healing' as not being within their competence."[1] On the other hand, some pastoral workers in some situations make health workers feel that the spiritual aspect of the patient is not theirs (health workers) to deal with. There is often a lack of proper coordination between the two teams supposedly working towards the same end—the spiritual, physical, and social well-being of the sick person. This attitude towards medical practice is at odds with indigenous medical practices and, indeed, biblical concepts of healing. Jesus did not only touch the sick to heal them, but also asked that they be fed (cf. Mt. 14:13ff; 15:29ff; Mk. 5:22-43).

Among the Akans, the involvement of the Church in the provision of health care services, as indicated earlier in this study, has been highly commendable. Hospitals and clinics that are found in rural and remote areas of Ghana are largely mission hospitals and clinics. And the better-staffed and -equipped hospitals, clinics and health centres in Ghana are usually mission ones. The quality of care given by doctors, nurses, technicians, and so on, to patients and their relatives, and the availability of medication, are often higher in the mission medical institutions than those of the government.

However, the approaches of the mission medical establishments to health, healing, and illness are inadequate. They tend to separate religion from medicine. Like their secular counterparts, the mission hospitals treat patients as though restoration of health pertains only to the physical body, "as though the human being is simply a collection of diseases to eradicate." Unlike the church-related and even governmental medical institutions in Europe and North America today where pastoral care departments or units have been established, in Ghana the mission hospitals, as well as the secular ones, have no pastoral care departments or units where the clergy comprehensively minister to patients. This reflects the sad fact that would-be clergy or Church ministers are not given the basics of clinical pastoral education in their training. There is an important need for such a department in the hospitals, and also the education of the clergy in clinical pastoral ministry, especially in Africa where religion is intrinsically bound with all of life, including particularly medicine.

Unlike the African Independent Churches, the mission churches in Ghana have failed to incorporate significant elements of traditional cultural and religious beliefs and practices into their evolving Christianity. In particular, the traditional medical beliefs and practices have been rejected in the mission churches' attempt to bring health care to the people. But for the large number of hospitals and clinics which they have established throughout Ghana to be more relevant, meaningful, acceptable and, thus, efficient in the provision of health care, the mission churches must integrate aspects of the traditional health beliefs, values, and practices into the practices of their medical institutions. The churches should run programs for indigenous practitioners to upgrade their skills, and also employ some of them to practice alongside the Western-trained practitioners in their medical institutions. They should contribute to research into the pharmacopoeia of traditional medicine, especially with regard to medicinal plants by way of morally and financially supporting existing research programs or establishing a research centre. These would make their health and healing activities more relevant to the people's understanding of health, healing and disease, enrich medical practices in Ghana, and reduce cost and, thus, make health care affordable to the poor majority. These would also contribute to the development of traditional medicine which is on the verge of extinction due to the churches' own activities in Ghana and other countries in Africa, Asia, and Latin America.

The mode of production analysis indicates that people resist, as well as accommodate, innovations. People resist innovations which tend to drastically change their mode of life for the worse. Specifically, they resist innovations which do not reflect or take into consideration their social, cultural, religious, legal, economic, medical, ethical beliefs and orientations. On the other hand, they accommodate innovations and changes which respect and/or are in consonance with their worldview. The Akans have resisted, and are still resisting, foreign versions of religious and therapeutic approaches which have been imposed upon them. They are doing so through significant references they make to their cultural and religious beliefs and practices. In other words, the cultural and religious elements which determine and give dynamism to all departments of the life of the people still persist despite centuries of social and religious change. This situation should bring Church leaders and health planners to realize the importance of inculturation in the life of the church in Africa in the areas of medical practices. It is through mutual respect and dialogue that peoples in different cultures will see the values in each other's beliefs and practices, and learn from each other.

Dialogue is necessary and important, this study has emphasized, because foreign conceptual frames are not necessarily better for the African in a number of important ways. In a similar way, it can be said that the ways of the African elites—political leaders, Church leaders, health planners, physicians, economic planners, academicians, etc.—are not the ways of the urban poor and the marginalized rural dwellers of Ghana. The people for whom projects are undertaken should be consulted to see if the projects are suitable, relevant, and necessary and meet their essential needs. To build a swimming pool, for example, for a village which rather needs a rest room[2] is a sign of mismanagement and lack of consultation at the grassroots level. To build a hospital in a village while the people have no access to good sanitation, adequate food and clean drinking water reflects lack of foresight. In the same way, to preach the need for love, equality, respect, and understanding in all situations to a people, and at the same time disregard their religious and cultural sensibilities, is poor spirituality and education. Conferences should be organized periodically for local leaders, Church leaders, pastoral agents, health and economic planners to communicate and discuss common concerns concerning their responsibilities to bring physical and spiritual well-being to the people.

The integration of foreign beliefs and practices and biomedical practice with Akan religio-cultural beliefs and practices and the traditional medical practice are bound to produce conflicts, as the concept of the articulation of modes of production illuminates. In fact, advocating the integration of traditional and modern carries with it an inherent danger of domination or even a destruction of cultural values. However, as the theology of inculturation also insists, there can be peaceful and beneficial co-existence if there is a mutual, fruitful, and critical dialogue and reconciliation among all concerned.

To recapitulate, the World Health Organization (WHO) has projected that, by the year 2000, peoples everywhere should have access to adequate health care services, nutrition and shelter. But, as this study has shown, the majority of Ghanaians, like many peoples in developing societies, have minimal or no access to clean and safe drinking water, food and shelter. The disparities in the distribution of health care services between the rich and the poor, the rural dweller and the urban dweller, and the developed and the underdeveloped societies, are widening. While "traditional" colonialism is collapsing, neocolonialism remains powerful. Indigenous therapeutic practices, in particular, which are comprehensive and inexpensive to indigenous peoples, are being destroyed and replaced with bio-medical practices which are often inadequate and costly. Bio-medical practitioners and indigenous practitioners are vying for recognition and prestige instead of working in cooperation with and learning from each other. Church health agents and public health planners are not working in collaboration with each other. The churches' theologies often place their faithful in dilemmas in terms of choices and reception of health care. Church leaders are interested in delivering bio-medical services and not the development of indigenous medicines. Health care facilities are established in some areas without proper and adequate feasibility studies; and health projects are often undertaken without follow-ups and maintenance. Millions of peoples in Africa, Asia, and Latin America are dying of diseases and malnutrition due to external and internal forms of oppression. Health care services are increasingly becoming expensive and inaccessible for the majority of the world population. The year 2000 is fast closing in on the WHO projection of health for all the end of this century. The contribution and cooperation of all—policy makers, Church agents, theologians, medical practitioners, governments, promoters and planners of health programs, social scientists, and the rest—are essential and important if health for all is to be achievable.

Modes of Production and Inculturation Approaches: New Tasks and Challenges

So far, the modes of production approach has been largely confined to analyzing political, social, religious, and economic relationships within societies and, also, between different societies. The analyses have pointed to tremendous impacts of relationships which are not based on respect, equality, and justice. What proponents of this approach, like those of inculturation, have failed to do, however, is to illuminate the impacts of asymmetric relationships on health and illness. In other words, this study challenges analysts to recognize issues of disease and healing at the heart of the clashes of different modes of production. Distorted modes of production produces conflicts which manifest themselves in physical, social, and psychological pathologies. These pathologies in turn call for the struggle for restoration and survival. Thus, at the heart of the clashes of modes of production are also the struggles of the victims for survival. They struggle to transform the distorted social systems—heirs of colonial and neo-colonial interventions and their marginal places in the contemporary world economy—in which they live.

For a better understanding of the medical and other situations in Ghana today, and for important and appropriate steps to be taken towards resolving the devastating conditions, there should be a new way of re-reading the history of Ghana. That is, colonialism and the history of missionary activities in Ghana should be re-read in the light of what is happening today. Modes of production approach has a task in this direction: rethinking the past to illumine the complexities of the present as well as possibilities for the future.

In their efforts at pointing out the asymmetric relationships, and thus the social, political, and economic inequalities inherent in the clashes of modes of production, thinkers should address the issues of health, healing, and illness and the general physical and spiritual well-being of the victims.

Recent trends in theology, specifically here liberation theology and the theology of inculturation, have ushered in new theological methodologies which radically challenge the traditional way of theologizing. They have gone beyond the traditional conceptual frames and methods of theology—abstract theology—into new frames which are characterized by "praxis". In other words, the proponents of these new trends in theology are reflecting on theological teachings in terms of human basic needs. They are emphasizing the need of theological thinking which leads to radical involvement with the poor and the suffering. This new way of looking at theology in turn raises challenges for the inculturation approach.

Inculturating the Gospel message with another culture, particularly an African culture, demands adequate knowledge and comprehension of the interrelatedness of elements of the whole culture. For this reason, advocates of the inculturation approach are challenged to study and see the individual parts of the doctrines and practices of the cultures as parts which are intimately related, and not as separate abstractions. The doctrines and practices must be seen as parts of dynamic cultural and religious wholes. For instance, the belief of Africans that the ancestors may inflict punishments in the form of sickness upon people who go against their will must not be seen in isolation of the people's religious and cultural systems. For the fear that the ancestors will inflict death (as a retribution) on a person if he or she kills another person helps to inhibit violence and to preserve harmony and social order. Thus, among Africans, cultural and religious beliefs and practices are a means of social control and cohesion. For example, the belief that Tuesday is a sacred day for Nana Bosompo and people fear that they will drown or see the monstrous Nana Bosompo (the ocean is seen as a spirit being) if they go to sea, keeps them from fishing on that day. Such a belief allows the fish and other creatures in the sea a period of "rest" and "tranquility". It also gives the fishermen a day of rest from their labours. It also checks over-fishing the sea, and guards productivity. Thus, religion (and culture more generally) must be seen in relation to political and economic systems. Indeed, it is impossible to understand, much less to evaluate, practices like polygamy or the honouring of ancestors or attitude towards barrenness apart from their embeddedness in social systems.

It is imperative, I will say, for theologians to recognize that the challenge of inculturation is a political and economic as well as cultural and religious challenge. The goodness in one cultural and religious system should be brought to challenge the weakness of another cultural and religious system, and vice versa. It is important for theologians to reaffirm that, in the end, what is important is not agreement on doctrines or ideologies but solidarity and collaboration in practice in transforming unjust and oppressive social systems. And in this process dialogue in mutual respect is absolutely fundamental, with no traces of triumphalism and great humility before the profound question of hope for survival in a hostile world tottering toward apocalypse in Africa and so many other parts of the so-called third world.

The roots of colonialism with its capitalism, Christianity, and also, Islam have been deeply embedded in the history of modern Africa, and there is no way that their impacts can be wished away. It is for this reason that this study has sought to point out theological and sociological effects of these impacts so that new choices can be made promising ways to transcend the continuous reproduction of the asymmetric relationships which characterize industrialized societies and African societies, and African elites and the urban poor and the marginalized rural dwellers of Africa. It is in this spirit of respect and equality that the material and the spiritual needs of Africans and peoples of other developing societies will be met.

Bibliography

Primary Sources

Ademuwagun, Z. A., '"Alafia"—The Yoruba Concept of Health: Implications for Health Education', *International Journal of Health Education*, Vol. XXI, No. 2, 1978, 89–97.

Anyinam, C. A. "Persistence with Change: A Rural-Urban Study of Ethno-Medical Practices in Contemporary Ghana." Unpublished Ph.D. Thesis. Kingston: Queen's University, 1987.

Appiah-Kubi, K., "Religion and Healing in an African Community: The Akan of Ghana". In: Sullivan, L. E. (ed.). *Healing and Restoring: Health and Medicine in the World's Religious Traditions*. New York: Macmillan Publishing, 1989, 203–224.

——— *Man Cures, God Heals: Religion and Medical Practice among the Akans of Ghana*. New York: Friendship Press, 1981.

Appiah-Kubi, K. and Sergio, T. (eds.). *African Theology En Route*. Maryknoll: Orbis Books, 1979.

Ashley, B. M. and O'Rourke, K. D. *Health Care Ethics: A Theological Analysis*. St. Louis: The Catholic Health Association of the United States, 1982.

Assimeng, M. *Religion and Social Change in West Africa*. Accra: Ghana University Press, 1989.

Azevedo, M. de Carvalho, "Inculturation and the Challenges of Modernity". In: Crollius, A. A. Roest, (ed.). *Inculturation: Working Papers on Living Faith and Cultures*, Vol. I. Rome: Pontifical Gregorian University, 1982, 1–63.

Baeta, C. G. *Christianity in Tropical Africa*. London: Oxford University Press, 1968.

——— *Prophetism in Ghana*. London: Oxford University Press, 1961.

Bandman, E. L. and Bandman, B., "Health and Disease: A Nursing Perspective". In: Caplan, A. L., Engelhardt, H. T. and Mcmartney, J. J. (eds.). *Concepts of Health and Disease: Interdisciplinary Perspectives*. Don Mills, Ontario: Addison-Wesley Publishing Company, 1981, 667–692.

178 *Bibliography*

Beckmann, D. M. *Eden Revival: Spiritual Churches in Ghana.* London: Concordia, 1975.

Bishaw, M., "Promoting Traditional Medicine in Ethiopia: A Brief Historical Review of Government Policy", *Social Science and Medicine*, Vol. 33, No. 2, 1991, 193–200.

Blum, H. L. *Planning for Health: Development and Application of Social Change.* New York: Human Sciences Press, 1974.

Boahene, A. Adu, "Politics in Ghana, 1800–1874". In: Ajayi, J. F. A. and Crowder, M., (eds.). *History of West Africa*, Vol. 2. New York: Columbia University Press, 1973.

Bonsi, S. K., "Foreign Impact on Precolonial Medicine". In: Falola, T. and Ityavyar, D., (eds.). *The Political Economy of Health in Africa.* Athens, Ohio: Ohio University Press, 1992, 49–64.

——— "Persistence and Change in Traditional Medical Practice in Ghana", *International Journal of Contemporary Sociology*, 14, January and April, 1977, Nos. 1 & 2, 27–38.

Callahan, D., "The WHO Definition of 'Health'", *The Hastings Center Studies*, Vol.1, No. 3, 1973, 77–88.

Caplan, A. L. et. al. *Concepts of Health and Disease: Interdisciplinary Perspectives.* Don Mills, Ontario: Addison-Wesley Publishing Co., 1981.

Chilcote, R. (ed.). *Dependency and Marxism: Toward a Resolution of the Debate.* Boulder, Colorado: Westview Press, 1982.

Chirban, J. T. (ed.). *Health and Faith: Medical, Psychological and Religious Dimensions.* Lanham, Md.: University Press of America, 1991.

Comaroff, J. *Body of Power, Spirit of Resistance: the Cultural and History of a South African People.* Chicago: University of Chicago Press, 1985.

——— "Healing and Cultural Transformation: The Tswana of Southern Africa [1]", *Social Science and Medicine*, Vol.15B, 1981, 361–378.

Cosminsky, S., "Traditional Midwifery and Contraception". In: Bannerman, R. H., Burton, J. and Wen-Chieh, C. (eds.). *Traditional Medicine and Health Care Coverage.* Geneva: World Health Organization, 1983, 142–162.

Crollius, A. A. R., "What is so New about Inculturation?" In: Crollius, A. A. Roest, (ed.). *Inculturation: Working Papers on Living Faith*, Vol. V. Rome: Pontifical Gregorian University, 1984, 1–18.

Crowder, M. *Colonial West Africa: Collected Essays.* London: Frank Cass, 1978.

——— *West Africa Under Colonial Rule.* London: Hutchinson & Co., 1968.

Dickson, K. A. *Theology in Africa.* New York: Orbis Books, 1984.

Dopamu, P. A., "Towards Understanding African Traditional Religion". In: Uka, E. M. (ed.). *Readings in African Traditional Religion: Structure, Meaning, Relevance, Future.* Bren: Peter Lang, 1991, 19–37.

Engelhardt, H. J., "Health and Disease: Philosophical Perspective". In: Reich, W. (ed.). *Encyclopedia of Bioethics*, Vol.2. New York: Macmillan Co., 1978, 599–606.

Fako, T. T., "The Dilemma of African Traditional Medicine: The Case of Botswana". In: du Toit, B. M. and Abdalla, I. H. (eds.). *African Healing Strategies.* New York: Trado-Medic Books, 1985, 190–229.

Falola, T. and Ityavyar, D. A. (eds.). *The Political Economy of Health in Africa.* Athens, Ohio: Ohio University Press, 1992.

Fink, H. E. *Religion, Disease and Healing in Ghana.* Munchen: Trickster Wissenschaft, 1990.

Fry, P. *Spirits of Protest.* Cambridge: Cambridge University Press, 1976.

Gbadegesin, S. *African Philosophy: Traditional Yoruba Philosophy and Contemporary African Realities.* New York: Peter Lang, 1991.

Geschiere, P. and Raatgever, R., "Introduction: Emerging insights and issues in French Marxist Anthropology". In: van Binsbergen, W. M. J. and Geschiere, P. (eds.). *Old Modes of Production and Capitalist Encroachment.* London: KPI, 1985, 1–38.

Graveyard, B. *African Theology in Social Context.* Maryknoll: Orbis Books, 1992.

Green, E. C., "Sexually Transmitted Disease, Ethnomedicine and Health Policy in Africa", *Social Science and Medicine*, Vol. 35, No. 2, 1992, 121–130.

Gyekye, K. *An Essay on African Philosophical Thought: The Akan Conceptual Scheme.* Cambridge: Cambridge University Press, 1987.

Hackett, R. I. J. (ed.). *New Religious Movements in Nigeria.* New York: The Edwin Mellen Press, 1987.

Henriot, P. J., "Africa and Structural Adjustment Programmes", *Sedos Bulletin 1994*, (Africa: The Kairos of a Synod), Vol. 26, No.3 & No. 4, Double Issue, 15th March–15th April, 1994, 108–109.

Human Development Report 1993. New York and Oxford: Oxford University Press, 1993.

Idowu, E. B. *African Traditional Religion: A Definition.* London: SCM Press, 1973.

Igun, U. A., "The Underdevelopment of Traditional Medicine in Africa". In: Falola, T. and Ityavyar, D. A. (eds.). *The Political Economy of Health in Africa.* Athens, Ohio: Ohio University Press, 1992, 143–162.

Janzen, J. M. *Ngoma: Discourses of Healing in Central and Southern Africa*. Los Angeles: University of California, 1992.

———— "Health, Religion, and Medicine in Central and Southern African Traditions". In: Sullivan, L. E. (ed.). *Healing and Restoring: Health and Medicine in the World's Religious Traditions*. New York: Macmillan Publishing, 1989, 225–254.

Kimble, D. *A Political History of Ghana: the Rise of the Gold Coast Nationalism, 1850–1928*. Oxford: Clarendon Press, 1963.

Kirby, J. P., "The Islamic Dialogue with African Traditional Religion: Divination and Health Care", *Social Science and Medicine*, Vol. 36, No. 3, February 1993, 237–247.

Lambo, J. O., "The Impact of Colonialism on African Cultural Heritage with Special Reference to the Practice of Herbalism in Nigeria". In: Singer, P. (ed.). *Traditional Healing: New Science or New Colonialism?* New York: Conch Magazine Limited, 1977, 123–135.

Latouche, S. *In the Wake of the Affluent Society: An Exploration of Post-Development*. Introduced and translated by O'Connor M. and Arnoux R. from the French. London and New Jersey: Zed Books Ltd, 1993.

Leys, C. *Underdevelopment in Kenya*. London: Heinemann, 1977.

Maduro, O. *Religion and Social Conflicts*. Translated from the Spanish by Robert R. Barr. Maryknoll: Orbis Books, 1982.

Manoukian, M. *Akan and Adangme Peoples of the Gold Coast*. London: Oxford University Press, 1950.

Mbiti, J. S. *Bible and Theology in African Christianity*. Nairobi: Oxford University Press, 1986.

———— *Introduction to African Religion*. Ibadan: Heinemann, 1981.

———— *Concepts of God in Africa*. London: SPCK, 1970.

———— *African Religions and Philosophy*. New York: Frederick Praeger, 1969.

Mburu, F. M., "The Impact of Colonial Rule on Health Development: The Case of Kenya". In: Falola, T. and Ityavyar, D. A. (eds.). *The Political Economy of Health in Africa*. Athens, Ohio: Ohio University Press, 1992, 88–106.

Milingo, E. *The World in Between: Christian Healing and the Struggle for Survival*. London: C. Hurst & Co., 1984.

Mobley, H. W. *The Ghanaians Image of the Missionary: An Analysis of the Published Critiques of Christian Missionaries by Ghanaians 1897–1965*. Leiden: E. J. Brill, 1970.

Moltmann, J. *God in Creation: An Ecological Doctrine of Creation*. Translated by Margaret Khol from the German. London: SCM Press, 1985.

Munro, J. F. *Colonial Rule and the Kamba: Social Change in the Kenya Highlands 1889–1939*. London: Clarendon Press, 1975.

Nazar, D. "Inculturation: Meaning and Method". Unpublished Doctoral Thesis. Ottawa: Saint Paul University, 1989.

Neil, S. *Colonialism and Christian Missions*. London: Lutherworth Press, 1966.

Nkéramihigo, T., "Inculturation and the Specificity of Christian Faith". In: Crollius, A. A. Roest. (ed.). *Inculturation: Working Papers on Living Faith and Cultures*, Vol. V. Rome: Pontifical Gregorian University, 1984, 21–29.

Obeng, E. A., "Inroads of African Religion into Christianity: the Case of the Spiritual Churches", *Africa Theological Journal*, Vol.16, No.1, 1986, 43–52.

Ocampo, J. F. and Johnson, D. L., "The Concept of Political Development". In: Cockcroft, J. D. et. al. *Dependence and Underdevelopment*. New York: Doubleday, 1972, 399–424.

Opoku, K. A., "Changes within Christianity: The Case of the Musama Disco Christo Church". In: Kalu, O. U. (ed.). *The History of Christianity in West Africa*. London: Longmans, 1980, 309–320.

Owoahene-Acheampong, S. "African Independent Churches in West Africa, with Particular Reference to their Theology and Practice of Healing." Unpublished Master's Thesis. Toronto: St. Michael's College, University of Toronto, 1991.

Parrinder, E. G. *African Traditional Religion*. London: Sheldon Press, 1974.

——— *West African Religion: A Study of Beliefs and Practices of Akan, Ewe, Yoruba, Ibo, and Kindred Peoples*. London: The Epworth Press, 1969.

Parsons, T., "Health and Disease: A Sociological and Action Perspective". In: Reich, W. (ed.). *Encyclopedia of Bioethics*, Vol. 2. New York: Macmillan Co., 1978, 590–599.

Parsons, R. T. *The Churches and Ghana Society 1918–1955*. Leiden: E. J. Brill, 1963.

Peel, J. D. Y. *Aladura: A Religious Movement among the Yoruba.* London: Oxford University Press, 1968.

Pinto, J. P. *Inculturation through Basic Communities*. Bangalore: Asian Trading Corporation, 1985.

Pobee, J. S. *Toward an African Theology*. Nashville: Partheon Press, 1979.

Provan, I. *Healing: A Limitational Approach to a Theology of Health*. London: Hodder & Stoughton, 1979.

Ranger, T. *Peasant Consciousness and Guerrilla War in Zimbabwe*. London: James Currey, 1985.

Saltonstall, R., "Healthy Bodies, Social Bodies: Men's and Women's Concepts and Practices of Health in Everyday Life", *Social Science and Medicine*, Vol. 36, No. 1, 1993, 7–14.

Sarpong, P. *Ghana in Retrospect: Some Aspects of Ghanaian Culture.* Accra-Tema: Ghana Publishing Corporation, 1974.

Sempebwa, J. W. "Religiosity and Health Behaviour in Africa", *Social Science and Medicine*, Vol.17, No. 24, 1983, 2033–2036.

Schineller, P. *A Handbook on Inculturation.* New York: Paulist Press, 1990.

Shamuyarira, N. *Crisis in Rhodesia.* London: Andre Deutsch, 1965.

Shorter, A. *Toward a Theology of Inculturation.* London: Geoffrey Chapman, 1988.

——— *African Christian Theology.* Maryknoll: Orbis Books, 1977.

Simonse, S., "African Literature between Nostalgia and Utopia: African Novels since 1953 in the Light of the Modes-Of-Production Approach". In: van Binsbergen, W. M. J. and Geschiere, P. (eds.). *Old Modes of Production and Capitalist Encroachment.* London: KPI, 1985.

Singer, P. (ed.). *Traditional Healing: New Science or New Colonialism?* New York: Conch Magazine Limited, 1977.

Sivalon, J. "Roman Catholicism and the Defining of Tanzanian Socialism 1953–1985." Toronto: Unpublished Ph.D. Thesis, University of St. Michael's College, 1990.

Starkloff, C. F., "Inculturation and Cultural Systems (Part 1)", *Theological Studies*, Vol. 55, No. 1, March 1994, 66–81.

Sullivan, L. E. (ed.). *Healing and Restoring: Health and Medicine in the World's Religious Traditions.* New York: MacMillan Publishing, 1989.

Sundkler, B., "The Challenge of the Independent Churches", *Missionalia*, Vol.12, No.1, 1984, 3–6.

Sundkler, B. G. M. *Bantu Prophets in South Africa.* London: Oxford University Press, 1970.

Taylor, J. C. *From Modernization to Modes of Production.* London: The MacMillan Press, 1983.

The Christian Medical Commission, World Council of Churches. *Healing and Wholeness: The Churches' Role in Health.* Geneva: CMC., 1990.

Turner, H. W. *Religious Innovation in Africa.* Boston: G. K. Hall & Co., 1979.

Turner, V. *The Forest of Symbols: Aspects of Ndembu Ritual.* London: Cornell University Press, 1967.

———(ed.). *Colonialism in Africa 1870–1960.* Vol. 3. Cambridge: Cambridge University Press, 1971.

Twumasi, P. A., "Colonial Rule, International Agency and Health: the Experience of Ghana". In: Falola, T. and Ityavyar, D. (eds.). *The Political Economy of Health in Africa*. Athens, Ohio: Ohio University Press, 1992, 107–120.

——— *Medical Systems in Ghana: A Study in Medical Sociology*. Accra-Tema: Ghana Publishing Corporation, 1975.

Uchendu, V. C. *Dependency and Underdevelopment in West Africa*. Leiden: E. J. Brill, 1980.

Uka, E. M. (ed.). *Reading in African Traditional Religion: Structure, Meaning, Relevance, Future*. Bren: Peter Lang, 1991.

Ulin, P. R. and Segall, M. H. (eds.). *Traditional Health Care Delivery in Contemporary Africa*. Syracuse: Maxwell School of Citizenship and Public Affairs, Syracuse University, 1980.

van Binsbergen, W. M. J. and Geschiere, P. (eds.). *Old Modes of Production and Capitalist Encroachment*. London: KPI, 1985.

van der Leeuw, G. *Religion in Essence and Manifestation*. Translated by J. E. Turner from the German. London: George Allen and Unwin, 1963.

Wall, L. L. *Hausa Medicine: Illness and Well-being in a West African Culture*. Durham: Duke University Press, 1988.

Ward, W. E. F. *A History of Ghana*. London: George Allen & Unwin, 1958.

——— *A Short History of the Gold Coast*. London: Longmans, 1935.

Warren, D. M. "The Techiman-Bono Ethnomedical System". In: Yoder, P. S. (ed.). *African Health and Healing Systems: Proceedings of a Symposium*. Los Angeles: Crossroads Press, 1982.

Webster, J. B., "Political Activity in British West Africa, 1900-1940". In: Ajayi, J. F. A. and Crowder, M. (eds.). *History of West Africa*. Vol.2. London: Longman, 1974, 568–595.

Welbourn, F. B., "Missionary Stimulus and African Responses". In: Turner, V. (ed.). *Colonialism in Africa 1870–1960*, Vol.3. Cambridge: Cambridge University Press, 1971, 310–345.

Westermann, D. *Africa and Christianity*. London: Oxford University Press, 1937.

Williamson, S. G. *Akan Religion and the Christian Faith*. Accra: Ghana University Press, 1965.

Wilson, B. (ed.). *The Social Impact of New Religious Movements*. New York: The Rose of Sharon Press, 1981.

Wilson, M. (ed.). *Explorations in Health and Salvation: A Selection of Papers by Bob Lambourne*. Birmingham: University of Birmingham, 1983.

————: *The Church is Healing*. London: SCM Press, 1966.

Wilson, R. N. *The Sociology of Health*. New York: Random House, 1970.

Wiredu, K. *Philosophy and an African Culture*. London: Cambridge University Press, 1980.

World Council of Churches, The Christian Medical Commission. *Healing and Wholeness: the Churches' Role in Health*. Geneva, 1990.

World Health Organization. *Report of a Consultation on the Coordination of Activities Relating to Traditional Medicine in the African Region*. Brazzavile, 1984.

Wiltgen, R. M. *Gold Coast Mission History 1471–1880*. Techny, Illinois: Divine Word Publications, 1956.

Other Sources

Ackerknecht, E. N. *Rudolf von Virchow, Arzt, Politiker, Anthropologe*. Stuttgart: 1957.

Adeloye, A. *African Pioneers of Modern Medicine*. Ibadan: University Press Limited, 1985.

Ademuwagun, Z. A., Ayoada, J. A. A., Harrison, I. E., and Warren, D. M. (eds.). *African Therapeutic Systems*. Waltham, Mass.: Crossroads Press, 1979.

Ahluwalia, R. and Mechin, B. *Traditional Medicine in Zaire: Present and Potential Contribution to the Health Services*. Ottawa: International Development Research Centre, 1980.

Aidoo, A. "Social Class, the State, and Medical Decolonization in Ghana: A Study in the Political Economy of Health Care." Unpublished Ph.D Thesis. Connecticut: The University of Connecticut, 1985.

Alavi, H. and Shanin, T. (eds.). *Introduction to the Sociology of "Developing Societies"*. New York: Monthly Review Press, 1982.

Alland, A. *Adaptation in Cultural Evolution*. New York: Columbia University, 1970.

Al-Safi, A. *Native Medicine in the Sudan: Sources, Conception, and Methods*. Sudan: University of Khartoum, 1970.

Anderson, S. and Staugard, F. *Traditional Medicine in Botswana: Traditional Midwives*. Gaborone: Ipelegeng Publishers, 1986.

Antubam, K. *Ghana's Heritage of Culture*. Leipzig: Koehler & Amelang, 1963.

Apostel, L. *African Philosophy: Myth or Reality?* Belgium: Scientific Publishers, 1981.

Azu, D. G. *The Ga Family and Social Change*. Leiden: Afrika Studie-centrum, 1974.

Balibar, E. *Race, Nation, Class: Ambiguous Identity*. London: Verso, 1991.

Bannerman, R. H., Burton, J. and Wen-Chieh, C. (eds.). *Traditional Medicine and Health Care Coverage*. Geneva: World Health Organization, 1983.

Baran, P. *The Political Economy of Growth*. New York: Monthly Review Press, 1957.

Barker, E. (ed.). *New Religious Movements: A Perspective for Understanding Society*. Toronto: The Edwin Mellen Press, 1982.

Bascom, W. R. and Herskovits, M. J.(eds.). *Continuity and Change in African Cultures*. Chicago and London: The University of Chicago Press, 1959.

Baum, G. *Religion and Alienation: a Theological Reading of Society*. New York: Paulist Press, 1975.

Berger, I. *Religion and Resistance: East African Kingdoms in the Precolonial Period*. Boston: African Studies Center, Boston University, 1981.

Berger, P. L. *The Capitalist Spirit: Toward a Religious Ethic of Wealth*. San Francisco, Calif.: ICS Press, 1990.

Best, K. Y. (ed.). *African Challenge: Major Issues in African Christianity*. Nairobi: Transafrica Publishers, 1975.

Birmingham, W., Neustadt, I. and Omaboe, E. N. (eds.). *A Study of Contemporary Ghana: Some Aspects of Social Structure*. London: Allen and Unwin, 1967.

Blake, J. W. *West Africa: Quest for God or Gold, 1454–1578 a Survey of the First Century of White Enterprise in West Africa*. London: Curson Press, 1977.

Bond, G., Johnson, W. and Walker, S. S. (eds.). *African Christianity: Patterns of Religious Continuity*. New York: Academic Press, 1979.

Bosman, W. *A New and Accurate Description of the Coast of Guinea*. New York: Barns and Noble, 1967.

Burrows, E. H. *A History of Medicine in South Africa: Up to the end of the Nineteenth Century*. Cape Town: A. A. Balkema, 1958.

Busia, K. A. *The Position of the Chief in the Modern Political System of Ashanti*. London: Oxford University Press, 1951.

Caldwell, J. C. *Population Growth and Family Change in Africa: The New Urban Elite in Ghana*. Canberra Australian National University Press, 1968.

Carlson, R. J. *The End of Medicine*. New York: John Wiley and Sons, 1975.

Carman, J. A. *A Medical History of the Colony and Protectorate of Kenya*. London: Rex Collings, 1976.

Carothers, J. C. *The African Mind in Health and Disease.* Geneva: World Health Organization, 1953.

Chaudhuri, B. (ed.). *Cultural and Environmental Dimensions on Health.* New Delhi: Inter-India Publications, 1990.

Chirban, J. T. (ed.). *Health and Faith: Medical, Psychological and Religious Dimensions.* New York: University Press of America, 1991.

Cockcroft, J. D., Frank, A. G. and Johnson, D. L. (eds.). *Dependence and Underdevelopment.* New York: Doubleday, 1972.

Dachs, A. J. *Livingstone: Missionary Explorer.* Salisbury: Central African Association, 1973.

DeBrunner, H. *A History of Christianity in Ghana.* Accra: Waterville Publishing House, 1967.

De Souza, A. R. and Porter, P. W. *The Underdevelopment and Modernization of the Third World.* Association of American Geographers: Commission on College Geography, 1974.

Dickson, K. *A Historical Geography of Ghana.* London: Cambridge University Press, 1969.

Doyal, L. *The Political Economy of Health.* London: Pluto Press, 1979.

Dudley, S. *Dependency Theory: a Critical Reassessment.* London: Francis Printer, 1981.

Durkheim, E. *The Elementary Forms of the Religious Life.* Translated by Joseph Ward Swain from the French. New York: Collier Books, 1961.

Durodola, J. I. *Scientific Insights into Yoruba Traditional Medicine.* Owerri, Nigeria: Trado-Medic Books, 1986.

Erinisho, O. A. and Bell, N. W. (eds.). *Mental Health In Africa.* Ibadan: Ibadan University Press, 1982.

Eboussi Boulaga, F. *Christianity without Fetishes: An African Critique and Recapture of Christianity.* Maryknoll: Orbis Books, 1981.

Feierman, S. and Janzen, J. M. (eds.). *The Social Basis of Health and Healing in Africa.* Los Angeles: University of California Press, 1992.

Field, M. J. *Religion and Medicine of the Ga People.* London: Oxford University Press, 1937.

Frank, A. G. *Capitalism and Underdevelopment in Latin America.* New York: Monthly Review Press, 1967.

———— *Latin America: Underdevelopment or Revolution?* New York: Monthly Review Press, 1969.

———— *Lumpenbourgeoise: Lumpendevelopment–Dependence, Class and Politics in Latin America.* New York: Monthly Review Press, 1972.

Frazer, J. G. *The Golden Bough*. New York: Macmillan, 1922.

Gill, R. (ed.). *Theology and Sociology, a Reader*. New York: Paulist Press, 1987.

Goodacre, D. (ed.). *World Religions and Medicine*. Oxford: The Institute of Religion and Medicine, 1983.

Goody, J. *Changing Social Structure in Ghana: Essays in the Comparative Sociology of a New State and Old Tradition*. London: International African Institute, 1975.

Grollig, F. X. and Haley, H. B. (eds.). *Medical Anthropology*. Paris: Mouton Publishers, 1976.

Harley, G. W. *Native African Medicine: With Reference to its Practice in the Mano Tribe of Liberia*. London: Frank Cass, 1970.

Hastings, A. C., Fadiman J. and Gordon, J. S. (eds.). *Health for the Whole Person*. Boulder, Colorado: Westview Press, 1980.

Hommond-Tooke, W. D. *Rituals and Medicines: Indigenous Healing in South Africa*. Johannesburg, South Africa: A. D. Donker, 1989.

Jaco, E. G. (ed.). *Patients, Physicians and Illness*. Glencoe, Illinois: The Free Press, 1958.

Janzen, J. M. *The Quest for Therapy in Lower Zaire*. Los Angeles: University of California Press, 1978.

———*Ngoma: Discourses of Healing in Central and Southern Africa*. Los Angeles: University of California Press, 1992.

Johnstone, R. L. *Religion in Society: A Sociology of Religion*. Englewood Cliffs, New Jersey: Prentice Hall, 1983.

Kiev, A. (ed). *Magic, Faith and Healing*. New York: The Free Press, 1966.

Kirwen, M. C. *The Missionary and the Diviner*. Maryknoll: Orbis Books, 1987.

Laider, P. W. and Gelfand, M. *South Africa, Its Medical History 1652-1898: A Medical and Social Study*. Cape Town: C. Struik, 1971.

Lambo, T. A. *African Traditional Beliefs: Concepts of Health and Medical Practice*. Ibadan: Ibadan University Press, 1963.

Landay, D. (ed.). *Culture, Disease, and Healing: Studies in Medical Anthropology*. New York: The Macmillan Co., 1977.

Lawson, E. T. *Religions of Africa*. San Francisco: Harper and Row, 1984.

Maclean, U. *Magical Medicine: a Nigerian Case-Study*. London: Allen Lane The Penguin Press, 1971.

Maier, D. J. E. *Priests and Power: The Case of the Dente Shrine in Nineteenth-Century Ghana*. Bloomington: Indiana University Press, 1983.

Makhubu, L. P. *The Traditional Healer*. Swaziland: The University of Botswana and Swaziland, 1978.

Malinowski, B. *Magic, Science and Religion*. New York: Anchor Books, 1954.

Marglin, F. A. and Marglin, S. A. (eds.). *Dominating Knowledge: Development, Culture, and Resistance*. Oxford: Clarendon Press, 1990.

Marret, R. R. *Sacrament of Simple Folk*. London: Oxford, 1833.

McElroy, A. and Townsend, P. K. *Medical Anthropology in Ecological Perspective*. San Francisco: Westview Press, 1989.

Moore, G. M., Van Arsdale, P. W., Glittenberg, J. E. and Aldrich, R. A. *The Biocultural Basis of Health: Expanding Views of Medical Anthropology*. Toronto: The C. V. Mosby Company, 1980.

Mullings, L. *Therapy, Ideology, and Social Change: Mental Healing in Urban Ghana*. Los Angeles: University of California Press, 1984.

———— "Healing, Religion and Social Change in Southeastern Ghana". Chicago: Ph.D. Dissertation, University of Chicago, 1975.

Mwamula-Lubandi, E. D. *Clan Theory in African Development Studies Analysis: Reconsidering African Development Promotive Bases*. New York: University Press of America, 1992.

Navarro, V. *Medicine Under Capitalism*. New York: Prodist, 1976.

Ngubane, H. *Body and Mind in Zulu Medicine: An Ethnography of Health and Disease in Nyuswa-Zulu Thought and Practice*. New York: Academic Press, 1977.

Olupona, J. K. (ed.). *African Religions in Contemporary Society*. New York: Paragon House, 1991.

Oosthuizen, G. C. *Post-Christianity in Africa*. Grand Rapids: Eerdmans Publishing, 1968.

Parrinder, G. *Africa's Three Religions*. London: Sheldon Press, 1976.

———— *Religion in Africa*. London: Cox & Wyman, 1968.

Parsons, R. T. (ed.). *Windows on Africa: A Symposium*. Leiden: E.J. Brill, 1971.

Patterson, K. D. *Health in Colonial Ghana: Disease, Medicine, and Socio-Economic Change 1900–1955*. Waltham, Mass.: Crossroads Press, 1981.

Payne, A. and Sutton, P. (eds.). *Dependency Under Challenge: The Political Economy of the Commonwealth Caribbean*. Manchester: Manchester University Press, 1984.

Payne, D. *African Independence and Christian Freedom*. London: Oxford University Press, 1965.

Peek, P. M. (ed.). *African Divination Systems: Ways of Knowing*. Bloomington & Indianapolis: Indiana University Press, 1991.

Provan, I. *Healing: A Limitational Approach to a Theology of Health*. London: Hodder & Stoughton, 1979.

Radcliffe-Brown, A. R. and Forde, D. *African Systems of Kinship and Marriage*. London: KPI, 1987.

Ranger, T. O. and Kimambo, I. N. (eds.). *The Historical Study of African Religion*. Los Angeles: University of California Press, 1972.

Reed, L. S. *The Healing Cults: A Study of Sectarian Medical Practice: Its Extent, Causes, and Control*. Chicago: Chicago University Press, 1932.

Reich, W. (ed.). *Encyclopedia of Bioethics*. Vol.2. New York: Macmillan Co., 1978.

Reindorf, C. *The History of the Gold Coast and Asante*. Accra: Ghana Universities Press, 1966.

Rosny, de E. *Healers in the Night*. New York: Orbis Books, 1985.

Rostow, W. W. *The Stages of Economic Growth*. Cambridge: Cambridge University Press, 1979.

Sarpong, P. *Girls' Nubility Rites in Ashanti*. Accra-Tema: Ghana Publishing Corporation, 1977.

Schapera, I. (ed.). *Livingstone's Missionary Correspondence 1841–1856*. London: 1961.

Shamuyarira, N. *Crisis in Rhodesia*. London: Andre Deutsch, 1965.

Shapiro, H. A. (ed.). *Medicine and Health in Developing Southern Africa*. Salt River, 1984.

Shorter, A. *African Culture and the Christian Church*. London: Geoffrey Chapman, 1979.

Smith, W. S. *African Beliefs and Christian Faith*. London: The United Society For Christian Literature, 1936.

——— *African Ideas of God*. London: Edinburgh House Press, 1950.

Steel, W. *Small-scale Employment and Production in Developing Countries: Evidence from Ghana*. New York: Praeger, 1977.

Sundkler, B. *The Christian Ministry in Africa*. London: SCM Press, 1962.

Sweezy, P. *The Theory of Capitalist Development*. New York: Monthly Review Press, 1942.

Szasz, T. *The Theology of Medicine: The Political-Philosophical Foundations of Medical Ethics*. New York: Harper and Row, 1977.

Tettey, C. *Ghana in Health and Disease 1957-77.* Accra: Library, University of Ghana Medical School, 1979.

The Christian Medical Commission, World Council of Churches. *Healing and Wholeness: The Churches' Role in Health.* Geneva: CMC., 1990.

Todd, J. M. *African Mission: A Historical Study of the Society of African Missions.* London: 1962.

Tovey, P. *Inculturation: The Eucharist in Africa.* Bramcote, Nottingham: Groves Books, 1988.

Tylor, E. B. *Primitive Culture.* New York: Henry Holt, 1889.

Waite, G. M. *A History of Traditional Medicine and Health Care in Pre-Colonial East-Central Africa.* Lewiston, New York: Edwin Mellen Press, 1992.

Wolfgang, G. J. *Indian Healing: Shamanic Ceremonialism in the Pacific Northwest Today.* Surrey, British Columbia: Hancock House Publishers Ltd., 1982.

World Health Organization. *Preamble of the Constitution of the WHO.* Geneva: World Health Organization, 1946.

Wright, W. *The Social Logic of Health.* News Brunswick, New Jersey: Rutgers University Press, 1982.

Yoder, P. S. (ed.). *African Health and Healing Systems: Proceedings of a Symposium.* Los Angeles: Crossroads Press, University of California, 1982.

Young, T. Kue, *Health Care and Cultural Change: the Indian Experience in the Central Subarctic.* Toronto: University of Toronto Press, 1988.

Zahan, D. *The Religion, Spirituality and Thought of Traditional Africa.* Chicago: The University of Chicago Press, 1970.

Articles in Books and Periodicals

Belshaw, W., "Church and State in Ashanti", *International Review of Mission*, Vol. 35, 1946, 408–415.

Berinyuu, A. A., "A Transcultural Approach to Pastoral Care of the Sick in Ghana", *African Theological Journal*, 16(1987)1, 53–59.

Christensen, J. B., "The Adaptive Functions of Fanti Priesthood", in: Bascom, W. R. and Herskovits M. J. (eds.). *Continuity and Change in African Cultures.* Chicago and London: The University of Chicago Press, 1959, 257–278.

Duhl, L. J., "Social Context of Health", in: Hastings, A. C., Fadiman, J. and Gordon, J. S. (eds.). *Health for the Whole Person*. Boulder, Colorado: Westview Press, 1980, 39–48.

Dunlop, D. W., "Alternatives to 'Modern' Health Delivery Systems in Africa: Public Policy Issues of Traditional Health Systems", in: Ademuwagun, Z. A. et al. *African Therapeutic Systems*. Waltham, Mass.: Crossroads Press, 1979, 191–196.

Engelhardt, H. T., "The Concepts of Health and Disease", in: Spicker, S. F. and Engelhardt, H. T. (eds.). *Philosophy and Medicine: Evaluation and Explanation in the Biomedical Sciences*. Vol.1. Boston: Reidel, 1975, 125–141.

Eriuwo, S. U., "Traditional Culture and Christianity", *African Ecclesial Review*, Vol.21, No.4, 1979, 216–222.

Good, C. M., "A Comparison of Rural and Urban Ethno-medicine Among the Kamba of Kenya", in: Ulin, P. R. and Segall, H. M. (eds.). *Traditional Health Care Delivery in Contemporary Africa*. Syracuse: Maxwell School of Citizenship and Public Affairs, Syracuse University, 1980, 13–56.

Good C. M. et. al. "The Interface of Dual Systems of Health Care in Developing Countries: Toward Health Policy Initiatives in Africa", *Social Science and Medicine*, Vol. 13B, 1979, 141–154.

Hunter, J. D., "The New Religions: Demodernization and the Protest against Modernity", in: Wilson, B. (ed.). *The Social Impact of New Religious Movements*. New York: The Rose of Sharon Press, 1981, 1–19.

Ityavyar, D. A. and Ogba, L., "Violence, Conflict, and Health in Africa", in: Falola, T. and Ityavyar, D. A. (eds.). *The Political Economy of Health in Africa*. Athens, Ohio: Ohio University Press, 1992, 163–183.

Ityavyar, D. A., "Health in Precolonial Africa", in: Falola, T. and Ityavyar, D. A. (eds.). *The Political Economy of Health in Africa*. Athens, Ohio: Ohio University Press, 1992, 35–48.

———— "The Colonial Origins of Health Care Services: The Nigerian Example", in Falola, T. and Ityavyar, D. A. (eds.). *The Political Economy of Health in Africa*. Athens, Ohio: Ohio University Press, 1992, 65–87.

Jules-Rosette, B. W., "Tradition and Continuity in African Religions", in: Olupona, J. K. (ed.). *African Traditional Religions in Contemporary Society*. New York: Paragon House, 1991, 149–165.

Kelman, S., "Social Organization and the Meaning of Health", *Journal of Medicine and Philosophy*, 5, 1980, 133–144.

Lan, D., "Spirit Mediums and the Authority to Resist in the Struggle for Zimbabwe", Seminar Paper, Institute of Commonwealth Studies, London, 14 January 1983.

Levin, J. S., "Religion and Health: Is there an Association, is it Valid, and is it Causal?" *Social Science and Medicine*, Vol. 38, No. 11, 1994, 1475–1481.

Madziyire, S. K., "The Heathen Practices in the Urban and Rural parts of Marandellas area and their effects upon Christianity", in Ranger, T. and Weller, J. (eds.). *Themes in the Christian History of Central Africa.* London: Heinemann, 1975, 76–82.

Matrion, U. and Madziga, Y., "The Training of Traditional Priests, Medicine-Men and Diviners", *Theological College of Northern Nigeria*, 5, 1980, 21–28.

McLeod, M., "On the Spread of Anti-Witchcraft Cults in Modern Asante", in: Goody, J. (ed.). *Changing Social Structure in Ghana: Essays in the Comparative Sociology of a New State and Old Tradition.* London: International African Institute, 1975, 107–117.

Mullings, L., "Religious Change and Social Stratification in Labadi, Ghana: The Church of the Messiah", in: Bond, G. et al. *African Christianity: Patterns of Religious Continuity.* New York: Academic Press, 1979, 65–88.

Okolo, C. B., "The Traditional African and the Christian Values", *AFER* Vol. 29, No.2, 1987, 81–93.

Onoge, O. M., "Capitalism and Public Health: A Neglected Theme in the Medical Anthropology of Africa", in: Ingman, S. R. and Thomas, A. (eds.). *Topias and Utopias in Health.* Hague: Mouton Publishers, 1975, 219–232.

Onunwa, U., "The Biblical Basis for some Healing Methods in African Traditional Society", *African Theological Journal*, Vol.15, No.3, 1986, 188–195.

Osborne, O. H., "Merging Traditional and Scientific Health Care Systems: Conceptual and Pragmatic Issues." Paper presented at the Annual Meeting of the Society for Applied Anthropology, San Diego, 1977.

Owoahene-Acheampong, S., "Theology and Healing Practices of African Independent Churches", *Kerygma*, Vol. 27, 1993, 93–109.

Patterson, K. D., "Health in Urban Ghana: The Case of Accra 1900–1940", *Social Science and Medicine*, Vol.13B, No. 4, 1979, 251–268.

Pearce, T. O., "Health Inequalities in Africa", in: Falola, T. and Ityavyar, D. A. (eds.). *The Political Economy of Health in Africa.* Athens, Ohio: Ohio University Press, 1992, 184–216.

Phillips, A., "The Concept of Development", *Review of African Political Economy*, No.8, 1977, 7–20.

Press, I., "Problems in the Definition and Classification of Medical Systems", *Social Science and Medicine*, Vol.14B, No.1, 1980, 45–57.

Schoffeleers, M., "The Resistance of the Nyau Societies to the Roman Catholic Missions in Colonial Malawi", in: Ranger, T. O. and Kimambo, I. N. (eds.). *The Historical Study of African Religion*. Los Angeles: University of California Press, 1972, 252–273.

Sharpston, M. J., "Uneven Geographical Distribution of Medical Care: A Ghanaian Case Study", *Journal of Development Studies*, Vol.8, No.2, 1972, 205–222.

Shorter, A., "Mediumship, Exorcism, and Christian Healing", *AFER*, Vol.22, No.1, 1980, 29–33.

Stock, R. and Anyinam, C. "National Governments and Health Service Policy in Africa". In: Falola, T. and Ityavyar, D. A. (eds.). *The Political Economy of Health in Africa*. Athens, Ohio: Ohio University Press, 1992, 217–246.

Stull, J. R., "From Illness to Health", in: Parsons R. T. (ed.). *Windows on Africa: A Symposium*. Leiden: E. J. Brill, 1971, 93–106.

Tillich, P., "The Meaning of Health", in: Belgum, D. (ed.). *Religion and Medicine*. Ames: Iowa State University Press, 1967, 3–12.

Twumasi, P. A. "Scientific Medicine—The Ghanaian Experience", *International Journal of Nursing Studies*, Vol.9, No.2, 1972, 63–75.

——— "Medicine: Traditional and Modern", *Insight and Opinion*, Vol.7, No.1, 1977, 20–50.

——— "A Social History of the Ghanaian Pluralistic Medical System", *Social Science and Medicine*, Vol.13B, No.4, 1979, 349–356.

——— "Ashanti Traditional Medicine and Its Relation to Present-day Psychiatry", in: Ademuwagun, Z. A. et al. *African Therapeutic Systems*. Waltham, Mass.: Crossroads Press, 1979, 235–242.

Ubot, I. S., "Social Science and Medicine in Africa", in: Falola, T. and Ityavyar, D. A. (eds.). *The Political Economy of Health in Africa*. Athens, Ohio: Ohio University Press, 1992, 123–142.

Uchendu, V. C., "Dependency Theory: Problems of Cultural Autonomy and Cultural Convergence", in: Uchendu, V. C. (ed.). *Dependency and Underdevelopment in West Africa*. Leiden: E. J. Brill, 1980, 78–96.

Wanjohi, R., "Medical and Spiritual Care among the Agikuyu", *Spearhead*, No.71, 1982, 38–45.

Warren, B., "Imperialism and Capitalist Industrialization", *New Left Review*, Vol. 81, 1973, 3–44.

Warren, D. M. et. al. "Ghanaian National Policy Toward Indigenous Healers: The Case of the Primary Health Training for Indigenous Healers (PRHETIH) Program", *Social Science and Medicine*, Vol. 16, 1982, 1873–1881.

Warren, D., "The Interpretation of Change in a Ghanaian Ethnomedical Study", *Human Organization*, Vol. 37, No. 1, 1978, 73–77.

——— "Indigenous Healers and Primary Health Care in Ghana", *Medical Anthropology Newsletter*, Vol. 11, No. 1, 1979, 11–13.

Wyllie, R. W., "Ritual and Social Change: A Ghanaian Experience", *American Anthropologist*, Vol. 70, No. 1, 1968, 21–33.

Yamsat, P., "The Need for Genuine Understanding of African Traditional Religion among Christians", *TCNN Research Bulletin*, Vol.18, 1987, 14–32.

Notes

Chapter 1

1   It is important to note from the onset that although our focus shall be on medical systems, institutions in African especially and other developing societies cannot be treated as separate abstractions; rather they are related intimately. Therefore this study shall refer to other institutions so as to maintain the wholeness of the social formations.

Chapter 2

1   Such a view has been expressed in a modified way by scholars like Rostow. See Rostow, W. W., *The Stages of Economic Growth*, Cambridge University Press, Cambridge, 1979.

2   This theory is judged by many to be inadequate in analyzing the transition of third world countries from 'tradition' to 'modernity'. Cf. Taylor, J. G., *From Modernization to Modes of Production*, The Macmillan Press, London, 1983. Also see Phillips, A., 'The Concept of Development', *Review of African Political Economy*, No. 8, 1977, pp. 7–20; Ocampo, J. F. and Johnson, D. L., "The Concept of Political Development", in: Cockcroft, J. D., Frank, A. G. and Johnson D. L. (eds.), *Dependency and Underdevelopment*, Doubleday, New York, 1972, pp. 399–424; De Souza, A. R. and Porter, P. W., *Underdevelopment and Modernization of the Third World*, Association of American Geographers, Commission on College Geography, 1974; Frank, A. G., "Sociology of Development and Underdevelopment of Sociology", in: Cockroft et. al., op. cit., pp. 321–397.
    Looking at it specifically in terms of the practical development and also the application of the theory in some African countries, critical analysts argue that almost all the countries did not tend to conform to the tenets of this ("modern—i.e western—ideal types") theory. As Geschiere and Raatgever put it: "In almost all the countries of Africa, within a few years of independence, democratic systems modelled on western examples made for one-party system or military dictatorships. And the relevance of a concept like nation-building to the understanding of, for instance, the complicated struggle between factions in the national politics of these countries has become increasingly question-

able." Geschiere, P. and Raatgever, R., "Introduction: Emerging insights and issues in French Marxist Anthropology", in: van Binsbergen, W. M. J. and P. Geschiere (eds.), *Old Modes of Production and Capitalist Encroachment*, KPI, London, 1985, p. 1.

3 Sweezy, P., *The Theory of Capitalist Development*, Monthly Review Press, New York, 1942; Sweezy, P. and Baran P., *Monopoly Capital*, Penguin, London, 1966.

4 Baran, P., *The Political Economy of Growth*, Monthly Review Press, New York, 1957; *Monopoly Capital* (with P. Baran) Penguin, London, 1966.

5 Frank, A. G., *Capitalism and Underdevelopment in Latin America*, Monthly Review Press, New York, 1967; *Latin America: Underdevelopment or Revolution?*, Monthly Review Press, New York, 1969; *Lumpenbourgeoise: Lumpendevelopment–Dependence, Class and Politics in Latin America*, Monthly Review Press, New York, 1972; *Dependence and Underdevelopment* (with J. Cokcroft and D. Johnson), op. cit.

6 Leys, C., *Underdevelopment in Kenya*, Heinemann, London, 1977, p. xiv. See p. 8 of same volume for an extensive bibliography on the theory.

7 Ibid.

8 Taylor, J. G., op. cit., pp. 97–98.

9 According to Taylor, this theory is inadequate in providing us with "any rigorous basis for analyzing the existence, or effects of the various types of capitalist penetration within societies dominated by non-capitalist modes of production." Ibid., p. 101. See same volume for an elaborate criticism. Also see Warren, B., 'Imperialism and Capitalist Industrialization', *New Left Review*, 81, 1973, pp. 3–44.

10 Uchendu, V. C., "Dependency Theory: Problems of Cultural Autonomy and Cultural Convergence", in: Uchendu, V. C. (ed.), *Dependency and Underdevelopment in West Africa*, E. J. Brill, Leiden, 1980, pp. 83, 84.

11 The theory has its original formulation in Economic Commission for Latin America (ECLA) "in the mid 1960's, although one can identify a continuity of both themes and methods long before that period in Latin American social science, e.g., S. Bagu: *Economia de la sociedad colonial* published in 1949, and even earlier in the writings of Mariategui, in 1920's." O'Brien, P. J., *Dependency Revisited*, Institute of Latin American Studies, University of Glasgow, Occasional Papers, 1984, No. 40, p. 1.

12 For some assessments of this theory, see Chilcote, R. H. (ed.), *Dependency and Marxism: Toward a Resolution of the Debate*, Westview Press, Boulder, Colorado, 1982; Hopkins, A. G., "Clio-Antics. The Horoscope for African Economic History," in: Fyte, C. (ed.), *African Stud-*

ies Since 1945: A Tribute to Basil Davidson, Longmans, London, 1976, pp. 31–44; Mahler, V. A., *Dependency Approaches to International Political Economy: a Cross-National Study*, Columbia University Press, 1980; O'Brien, P. J., *Dependency Revisited*, op. cit; Uchendu, V. C. (ed.), op. cit; Rapley, J., *Dependency Theory Re-examined: Economic Development in Cote d'Ivoire*, Queen's University, Department of Political Studies, 1987; Payne, A. and Sutton, P. (eds.), *Dependency Under Challenge: The Political Economy of the Commonwealth Caribbean*, Manchester University Press, 1984; Dudley, S. (ed.), *Dependency Theory: a Critical Reassessment*, Frances Printer, London, 1981; Palma, G., 'Dependency: A Formal Theory of Underdevelopment or a Methodology for the Analysis of Concrete Situations of Underdevelopment?' *World Development*, (July–August), 1978, pp. 881–912; Leys, C., 'Underdevelopment and Dependency: Critical Notes', *Journal of Contemporary Asia*, 7, No. 1, 1977; Kennedy, P., 'Indigenous Capitalism in Ghana', *Review of African Political Economy*, No. 8, 1977, pp. 21–38.

13   Geschiere, P. and Raatgever, R., op. cit., p. 4.

14   Taylor, J. G., op. cit., pp. 221–222.

15   Simonse, S., "African literature between nostalgia and utopia: African novels since 1953 in the light of the modes-of-production approach," in: van Binsbergen, W. M. J. and Geschiere, P. (eds.), op. cit., p. 151.

16   Ibid.

17   Comaroff, J., *Body of Power, Spirit of Resistance: the Culture and History of a South African People*, University of Chicago Press, Chicago, 1985, p. 2.

18   I want to note here that, in this work, I am not arguing for either capitalism or socialism. I am rather using the framework which, to my mind, can help us better analyze and understand what is taking place in third world societies. For our case, this is a neo-Marxian framework.

19   Taylor, J. G., op. cit., p. 101.

20   Geschiere, P. and Raatgever, R., op. cit., p. 7.

21   Maduro, O., *Religion and Social Conflicts*, Orbis Books, Maryknoll, 1982, p. 20.

22   Ibid., p. 136.

23   Ibid.

24   Maduro cautions that a religion's potential and "favorable influence on the autonomic strategy of a subordinate group is not, in spite of what may appear from what we have said, reducible to the level of a

worldview. A religion has potential influence at any one or more of the [following] three levels at which the degree of a class's autonomy can be analyzed." (1) the degree of *class consciousness* of a given subordinate class; (2) its degree of *class organization*; and (3) its degree of *class mobilization*.

Class consciousness in subordinate classes is defined by Maduro as "a dominated group's perception of itself *as* a dominated group distinct from dominating groups." Class organization is understood, in the case of subordinate classes, as "the continuous existence and periodically repeated collective utilization of spaces and times exclusively common to those in a dominated social position." And class mobilization, as regards subordinate classes, refers to "collective actions of explicit confrontation with the power of dominant classes." Ibid., pp. 137–138.

25   Ibid., p. 116.

26   Ibid., pp. 116–117.

27   Ibid., p. 52.

28   Ranger, T., *Peasant Consciousness and Guerrilla War in Zimbabwe*, James Currey, London, 1985, p. 188.

29   In his field work done among the Dande, Lan reports that when political authority had "progressively shifted from the chiefs" (who, in African traditional societies, are the political authorities) "to the mediums to the guerillas and, finally, to the newly established ZANU (PF) political committees. . . the interference of the white administration in the appointment of the chiefs and in the operation of their traditional duties had the effect of delegitimising their 'ancestral' authority. . .willingly or otherwise, the chiefs became intimately associated with the white government. The mediums rejected it and demonstrated their rejection by their 'ritual' of avoidance. . . Mediums may not ride in buses or cars. The smell of petrol is so dangerous that the medium of Mutota is said to have died of it. They may not enter shops or eat food produced by mechanical means. . .It is inconceivable that mediums would accept employment from a white person. . .Many mediums refuse to see white at all. . . The shift of 'traditional' political authority from the chiefs to the independent, nationalist *mhondoro* mediums provided the thousands of deeply discontented villagers in Dande with the authority to do what the ancestors required of them. They received the authority to resist." Lan, D., 'Spirit Mediums and the authority to resist in the struggle for Zimbabwe', seminar paper, Institute of Commonwealth Studies, London, 14 January 1983. Quoted in: Ranger, T., op. cit., p. 202.

30   Ibid., p. 189.

31 Ranger recounts the views of Diki Rukadza, a medium of the Nyawada spirit, an ex-labour-migrant, to illustrate the consciousness of radical peasant nationalists. "According to Diki Rukadza, his spirit disapproves of certain developments introduced in modern days. For instance, it does not care for contour ridging because it causes too much work and has introduced features that were not in the landscaping in former days. His spirit declares that there is no pleasure in walking the fields or bush as the contours make movement difficult. This innovation makes the spirit angry and as a result people are short of food. The tribal spirit, he says, dislikes the rising rates levied by rural councils in the TTLs [Tribal Trust Lands]. . .The tribal spirit gave people soil on which to grow their crops and enough water to enable them to flourish. But nowadays they were being told to plough here and not there, only in particular places, unlike the instructions of the tribal spirit, which were merely to plant and water would be provided." Ibid., p. 191.

32 Ibid., p. 189.

33 Maduro, O., op. cit., p. 137.

34 Ibid., p. 140.

35 Fry, P., *Spirits of Protest*, Cambridge University Press, Cambridge, 1976, p. 110.

36 Ibid., p. 111.

37 Shamuyarira, N., *Crisis in Rhodesia*, Andre Deutsch, London, 1965, quoted in Fry, P., op. cit., p. 110.

38 Ibid., p. 112.

39 Ibid., p. 114.

40 Ackerknecht, E. H., *Rudolf von Virchow, Artz, Politiker, Anthropologe*, Stuttgart, 1957, quoted in: Fink, H. E., *Religion, Disease and Healing in Ghana*, Trickster Wissenschaft, Munchen, 1990, p. 30.

41 Ibid.

42 Ibid.

43 Comaroff, J., op. cit., p. 3.

44 Kirby, J. P., "The Islamic Dialogue with African Traditional Religion: Divination and Health Care", *Social Science and Medicine*, Vol. 36, No. 3, February 1993, p. 237.

45 Ibid.

46 Ibid.

47   Ibid.

48   Ibid.

49   Bonsi, S. K., "Persistence and Change in Traditional Medical Practice in Ghana", *International Journal of Contemporary Sociology*, 14, January and April, 1977, Nos. 1 & 2, 27–38.

50   Ibid., p. 27.

51   Ibid., pp. 29–30.

52   Ibid., p. 30. I claim the indulgence of the reader for the use of sexually exclusive language in some parts of this work. I am quite sensitive to this issue myself. Therefore, I have tried as much as I can to avoid them. Whenever they appear in this study, they do so in materials I have quoted directly from other sources. The use of sexually exclusive language is part of the problem we are dealing with in this project. It is the problem of domination and suppression of ideas, knowledge, beliefs, cultures, genders, etc. of the large human society by an exclusive group or groups of people.

53   Maduro, O., op. cit., p. 136.

54   Cf. Comaroff, J., *Body of Power, Spirit of Resistance*.

55   Sivalon, J., "Roman Catholicism and the Defining of Tanzanian Socialism 1953-1985", Unpublished Ph.D. Thesis, University of St. Michael's College, Toronto, 1990, p. 7.

56   Fink, H. E., op. cit., p. 35.

57   Recently attempts are being made in this direction by some scholars. See, for example, *The Political Economy of Health in Africa*, edited by Falola, T. and Ityavyar, D. A., Ohio University Press, Athens, 1992.

58   Comaroff, J., op. cit., pp. 1–2.

59   Lambo, J. O., "The Impact of Colonialism on African Cultural Heritage with Special Reference to the Practice of Herbalism in Nigeria", in: Singer, P. (ed.), *Traditional Healing: New Science or New Colonialism?* Conch Magazine, New York, 1977, pp. 125–126.

60   Ibid., p. 126.

61   Ibid.

62   Bonsi, S. K., op. cit., pp. 28–29.

Chapter 3

1   Cf. for example AG 22, SC 38ff., GS 44. According to Roest Crollius, in employment and meaning, the two terms can be considered identi-

cal. Crollius, A. A. R., (ed.), "What is so New about Inculturation?" in *Inculturation: Working Papers on Living Faith and Cultures*, V, Pontifical Gregorian University, Rome, 1984, p. 3.

2   Pinto, J. P., *Inculturation through Basic Communities*, Asian Trading Corporation, Bangalore, 1985, p. 9.

3   Shorter, A., *African Christian Theology*, Orbis Books, Maryknoll, 1977, p. 150. David Nazar neatly delineates the affects of 'adaptation' ('accommodation') on both the evangelizer and the evangelizee. Affect on Evangelizer: retains control of meaning; no change in theology or structure; "the faith" is "being brought" to these people; the "individual" is the focus: culture is superficial and irrelevant to faith. Affect on Evangelizee: Christianity remains foreign in its thought and structure; an already enculturated Christianity is being grafted onto the culture; local faith and experience are denied value *a priori*, unless they accord with foreign terms. Nazar, D., "Inculturation: Meaning and Method", Unpublished Doctoral Thesis, Saint Paul University, Ottawa, 1989, p. 183.

4   Schineller, P., *A Handbook on Inculturation*, Paulist Press, New York, 1990, p. 19.

5   Ibid.

6   Nazar, D., op. cit., p. 186.

7   Schineller, P., op. cit., pp. 19–20. Nazar indicates its affects. Affects on Evangelizer: very open to local culture and religion; evangelizes by means of the gospel, not dogmatics; much more is negotiable structurally and theologically; everything but "faith" is negotiable; identifies "culture" as something to be dealt with in the process of evangelization. Affects on Evangelizee: the faith of the gospel is brought to local experience and issues; local culture is valued in the expression of faith; local thoughts and feelings mean something in the dialogue; local faith is undervalued. Nazar, D., op. cit., p. 186.

8   Schineller, P., op. cit., p. 18.

9   Pinto, J. P., op. cit., p. 9.

10   Schineller, P., op. cit.

11   Ibid., p. 20.

12   Ibid.

13   Pinto, J. P., op. cit., p. 10.

14   Ibid.

15   Aylward Shorter sees the terms 'acculturation' and 'enculturation' as sociological concepts while Roest Crollius and others see them as an-

thropological. See for example, Shorter, A., *Toward a Theology of Inculturation*, Geoffrey Chapman, London, 1988, p. 5ff.; Crollius, A. A. R., op. cit., p. 4ff.

16   Quoted by Herskovits, M. J., *Man and His Works*, New York, 1952, p. 523. See Also Crollius, A. A. R., op. cit., p. 4; Pinto, J. P., op. cit., p. 10.

17   Crollius, A. A. R., op. cit., p. 4.

18   Ibid. Cf. Schineller, P., op. cit., p. 22.

19   Pinto, J. P., op. cit.

20   Shorter, A., op. cit., p. 5.

21   Ibid.

22   J. Masson is said to be the first person to use the term in the theological sense. In 1962, he wrote: "Today there is a more urgent need for a Catholicism that is *inculturated* in a variety of forms (*d'une façon polymorphe*)." Quoted in ibid., p. 10. Cf. also Roest Crollius, op. cit., p. 2, fn. 3. In their Final Statement at the First Plenary Assembly of the Federation of Asian Bishops' Conference in Taipei in 1974, the bishops spoke of "a church indigenous and inculturated." Ibid. During the 32nd General Congregation of the Society of Jesus which took place from December 1, 1974 to April 7, 1975, the term 'inculturation' gained wider acceptance. Ibid., p. 2, fn. 4. According to Congar, the term 'inculturation' was coined in Japan as a modification of the term 'acculturation'. Congar, Y., "Christianisme comme foi et comme culture", in *Evandelizzazione e culture: Atti del concresso internazionale scientifico di missiologia*, Roma, 5–12 Ottobre 1975. For the English translation of same text, cf. *East Asian Pastoral Review*, Vol. 18, 1981, 304–319, p. 315. The first time the term appeared in a Church document meant for the universal church was at the close of the Synod of bishops in 1977. Cf. "Message of Synod of Bishops to the People of God", *L'Osservatore Romano*, English Edition, 3.11.1977. It also appeared for the first time in an official papal document (Apostolic Exhortation on Catechesis) by John Paul II in October 1979. Cf. *Catechesi Tradendae*, 53.

23   Crollius, A. A. R., op. cit., p. 6.

24   Ibid.

25   Ibid., p. 7. Concerning similarities in both concepts, and the theological relevance of the concept of inculturation, see same volume.

26   Ibid., pp. 15–16.

27   Azevedo, M. de Carvalho, "Inculturation and the Challenges of Modernity", in: Crollius, A. A. R., (ed.), *Inculturation: Working Papers on*

Living Faith and Cultures, I, Pontifical Gregorian University, Rome, 1982, p. 11.

28 Nazar, D., op. cit., p. 187.

29 Ibid.

30 Nkéramihigo, T., "Inculturation and the Specificity of Christian Faith", in: Crollius, A. A. R., (ed.), *Inculturation: Working Papers and Living Faith and Cultures*, V, op. cit., pp. 22–23.

31 Some attempts have been made in relating the concept of articulation of modes of production to medical practice, but it has not been done on a considerable scale. See for example the works of S. K. Bonsi in the bibliographic literature below.

32 Schineller mentions possible areas—healing, marriage, baptism, eucharistic liturgy, catechesis, and the rest—where inculturation can take place in Africa. Schineller, P., op. cit., pp. 83ff.

33 Shorter, A., op. cit., p. 13.

34 Crollius, A. A. R., op. cit., p. 7.

35 Starkloff, C. F., "Inculturation and Cultural Systems (Part 1)", *Theological Studies*, Vol. 55, No. 1, March 1994, p. 76.

Chapter 4

1 This is the division given by Sarpong, P., *Girl's Nubility Rites in Ashanti*, Ghana Publishing Corporation, Accra-Tema, 1977, p. 1. For other slightly different divisions, see Manoukian, M., *Akan and Adangme Peoples of the Gold Coast*, Oxford University Press, London, 1950, pp. 9–10; Antubam, K., *Ghana's Heritage of Culture*, Koehler & Amelang, Leipzig, 1963, p. 32.

2 Twumasi, P. A., *Medical Systems in Ghana: A Study in Medical Sociology*, Ghana Publishing Corporation, Accra-Tema, 1975, p. 16.

3 Ibid., p. 19. See also Manoukian, M., op. cit., p. 26ff.

4 Bishop Sarpong notes some exceptions to this rule. He says male children, for example, succeed their fathers to offices such as that of drummers, warriors and spokesmen. Sarpong, P., op. cit., p. 4, fn. 18.

5 Manoukian, M., op. cit., p. 51. See also Fink, H., op. cit., p. 108ff.

6 Appiah-Kubi, K., *Man Cures, God Heals: Religion and Medical Practice among the Akans of Ghana*, Friendship Press, New York, 1981, p. 10.

7 Sarpong, P., op. cit., p. 5.

8 Manoukian, M., op. cit., p. 27.

9   Fink, H., op. cit. p. 106.

10 Appiah-Kubi, K., op. cit., pp. 5–7.

11 Manoukian, M., op. cit., p. 39.

12 Appiah-Kubi, K., op. cit., p. 7.

13 Ibid.

14 Idowu, E. B., *African Traditional Religion: A definition*, SCM Press, London, 1973, p. 103. See also Dopamu, P. A., "Towards Understanding African Traditional Religion", in: Uka, E. M., (ed.), *Readings in African Traditional Religion: Structure, Meaning, Relevance, Future*, Peter Lang, Bren, 1991, pp. 19ff; Nadal, S. F., *Nupe Religion*, 1954, pp. 1ff.

15 Pobee, J. S., *Toward an African Theology*, Partheon Press, Nashville, 1979, p. 18.

16 Assimeng, M., *Religion and Social Change in West Africa*, Ghana University Press, 1989, pp. 39–40.

17 Idowu, E. B., op. cit., p. 137.

18 Assimeng, M., op. cit., p. 54.

19 Idowu, E. B., op. cit., p. 137.

20 Ibid.

21 Mbiti, J. S., *African Religions and Philosophy*, Frederick Praeger, New York, 1969, pp. 7–8.

22 Idowu, E. B., op. cit., p. 138.

23 Ibid., p. 139.

24 See Assimeng, M., op. cit., p. 53 for an elaborate illustration of 'The Cosmic Structure of Traditional Ghanaian Religion'.

25 Smith, E. W., *African Ideas of God*, Edinburgh House Press, London, 1950, p. 246.

26 Pobee, J. S. op. cit., p. 46.

27 Cf. Mbiti, J. S., *Concepts of God in Africa*, SPCK, London, 1970, p. 4ff.

28 Cf. for example, Nketia, J. H., "The Poetry of Drums", in: *Voices of Ghana: Literary Contributions to the Ghana Broadcasting System 1955–57*, The Government Printer, Accra, 1958, p. 20.

29 Smith, E. W., op. cit., p. 249.

30 Ellis, A. B., *Twi-Speaking Peoples of the Gold Coast*, quoted in: Smith, E. W., *African Ideas of God*, op. cit., p. 162.

31 Mbiti, J. S., *African Religions and Philosophy*, op. cit., p. 162.

32 Van der Leeuw, G., *Religion in Essence and Manifestation*, George Allen and Unwin, London, 1963, pp. 128–129.

33 Mbiti, J. S., *African Religions and Philosophy*, op. cit., p. 83.

34 Ibid.

35 Sarpong, P., *Ghana in Retrospect*, Ghana Publishing Corporation, Accra-Tema, 1974, pp. 41–42.

36 Van der Leeuw, G., op. cit., p. 128.

37 Shorter, A., *African Christian Theology*, op. cit., p. 126.

38 Sarpong, P., *Ghana in Retrospect*, op. cit., pp. 35–36.

39 Shorter, A., *African Christian Theology*, op. cit., pp. 125–126.

40 Ibid.

41 Williamson, S. G., *Akan Religion and the Christian Faith*, Ghana, University Press, 1965, p. 89.

42 Pobee, J. S., op. cit., p. 47.

43 Ibid.

44 Mbiti, J. S., *Concepts of God in Africa*, op. cit., p. 233.

45 Pobee, J. S., op. cit., p. 48.

46 Assimeng, M., op. cit., p. 60.

47 Ibid., p. 61.

48 Cf. Owoahene-Acheampong, S., "Theology and Healing Practices of African Independent Churches", *Kerygma*, 27 (1993), pp. 93–109.

49 See Frazer, J. G., *The Golden Bough*, Macmillan, New York, 1922; Durkheim, E., *The Elementary Forms of the Religious Life*, translated by Swain, J. W. from the French, Collier Books, New York, 1961; Malinowski, B., *Magic, Science and Religion*, Anchor Books, New York, 1954; Tylor, E. B., *Primitive Culture*, Henry Holt, New York, 1889.

50 Idowu, E. B., op. cit., p. 196.

51 Ibid., pp. 195–196.

52 Ibid., pp. 196–197.

53 Parrinder, E. G., *African Traditional Religion*, Sheldon Press, London, 1974, p. 113.

54 Parrinder, E. G., *West African Religion: A Study of Beliefs and Practices of Akan, Ewe, Yoruba, Ibo, and Kindred Peoples*, The Epworth Press, London, 1969, pp. 157–158.

55 Mbiti, J. S., *African Religions and Philosophy*, op. cit., 198.

56   Ibid., p. 201.

57   Cf. Parrinder, E. G., *African Traditional Religion*, op. cit., pp. 113ff;. *West African Religion*, op. cit., pp. 156ff. For some vivid account of experiences of mystical powers, see for example, Neal J. H., *Ju-Ju in My Life*, London, 1966; Bloomhill, G., *Witchcraft in Africa*, Cape Town, 1962; Mbiti, J. S., *African Religions and Philosophy*, op. cit.

58   Cf. Manoukian, M., op. cit., p. 57.

59   Appiah-Kubi, K., op. cit., p. 36.

60   Parrinder, E. G., *African Traditional Religion*, op. cit., p. 100.

61   Parrinder, E. G., *West African Religion*, op. cit., p. 75.

62   Mbiti, J. S., *African Religions and Philosophy*, op. cit., pp. 166ff.

63   Fink, H. E., op. cit., p. 227.

64   Appiah-Kubi, K., op. cit., p. 36.

65   Ibid., pp. 35–36.

66   Fink, H. E., op. cit., p. 237. For the training of the priest-healers or healers, see same volume, pp. 239ff.; also Appiah-Kubi, op. cit., pp. 37ff.; Parrinder, E. G., *African Traditional Religion*, pp. 100ff.; Mbiti, J. S., *African Philosophy and Religions*, pp. 166ff.

67   Parrinder, E. G., *West African Religion*, op. cit., p. 137.

68   Appiah-Kubi, K., op. cit., p. 35.

69   Parrinder, E. G., *West African Religion*, op. cit., p. 137.

70   Mbiti, J. S., *African Religions and Philosophy*, op. cit., p. 177.

71   Cosminsky, S., "Traditional Midwifery and Contraception" in: Bannerman, R. H., Burton, J. and Wen-Chieh, C. (eds.), *Traditional Medicine and Health Care Coverage*, World Health Organization, Geneva, 1983, pp. 142–143.

72   Ibid.

73   Appiah-Kubi, K., op. cit., p. 36.

74   Cf. Ibid., p. 36 and pp. 58ff.

75   For the Akan concepts of illness and misfortune, see the Chapter 6 below.

76   Parrinder, E. G., *African Traditional Religion*, op. cit., p. 106.

77   Ibid.

78   Appiah-Kubi, K., op. cit., p. 36.

Chapter 5

1 Crowder, M., *Colonial West Africa: Collected Essays*, Frank Cass, London, 1978, p. 1.

2 Ibid.

3 Ward, W. E. F., *A History of Ghana*, George Allen and Urwin, London, 1958, p. 66.

4 The first English voyage to the Gold Coast may have taken place in 1479, but they could not settle there because of an official protest the Portuguese made to Edward IV. The English resumed voyages to the Gold Coast in 1553. It was only in 1662 that they settled there. Cf. ibid., pp. 72ff.

5 Ward, W. E., *A Short History of the Gold Coast*, op. cit., p. 143.

6 Cf. Ward, W. E. F., *A History of Ghana*, op. cit., pp. 187ff.

7 Ibid., p. 193.

8 Ibid., pp. 194–195.

9 Ibid., p. 196.

10 Ibid., pp. 196–197.

11 Ibid., pp. 197–198. For thorough details of the Poll Tax Ordinance see also Kimble, D., *A Political History of Ghana: The Rise of Gold Coast Nationalism, 1850-1928*, Clarendon Press, Oxford, 1963, pp.168ff; Boahen, A. Adu, "Politics in Ghana, 1800-1874", in Ajayi, J. F. A. and Crowder, M., (eds.), *History of West Africa*, Vol.2, Columbia University Press, New York, 1973, pp. 218–224.

12 This is a union of independent Chiefs who came together under the leadership of Osei Tutu and his priest, Okomfo Anokye. They developed their own political and military organization. Their unity is symbolized by the Golden Stool, a sacred stool, which had been called down from heaven by Okomfo Anokye. The people were united under the sacred Golden Stool. So the role of religion or a religious belief as a force, in this case, a dynamic force, in uniting a people and also shaping their consciousness and sense of direction is underlined here.

13 Kimble, D., op. cit., p. 270.

14 It must be noted, as Crowder has indicated, that the defeat of the Ashantis also meant the annexation of the coastal peoples to the crown. The willingness of the Fantis to join arms with the British against the Ashantis "was a result of their own fear that if the Ashanti were unchecked they would be the sufferers. The coastal peoples had in fact

tried their best to secure their independence from both the British and Ashanti." Crowder, M., *West Africa under Colonial Rule*, Hutchinson & Co., London, 1968, p. 147.

15 Confidential Dispatch of 11 Apr. 1900, from Hodgson to Chamberlain; CO/96/359, quoted in ibid., p. 318.

16 Letter of 7 May 1891, from King of Ashanti to Brandford Griffith, enclosed in his Dispatch of 3 June 1891, to Knutsford. To a letter which the Governor had sent to Prempeh on the same request—"asking him to accept a British officer stationed at Kumasi 'as the Agent of this Government, and as your friend and advisor'"—and which he needed an urgent reply, the King replied that he was "deferring a formal reply until his 'District Kings, Chiefs and principal men' arrived in Kumasi, when they could discuss 'the subject of the British Government, which is not a small case.'" Kimble, D., op. cit., p. 283.

17 *The Gold Coast Chronicle*, December 12, 1895, quoted in Kimble, D., op. cit., p. 295.

18 Minute of 21 Dec. 1893, by Bramston, quoted in ibid., p. 282.

19 *The Gold Coast Chronicle*, 30 Nov. 1894, quoted in ibid., p. 285.

20 Ibid., p. 296.

21 Ibid.

22 Boahen, A. Adu, op. cit., p. 261.

23 Munro, J. F., *Colonial Rule and the Kamba: Social Change in the Kenya Highlands 1889–1939*, Clarendon Press, London, 1975, p. 53.

24 Ibid.

25 Crowder, M., *Colonial West Africa*, op. cit., p. 209.

26 Munro, J. F., op. cit., pp. 53–54.

27 Cf. Crowder, M., *West Africa Under Colonial Rule*, op. cit., p. 168ff.

28 Kimble, D., op. cit., p. 461.

29 Ibid.

30 Webster, J. B., "Political Activity in British West Africa, 1900-1940", in: Ajayi, J. F. A. and Crowder, M. (eds.), *History of West Africa*, Vol.2, Longman, London, 1974, p. 570.

31 Ibid., p. 571.

32 Ibid., p. 578.

33 Ibid., pp. 571–572.

34 Kimble, D., op. cit., pp. 485–486.

35 Quoted in ibid., p. 487.

36 Ibid.

37 Dickson, K. A., *Theology in Africa*, Orbis Books, New York, 1984, p. 77.

38 Kimble, D., op. cit., p. 457.

39 Ibid. For some accounts of missionary intervention and their work toward the abolition of slave trade, see Wiltgen, R. M., *Gold Coast Mission History 1471–1880*, Divine Word Publications, Techny, Illinois, 1956, p. 93ff.

40 Welbourn, F. B., "Missionary Stimulus and African Responses", in: Turner, V. (ed.), *Colonialism in Africa 1870-1960*, Vol. 3, Cambridge University Press, Cambridge, 1971, p. 310. For some elaborate positive aspects of Christian missions, see Neill, S., *Colonialism and Christian Missions*, Lutterworth Press, London, 1966.

41 Orchard, R. K., *The Ghana Assembly of the I.M.C.*, 1958, p. 148, quoted in: Mobley, H. W., *The Ghanaian's Image of the Missionary*, E. J. Brill, Leiden, 1970, p. 24.

42 Welbourn, F. B., op. cit., p. 311.

43 Kimble, D., op. cit., p. 151.

44 Ibid.

45 Cf. ibid.

46 Parsons, R. T., *The Churches and Ghana Society 1918–1955*, E. J. Brill, Leiden, 1963, p. 3.

47 Barbot, J., *A Description of the Coasts of North and South Guinea*, Churchill's Collection of Voyages and Travels, Vol. V, London, 1732, quoted in Mobley, H. W., op. cit., p. 17.

48 Ibid.

49 Ibid., p. 20.

50 Casely, Hayford, J. E., *Gold Coast Native Institutions*, 1903, quoted in ibid., p. 105.

51 Welbourn, F. B., op. cit., p. 310.

52 Opoku, K. A., "Changes within Christianity: the case of the Musama Disco Christo Church", in: Kalu, O. U. (ed.), *The History of Christianity in West Africa*, Longman, London, 1980, p. 309.

53 Bujo, B., *African Theology in Social Context*, Orbis Books, Maryknoll, 1992, p. 44.

54 On the other hand, it must be noted that it is not uncommon for women to advise their husbands to find other wives so that they help them on the farms and in family and household activities.

55 Dickson, K. A., op. cit., pp. 104–105.

56 Ibid., p. 105.

57 Graveyard, B., op. cit., p. 48.

58 Mobley, H. W., op. cit. p. 73.

59 Danquah, J. B., *Akim Abuakwa Handbook*, 1928, quoted in ibid., p. 75.

60 Quoted in ibid.

61 Busia, K. A., *The Position of the Chief in the Modern Political System of Ashanti*, 1951, quoted in ibid., p. 76.

62 For instance, Kwesi A. Dickson says that: "It may be remarked, incidentally, that in some ways missionary activity contributed to the expansion of European interests in Africa. The missionaries often inculcated a policy which paralleled that colonial policy which. . .assumed a necessary precondition for the development of Africa the creation of an African middle class which would fit into the world of the European. Thus, for example, the training of Africans for the Church's ministry in the early days of missions in West Africa aimed at creating an African ministry that had a European approach to the Gospel and as much as possible adopted a European mode of life; and as late as 1971, Portuguese bishops in Angola issued a pastoral letter in which, among other things, they noted: 'What is absolutely necessary is that we build an African middle class. . .for only in this way can we fulfil our mission and justify the laws which we obey.' Also, active support was lent to the missionary effort by the home governments. This was true, for example, of British missionary effort in West Africa in the last century." Dickson, K. A., op. cit., pp. 78–79.

63 Deng, F. M., "The impact of alien religions among the Dinka", Institute of African Studies, University of Ife, Seminar on *The High God in Africa*, 1964, quoted in Welbourn, op. cit., p. 328.

64 Ibid., p. 329.

Chapter 6

1 Wilson, R. N., *The Sociology of Health*, Random House, New York, 1970, p. 11.

2 Moltmann, J., *God in Creation: An Ecological Doctrine of Creation*, SCM Press Ltd., London, 1985, p. 270.

3   Blum, H. L., *Planning for Health: Development and Application of Social Change*, Human Sciences Press, New York, 1974, p. 77.

4   For a shorter summary of the definitions proposed by Blum, see Ashley, B. M. and O'Rourke K. D., *Health Care Ethics: A Theological Analysis*, The Catholic Health Association of the United States, St. Louis, 1982, pp. 22–23.

5   Blum, H. L., op. cit., p. 77.

6   Ibid.

7   Ibid., p. 79.

8   Ibid., p. 81.

9   Ibid., p. 83.

10   Ibid., p. 85.

11   Ibid., p. 86.

12   Ibid., p. 87.

13   Ibid., p. 88.

14   Armstrong, J. E., et al., "Another Value-Belief System: The Third World Concept of Health", School of Public Health, University of California, Berkeley, August 1971, mimeographed, quoted in ibid., p. 90.

15   Ibid., p. 91.

16   Ibid., p. 93.

17   Ashley, B. M. and O'Rourke, K. D., op. cit., p. 22.

18   World Health Organization, *Preamble of the Constitution of the WHO*, World Health Organization, Geneva, 1946.

19   Cf. Parsons, T., "Health and Disease: A Sociological and Action Perspective", in: Reich, W., (ed.), *Encyclopedia of Bioethics*, Vol. 2, Macmillan Co., New York, 1978, p. 590–599.

20   Engelhardt, H. J., "Health and Disease: Philosophical Perspective", in: Reich, W, (ed.), *Encyclopedia of Bioethics*, op. cit., p. 605.

21   Callahan, D., "The WHO Definition of 'Health'", *The Hastings Center Studies*, Vol. 1, No. 3, 1973, p. 78.

22   Ibid., p. 80.

23   Ibid., pp. 82–83.

24   Ibid., p. 83.

25 Duhl, L. J., "Social Context of Health", in Hastings, A. C., Fadiman, J. and Gordon, J. S. (eds.), *Health for the Whole Person*, Westview Press, Boulder, Colorado, 1980, p. 44.

26 Callahan D., op. cit., p. 87.

27 Contrast Callahan's view with that of Rudolf Virchow, who said in 1849: "In reality, if medicine is the science of the healthy as well as of the ill human being (which is what it ought to be), what other science is better suited to prepare laws as the basis of the social structure, in order to make effective those which are inherent in man himself?. . .Medicine is a social science in its very bone and marrow. . ." *Disease, Life and Man, Selected Essays by Rudolf Virchow*, Helfand Rather (trans.), Standford University Press, Standford, 1958, quoted in: Carlson, R. J., *The End of Medicine*, John Wiley and Sons, New York, 1975, p. 192.

28 Parsons T., op. cit.

29 Ibid., p. 598.

30 Ibid.

31 Moltmann, J., op. cit., p. 271.

32 Ibid., pp. 271–272.

33 See also Callahan, D., op. cit., p. 82ff.

34 Moltmann, J,. op. cit., p. 272.

35 Ibid., p. 272–273.

36 Ibid., p. 273.

37 Ibid.

38 Ibid., p. 274.

39 Ibid.

40 Provan, I., *Healing: A Limitational Approach to a Theology of Health*, Hodder & Stoughton, London, 1979, p. 8.

41 The Christian Medical Commission, World Council of Churches, *Healing and Wholeness: The Churches' Role in Health*, Geneva: CMC., 1990, p. 21.

42 Saltonstall, R., "Healthy Bodies, Social Bodies: Men's and Women's Concepts and Practices of Health in Everyday Life", *Social Science and Medicine*, Vol. 36, No. 1, 1993, p. 7.

43 Ibid.

44 Ibid., p. 8.

45   Ibid., p. 12.

46   Bandman, E. L. and Bandman B., "Health and Disease: A Nursing
      Perspective", in: Caplan, A. L., Engelhardt, H. T. and McCartney, J. J.,
      Concepts of Health and Disease: Interdisciplinary Perspectives, Addison-
      Wesley Publishing Company, Don Mills, Ontario, 1981, p. 686.

47   Ibid., p. 687.

48   Wilson, M. (ed.), *Explorations in Health and Salvation: A Selection of
      Papers by Bob Lambourne*, University of Birmingham, Birmingham, 1983,
      p. 28.

49   Onions, C. T., (ed.), *The Shorter Oxford English Dictionary*, Vol. 1, The
      Clarendon Press, Oxford, 1973.

50   Cayne, B. S., Lechner, D. E., et. al., *The New Lexicon Webster's Encyclo-
      pedic Dictionary of the English Language*, Canadian Edition, Lexicon
      Publications, New York, 1988.

51   Ibid.

52   Wilson, M., *The Church Is Healing*, SCM Press Ltd., London, 1966, p.
      16.

53   Ibid., p. 17.

54   Emphasis mine. Although Michael Wilson made this observation over
      thirty years ago, contrast his view with later views of Callahan, Blum,
      and others.

55   Wilson, M., *The Church Is Healing*, op. cit., p. 18.

56   Appiah-Kubi, K., "Religion and Healing in an African Community:
      The Akan of Ghana", in: Sullivan, L. E., (ed.), *Healing and Restoring:
      Health and Medicine in the World's Religious Traditions*, Macmillan Pub-
      lishing Company, New York, 1989.

57   Ibid., p. 216.

58   Wilson, M. (ed.), *Explorations in Health and Salvation*, op. cit.

59   Ibid., p. 28.

60   Ibid.

61   Caplan, G., *An Approach to Community Mental Health*, Tavistock, 1961,
      quoted in ibid., p. 30.

62   Ibid.

63   Ibid., p. 28.

64   Ibid., p. 29.

65   Ibid., p. 30.

66   Comaroff, J., "Healing and Cultural Transformation: The Tswana of Southern Africa [1]", *Social Science and Medicine*, Vol. 15B, 1981, p. 368.

67   Ibid.

68   Ibid.

69   Ibid.

70   Ibid., p. 369.

71   Ibid.

72   I use the terms "illness" and "disease" interchangeably in this work, but with the awareness that there is a core distinction between them, as I shall point out below.

73   Mbiti, J. S., *African Religions and Philosophy*, op. cit., p. 2.

74   Pobee, J. S., *Toward an African Theology*, Partheon Press, Nashville, 1979, p. 44.

75   It must be noted here that the pervasiveness of religion in the traditional institutions of the Akans does not mean that the states are theocratic ones. As indicated above, the rulers in Akanland are regarded sacred, but they are not regarded nor do they claim to rule by divine authority. It means, however, that the elements in the society derive their values from the traditional religion.

76   Appiah-Kubi, K., "Religion and Healing in an African Community: The Akan of Ghana", op. cit., p. 215.

77   For a classical example of symbolic interpretation of rituals (of healing) in an African culture, see Turner, V., *The Forest of Symbols: Aspects of Ndembu Ritual*, Cornell University Press, Ithaca and London, 1967.

78   Mbiti, J. S., *African Religions and Philosophy*, op. cit., p. 196.

79   Appiah-Kubi, K., "Religion and Healing in an African Community: The Akan of Ghana", op. cit., p. 211.

80   Ibid., p. 212.

81   See Gyekye, K., *An Essay on African Philosophical Thought: The Akan Conceptual Scheme*, Cambridge University Press, Cambridge, 1987, p. 154ff.

82   Ibid., p. 156.

83   Appiah-Kubi, K., "Religion and Healing in an African Community: The Akan of Ghana", op. cit., p. 212.

84   Radcliffe-Brown, A. R. and Forde, D. (eds.), *African Systems of Kinship and Marriage*, KPI, London, 1987, p. 262.

85   Ibid.

86   Ademuwagun, Z. A., '"Alafia"—The Yoruba Concept of Health: Impli-
      cation for health education', *International Journal of Health Education*,
      XXI, 2, 1978, p. 89.

87   Wall, L. L., *Hausa Medicine: Illness and Well-being in a West African
      Culture*, Duke University Press, Durham and London, 1988, p. 334.

88   Ademuwagun, Z. A., op. cit., p. 90.

89   Appiah-Kubi, K., "Religion and Healing in an African Community:
      The Akan of Ghana", op. cit., p. 212.

90   Twumasi, P. A., *Medical Systems in Ghana*, op. cit., p. 23.

91   Appiah-Kubi, K., "Religion and Healing in an African Community:
      The Akan of Ghana", op. cit., p. 218.

92   Ibid.

93   Sarpong, P., *Ghana In Retrospect*, op. cit., p. 18.

94   Ibid.

95   Appiah-Kubi, K. "Religion and Healing in an African Community:
      The Akan of Ghana", op. cit., p. 211.

96   Wall, L. L., op. cit., p. 172.

97   Gbadegesin, S., *African Philosophy: Traditional Yoruba Philosophy and
      Contemporary African Realities*, Peter Lang, New York, 1991, p. 128.

98   Reading, A., "Illness and Disease", *Medical Clinics of North America*,
      61, 1977, quoted in Wall, L. L., op. cit., pp. 172–173.

99   Ibid., p.173. The treatment of a medical "problem" or "ailment" with
      its own "medicine" or "remedy" (*magani*) here means treating an ail-
      ment comprehensively—physical, spiritual, emotional, psychological,
      etc. For example, a leaf of a particular plant may be used to cure a
      particular boil, but the patient is not considered completely cured
      until some ritual(s) or sacrifice(s) is performed to wholly cleanse the
      individual and integrate him or her into the family or community. In
      other words, the use of "medicine" or "remedy" implies physical and
      spiritual curing.

100   Cf. Fink, H. E., op. cit., p. 223.

101   Ademuwagun, Z. A., op. cit., pp. 90–91.

102   Warren, D. M., "The Techiman-Bono Ethnomedical System", in Yoder,
      P. S. (ed.), *African Health and Healing Systems: Proceedings of a Sympo-
      sium*, Crossroads Press, Los Angeles, 1982, p. 89.

103   Cf. Appiah-Kubi, K., "Religion and Healing in an African Commu-
      nity: The Akan of Ghana", op. cit., p. 217.

104 Gbadegesin, S., op. cit., pp. 129–130.

105 Ibid., p. 213.

106 Janzen, J. M., "Health, Religion, and Medicine in Central and Southern African Traditions", op. cit., pp. 241–242.

Chapter 7

1 Fako, T. T., "The Dilemma of African Traditional Medicine: The Case of Botswana", in: du Toit, B. M. and Abdalla, I. H. (eds.), *African Healing Strategies*, Trado-Medic Books, New York, 1985, p. 226.

2 Bishaw, M., "Promoting Traditional Medicine in Ethiopia: A Brief Historical Review of Government Policy", *Social Science and Medicine*, Vol. 33, No. 2, 1991, pp. 195–196.

3 Cf. Anyinam, C. A., "Persistence with Change: A Rural-Urban Study of Ethno-Medical Practices in Contemporary Ghana", Unpublished Ph.D. Thesis, Queens University, Kingston, 1987, p. 130, fn. 30.

4 Cf. ibid., p. 124.

5 Ibid., p. 125.

6 For example, in 1982, the government reaffirmed that: "Traditional healers form an important source of medical care, with a profound herbal knowledge which cannot any longer be neglected or ignored by our government. As specialists in traditional and herbal medicine and as custodians of our culture and tradition they can and they should contribute to the improvement of rural health." Ministry of Health, National Advisory Council, Accra, Ghana, 1982, p. 2.

7 Fink, H. E., op. cit., p. 17.

8 Anyinam, C. A., op. cit., pp. 126–127. Emphasis mine.

9 They do so, I think, not without inner conflicts since, as Africans, they cannot rid themselves altogether of their African worldview.

10 Bonsi, S. K., "The Foreign Impact on Precolonial Medicine", in: Falola, T. and Ityavyar, D. A. (eds.), *The Political Economy of Health in Africa*, Ohio University Press, Athens, Ohio, 1992, p. 59. Also see Heinecke, P., "Sickness is Wealth", *The Nigerian Standard*, Jos, Nigeria, April 20, 1982.

11 Ibid.

12 Faith-healers are classified in this study as leaders of the African Independent Churches—priests, priestesses, prophets, and prophetesses.

13 Anyinam, C., op. cit., p. 179.

14 In 1960, 23% of Ghana's total population lived in urban areas. In 1991, the percentage was 33%. It is estimated that by the year 2000, urban population will increase to 38%. The annual urban population growth rate was 3.9% in 1960–91. It is estimated that 1991–2000 annual growth rate will be 4.6%. *Human Development Report 1993*, Oxford University Press, Oxford and New York, 1993, p. 179.

15 Anyinam, C. A., op. cit., p. 182.

16 Quoted in ibid., p. 180.

17 Cf. ibid.

18 Accra, March 1989.

19 Fako, T. T., op. cit., p. 227.

20 Ibid.

21 Anyinam, C. A., op. cit.

22 Ibid., p. 206.

23 This information is based on two separate conversations I had with two members of the Association in Kumasi in 1989.

24 Singer, P., "Introduction: From Anthropology and Medicine to "Therapy" and Neo-Colonialism", in: Singer, P. (ed.), *Traditional Healing: New Science or Neo-Colonialism?* (Essays in Critique of Medical Anthropology), Conch Magazine Limited (Publishers), New York, 1977, p. 22.

25 Ityavyar, D. A., "A Traditional Midwife Practice, Sokoto State, Nigeria", *Social Science and Medicine*, Vol. 18, No. 6, 1984, p. 500.

26 According to Fako, in Botswana, the missionaries originally intended to keep European medicine for themselves. It "was only extended to Africans as an inducement to accept Christianity, after years of personal efforts to evangelize had failed." Fako, T. T., op. cit., p. 198.

27 Cf. Anyinam, C. A., op. cit., p. 100.

28 Gold Coast Medical Report, "Report of the Ministry of Health", (Mimeo), 1954. Cf. also Anyinam, C. A., op. cit., p. 101.

29 Twumasi, P. A., *Medical Systems in Ghana*, op. cit., p. 64.

30 Anyinam, C., op. cit., pp. 100–101.

31 Twumasi, P. A., *Medical Systems in Ghana*, op. cit., p. 65.

32 Ghana Government, National Physical Development Plan 1963–70, Town and Country Planning Division, September 1965.

33 Anyinam, C., op. cit., p. 103.

34   *The Europa World Year Book* 1993, Vol. 1, Europa Publications Limited, London, 1993, p. 1257.

35   The children are weak because of disease, malnutrition and poor drinking water.

36   The growth of the children is hindered because of malnutrition and poor drinking water.

37   Ghana Demographic and Health Survey 1988, Ghana Statistical Service, May 1990, p. 18.

38   Ibid., p. 17.

39   "No Food at the Korle-Bu Hospital", *Ghana Drum*, Vol. 3, No. 3, March 1994, p. 18.

40   Ibid.

41   Cf. Henriot, P. J., "Africa and Structural Adjustment Programmes", *Sedos Bulletin 1994*, (Africa: The Kairos of a Synod), Vol. 26, No. 3 & No. 4, Double Issue, 15th March–15th April, 1994, pp. 108–109.

42   Ghana Demographic and Health Survey 1988, op. cit., p. 18.

43   Green, E. C., "Sexually Transmitted Disease, Ethnomedicine and Health Policy in Africa", *Social Science and Medicine*, Vol.35, No.2, 1992, p. 127.

44   Ibid., p. 124. Cf. also Anyinam, C., op. cit., p. 194, for the utilization of bio-medical and traditional medical practices by the Akans.

45   Cf., for example, Lanternari, V., *Religions of the Oppressed*, New American Library, New York, 1965, p. 19ff.

46   Cf., for example, Nwanunobi, O. C., "Sects as an Urban Phenomenon in Contemporary Eastern Nigeria", *Anthropos International Review of Ethnology and Linguistics*, No.71, 1980, pp. 117–28.

47   Cf., for example, Appiah-Kubi, K., "Indigenous African Christian Churches: Signs of Authenticity", in: Appiah-Kubi K. and Torres, S. (eds.), *African Theology en Route*, Orbis Books, Maryknoll, 1979, pp.117–118.

48   Acta Apostolici Sedis, 59, 1967, quoted in: Milingo, E., *The World in Between: Christian Healing and the Struggle for Survival*, C. Hurst & Co., London, 1984, pp. 12–13.

49   Wyllie, R. W., *Spiritism in Ghana*, Scholars Press, Montana, 1980, p. 49.

50   Cf., for example, Anyinam, C., op. cit., p. 117ff.

51   Owoahene-Acheampong, S., "African Independent Churches in West Africa, with Particular Reference to their Theology and Practice of Healing", Unpublished Master's Thesis, St. Michael's College, University of Toronto, Toronto, 1991.

52   Sundkler, B. G. M., *Bantu Prophets in South Africa*, Oxford University Press, London, 1970, p. 226.

53   Ibid., pp. 226–227.

54   Peel, J. D. Y., *Aladura: a Religious Movement among the Yourba*, Oxford University Press, London, 1968, p. 134.

55   Turner, H. W., *Religious Innovation in Africa*, G. K. Hall & Co., Boston, 1979, p. 228.

56   Ibid.

57   Onibere, S. G. A. Ose, "The Phenomenon of African Religious Independency: Blessing or Curse on the Church Universal?", *African Theological Journal*, Vol.10, No.1, 1981, p .21.

58   Sundkler, B. G. M., op. cit., pp. 227–228.

Chapter 8

1   Wilson, M., *The Church Is Healing*, op. cit., p. 94.

2   Appiah-Kubi recounts a story in which through the advice of a social worker, he and a team of young voluntary work-campers built a swimming pool for a village, only to come two years later to find the pool turned into a toilet. Appiah-Kubi, K., *Man Cures, God Heals: Religion and Medical Practice among the Akans of Ghana*, op. cit., p. 141.

Index